Financial Speculation in Victorian Fiction

Financial Speculation in Victorian Fiction

*Plotting Money and the Novel Genre,
1815–1901*

Tamara S. Wagner

The Ohio State University Press • Columbus

Copyright © 2010 by The Ohio State University.
All rights reserved.

Library of Congress Cataloging-in-Publication Data
Wagner, Tamara S., 1976–
Financial speculation in Victorian fiction : plotting money and the novel genre, 1815–1901 / Tamara S. Wagner.
p. cm.
Includes bibliographical references and index.
ISBN 978-0-8142-1119-9 (cloth : alk. paper)—ISBN 978-0-8142-9217-4 (cd-rom) 1. English fiction—19th century—History and criticism. 2. Finance in literature. 3. Money in literature. I. Title.
PR468.F56W34 2010
823.'8093553—dc22
2009039277

Cover illustration: "Celebrated Comic Scene Between the Railway Clown (Hudson) and the Indignant Shareholders," from *Punch* (artist unknown), 1849. Courtesy of The Ohio State University Billy Ireland Cartoon Library & Museum.

This book is available in the following editions:
Cloth (ISBN 978-0-8142-1119-9)
CD-ROM (ISBN 978-0-8142-9217-4)
Paper (ISBN: 978-0-8142-5698-5)
Cover design by Laurence Nozik
Text design by Juliet Williams
Type set in Adobe Minion Pro

Contents

Acknowledgments	vii
Introduction	1
Plotting Financial Speculation: The Making of Stock-Market Villains	3
Narrating Financial and Emotional Instabilities	7
Bubbles of the Past: The Stock Market's Literary History	13
Mapping Plots of Financial Speculation	24
One • Silver-Fork Speculation and the Making of Financial Fiction	31
Silver-Fork Enterprise	34
In the Great Scheme of Commerce	48
Two • The Sensational Stock-Market Novel	61
The Plagiarisms of Commerce: Rewriting the Figure of the Speculator	63
The Miser's New Notes: Plotting the Magic of Paper Money	78
Three • Speculators Abroad	89
The Conversion of Colonial Legacies	92
Hard Cash and Paper Diamonds	113
Four • Speculators at Home	126
Building Speculation at Home	131
Romancing the Stock Market	146
Conclusion	173
Notes	179
Bibliography	210
Index	225

Acknowledgments

These acknowledgments can only begin to express the enormous debt of gratitude for the emotional as well as intellectual support freely given by the many people, scattered over the globe, who have helped to make this book possible—a debt accumulated in uncountable ways as well as across time and space. In particular, I am indebted to Heather Glen, Grace Moore, Kristine Moruzi, and Graham Pechey for so kindly offering detailed comments on several chapters, parts of chapters, and related material, in all their different incarnations. Equally important was and always will be the generous advice and much-valued friendship, often extended over vast distances, despite lengthy separations, and during particularly unsettling times, of Neil Murphy, Talia Schaffer, Lim Lee Ching, Geraldine Song, Julia Kuehn, and Rosie Sykes. I am also grateful to the numerous international scholars and especially fellow Victorianists who have not just commented on various ideas in their different stages of germination and fermentation, but have also shared both the joys and the challenges of making and trying to perfect a manuscript. Likewise spanning the globe, they include Terence Dawson, Monika Elbert, Michael Flowers, Deborah Madsen, Deborah Denenholz Morse, John Whalen-Bridge, and indeed the international community of Victorian scholars facilitated by the VICTORIA discussion list (VICTORIA@LISTSERV.INDIANA.EDU). Above all, I would like to thank Sandy Crooms, my editor at The Ohio State University Press, for believing in the book and being so unfailingly patient and helpful, always there to lend cheerful advice. Likewise, nothing can repay the continued patience and especially the practical support of my husband, Chai Kah Hin, whose detailed knowledge of financial processes, past and present, has moreover fed into my research on every level.

Finally, this study has benefited greatly from the rigorous readers' reports provided by the Press and also by the academic journals that have considered the various outgrowths of my research over the years. Earlier versions of material in chapter 2 were in parts first published as "The Miser's New Notes and the Victorian Sensation Novel: Plotting the Magic of Paper Money" in a special issue of the *Victorian Review* on "Literature and Money" 31.2 (2005): 79–98, and as "Speculators at Home in the Victorian Novel: Making Stock-Market Villains and New 'Paper Fictions'" in *Victorian Literature and Culture* 36.1 (2008): 43–62. Some of the material on Victorian suburbia as well as references to Margaret Oliphant's reworking of literary sensationalism in chapter 4 have appeared, in different forms, in "London's Great Starfish: The Construction of Mid-Victorian Suburban Fiction," *Cahiers Victoriens & Edouardiens* 69 (2009): 151–67, and in "'Very saleable articles, indeed': Margaret Oliphant's Repackaging of Sensational Finance," *Modern Language Quarterly* 71.1 (March 2010).

Introduction

> No one knows who they are, or where they came from, or what they'll turn to.
> —Anthony Trollope, *The Way We Live Now*

In *The Way We Live Now* (1875), the Melmottes' origins remain a mystery that becomes increasingly irrelevant. Few of M. Melmotte's business partners venture to inquire too closely into the specious public faith in his financial integrity even as they prepare to profit from his enterprises. On the contrary, a suspicion that their seemingly stable investments are as unsafe as they are spurious, that they bear the marks of risky speculation, accompanies the rise of the commercial Melmotte empire from its beginnings. Detailed investigation is not so much guarded against by the speculator as shirked by those who consider it financially advantageous to believe in him. When aristocratic would-be investors scramble for a seat on the boards of this financial "New Man," they are guilty of countenancing more than simply a fraudulent financier of whose history as a swindler they are well apprised, for Melmotte's connection to scams abroad is notorious. Rather, they are building on fluctuating attitudes to the seemingly successful speculator. Financial instability becomes the key to an immensely popular set of motifs in the nineteenth century. In Trollope's novel, the most common plotline is already evoked as deeply familiar, even typecast. Precisely as the uncertainties associated with speculation are conveniently embodied by an international man of mystery, they may then be exorcised as straightforwardly by his self-destruction. But what happens if the threat comes from within, if the stock-market villain really is a born English gentleman instead of simply posing as one? By mid-century, Victorian fiction had already brought forth better camouflaged and hence all the more invidious stock-market villains. Embedded in the society they set out to cheat, these villains acquired sets of attributes that were to stereotype fictional financiers for decades. They featured in financial plots that became crucial to the development of the novel genre in the nineteenth century.

In capitalizing on social and cultural shifts to which it contributed as a formative influence, the Victorian novel was indeed significantly shaped by financial speculation. It is not only that its engagement with finance capitalism as a source of plots belies concepts of a unidirectional effect that have traditionally dominated discussions of the impact of market forces on literature. Awareness of this complex relationship ensured that financial narratives became characterized by a self-reflexivity that built on a fascination with cultural myths, or fictions, of various, at times peculiarly identified, "papers." In an ongoing restructuring of plotlines and metaphorical constructions, these papers were seen to stretch from banknotes and stock-market shares to popular fiction itself. Although Victorian writers took a deeply ambiguous stance towards financial speculation, the interchanges between literary productions and the credit economy's new instruments became intricately worked into fiction. In reassessing their representation, I shall show that the resulting narratives necessitate and assist in a revaluation of the role of fiscal relationships in nineteenth-century literature. Before analyzing a number of key texts, both canonical and noncanonical, I shall begin by stressing the ways in which financial difficulties function as an expression of concerns with indeterminacy and inscrutability, with a sense of instability that encompasses the individual's experience of a changing economic system and, by extension, a speculating society thriving on such fluctuations.

Financial instability serves as an indicator of social, cultural, and literary change and as a conduit for the adaptation of fiscal metaphors to emotional as well as epistemological uncertainties. Hence a close look at the impact of the pervading cultural preoccupation with financial speculation on Victorian fiction also helps to clear up some of the most persistently elusive complexities in the formation and differentiation of newly evolving subgenres. As exponents of divergent modes of writing engage with the same constellation of events, but in distinct groupings of ways of turning them into narratives, they invite comparison of these different versions of a single, yet increasingly variegated, narrative. An account of emergent fictions of finance that takes seriously this shaping influence on literary culture compels a new look at their structures. This critical inquiry is necessarily as much formal as it is historically inflected. More than a cultural or literary history of Victorian financial fiction, this study seeks to explore the making and adaptation of specific motifs, of variously adapted tropes, extended metaphors, and recurring figures, and how they turn a series of crises into narratives. Since the described crises are often personal and emotional as well as financial, the new plots of speculation outline maps of some of the major themes of nineteenth-century literature. These maps lead across overlapping categories of literary culture, generating zones of intersection between subgenres in which financial plots operate as the intersecting points.

Plotting Financial Speculation: The Making of Stock-Market Villains

Although much has been written on the economic circumstances that framed the production of nineteenth-century popular writing, the analysis of Victorian financial fiction rarely has ranged beyond the most obvious swindles and swindlers. Dickens's Merdle in *Little Dorrit*, serialized in 1855–57, and Trollope's Melmotte in *The Way We Live Now*, published nearly two decades later, are both based on railway and company speculators of the time. Similarly, the West Diddlesex Assurance Company of Thackeray's 1841 *Great Hoggarty Diamond* and the Anglo-Bengalee Disinterested Loan and Life Assurance Company in Dickens's 1844 *Martin Chuzzlewit* share the same origins. But these examples have been discussed predominantly with the intention to illustrate the historical processes of nineteenth-century economic ideologies and practices and not to analyze their transformation in literature.[1] This hardly does justice to the fascination with which the Victorians took up this source of plots. As John Butt stressed in 1959 in "The Topicality of *Little Dorrit*," Dickens did not need specific financial scandals to create fictional speculators: "it is rather that he had already taken imaginative stock of the situation when some fresh event occurred to confirm his diagnosis and to supply him with an illustrative example."[2] There is much more to literature's use of the stock market than a mere reflection of contemporary financial crises alone. It formed a new cultural imaginary that expressed changing ideas of moral probity and indeterminate identity, creditworthiness and the management of financial risks, the experience of instability and the contesting strategies to consider its repercussions at home and abroad.[3]

Pressing anxieties, in other words, yielded new narrative structures. As Gillian Beer has emphasized in her reassessment of studies that read scientific and literary discourses side by side, the function of science in literature is not "a one-way traffic, as though literature acted as a mediator for a topic (science) that precedes it and that remains intact after its re-presentation."[4] Instead, the relationship is one of interchange and transformation.[5] The intersections of economic and literary discourses have now begun to be explored as a source of cultural fictions in the nineteenth century, much as the intersections between science and literature have long been. The influential work of Marc Shell and Jean-Joseph Goux has paved the way for studies of what has nonetheless repeatedly been called the oxymoronic relationship of money and art or literature.[6] John Vernon has pointed out that banks and realist novels are both fictions with their "roots in the actual—but a fiction nonetheless."[7] Cedric Watts refers to "modes of 'mystification' (obfuscation) of finance, commerce and class relations" in literature.[8] There are occasions when the mystifications of money "are not on holiday but are working hard; striving to be mistaken for the empirical, the factual, so that the world may be recast in their image."[9] This is of special relevance when these narratives seek to question perceptions of money beyond the confines of social critique. As Gail Turley Houston has pointed out, it has become a critical commonplace that "it is no coincidence that fiction became the most popular genre at the same time that capitalism's construction of reality required that a new discourse be developed around 'the economy.'"[10] Since this increasingly pressing issue generated a proliferation of various circulating "paper fictions"—advertisements touting investment opportunities and warnings against reckless reliance on these papers—it is not surprising that popular fiction tapped into the narrative potential of this excess.

Economic uncertainty, the loss of a stable home or fixed community, and the emotional fragility of the socially and geographically mobile protagonist created new motif-structures. The newly emergent plots of financial speculation consequently became much more than a variation of property plots, which had previously determined fictionalizations of financial issues. Narratives of inheritance and courtship became incorporated into the literary representation of a world that was seen to be driven by speculative ventures to a new extent. As Barbara Weiss has already put it in her pointedly titled *The Hell of the English: Bankruptcy and the Victorian Novel*, traditional narrative structures, or mythic patterns, took on new resonance when they were set against the volatile economic conditions of the mid-century. Bankruptcy emerged as "the perfect structural metaphor for the vulnerability of the individual."[11] Jeff Nunokawa speaks of the "afterlife" of property: by mid-century, property had become subjected to the fluctuations of a speculative economy, annulling "the dream of stable estate" by introducing concerns that could not be further removed from the restoration of inheritance as the resolution commonly offered in the fiction of the previous century.¹² The continued centrality of the estate and often of disputed inheritance shows that these traditional plotlines were not so much replaced as co-opted. This is not to say, of course, that they did not undergo changes at times so profound that the original structures could become almost unrecognizable. This transformation was about much more than interrogations of an over-reliance on uncertain expectations. Pecuniary instability formed an organizing motif that connected divergent developments across nineteenth-century literature, and I wish to discuss its specific functions in financial speculation plots in more detail. The uncertainties caused by impending bankruptcy, a stock-market crash, or the exposure of an unreliable currency or of the devalued shares of a possibly fraudulent company could operate as an easily realizable way of articulating instability.

Beyond this critical articulation of prevailing concerns with economic change, Victorian culture's engagement with the fictional potential of financial narratives became intriguingly complex. This was not only because it was never unidirectional. Recent research on the interrelationship between literature and finance has given more attention to what was perceived as a "magicality" of "paper fictions" that could "refer equally to pound notes and to novels, to scrip and to script," in a struggle over the issue of value (and values).¹³ The attendant fascination with issues of representation itself militated against the appropriation of fictional texts as mere mouthpieces for new economic ideas. Fictional papers of various kinds were an integral part of the market, not only within an increasingly complex "economics of authorship."¹⁴ Novelists transferred their anxieties about manipulated popularity on to stock-market plots in which the devaluation of financial papers such as paper money or stock-market shares stood in for similarly circulating popular fiction. Money, Peter Brooks emphasizes in a recent discussion of the emergence of nineteenth-century realism, became "the representation of representation itself."¹⁵ As critics have remarked, this is perhaps the most intriguing manifestation of the Victorians' prevailing preoccupation with money matters. In a recent review essay, Jonathan Rose has even raised the provocative question of whether the capitalist economy was good for nineteenth-century literature, despite the fact that "every important Victorian author deeply distrusted speculative capitalism."¹⁶ Patrick Brantlinger has symptomatically entitled the chapter on Victorian literature in his analysis of the rise of the credit economy "Banking on Novels," and Paul Delany has added that novelists, like bankers, hoped "to convince everyone that their tokens can be cashed out on demand—in other words, that they have endowed the conventional with all the functional attributes of the essential."[17] This exchangeability provided a recurrent narrative structure in popular fiction. Overall, as financial narratives became increasingly self-reflexive in engaging with the inextricability of aesthetic, moral, and commercial discourses on value, the representation of getting and spending became crucial to the novel genre's formation.

Whereas the complexities of this formation through critical engagements with various, intersecting interests in speculation have largely remained unexplored, much important work has been done over the last decades to elucidate the economic contexts of Victorian culture, to interrogate the impact of emergent economic theories on popular writing, and to read finance journalism side by side with its appropriation and reworking by fiction.[18] Mary Poovey has detailed how journalists and novelists alike "turned the national fixation [with money] into some of the most engaging fictions of the century."[19] In creating imaginative substance out of the intangible, nineteenth-century novelists—as much as the emergent finance journalism and what came to be established as the discipline of economics—made up part of a concerted effort to establish the financial system as reliable.[20] Financial narratives of the century's first half were regularly concerned with marking out anything fraudulent or unstable as an exception, a mere fluke, or, even more conveniently, an infesting element that could then be extricated. Such projections were to effect a convenient closure. Whenever financiers turned out to be criminals in popular fiction, they could be expunged from the system.[21] As it became more common to measure worth by disembodied capital instead of landed wealth, novelists simultaneously began to abandon providential inheritance plots in favor of financial plots that allowed them to "explore matters involving personal agency and individual will, like financial temptation and fiscal responsibility."[22] This apparent replacement of what John Reed has termed "the subject of inheritance," a convention "so familiar as to be almost offensive" to the reader of nineteenth-century fiction,[23] by new fictional engagements with economic systems necessarily implied a complex renegotiation of the "classic" British novel's underlying structures. Yet it was primarily this adaptation of traditional plotlines to the demands of a changing literary marketplace that ensured that financial speculation had such an important impact on the form and content of the Victorian novel. The growing fascination with speculative ventures entered the novel genre at the level of plot-structure and as figurative language, shaping its development in intricate ways that went far beyond mere reflection, commentary, or wish fulfillment.

While acknowledging my debt to recent scholarship on Victorian economics, I wish to direct new attention to considerations of form and literary influence. In the introduction to *The New Economic Criticism*, Mark Osteen and Martha Woodmansee have already pinpointed a growing "body of literary and cultural criticism founded upon economic paradigms, models and tropes."[24] So far, however, "productionist" or "contextualist" approaches still predominate, and while cautioning against a potential promiscuity in "metatheoretical" accounts, they stress the importance of a move away from a purely "extratextual" as well as from a purely formalist approach alone.[25] The analysis of the novel genre's creative investment in nineteenth-century finance capitalism lends itself particularly well to this breaking away from the idea of "a one-way traffic." The invigorating impetus of interdisciplinary critical discourses has begun to converge with an important development that James Phelan has termed a "narrative turn": by foregrounding "the nature and power of story and storytelling," we shall best contribute to an interdisciplinary study of narrative.[26] The divergent ways in which texts "narratively," "that is, in and through their plots and characters," as Susan Griffin has put it in a recent study, explore cultural ideas and problems as well as epistemological concerns at once demand and facilitate a reassessment of the interaction between literary forms and social formations.[27] In response to the pressing need to proceed beyond purely contextual studies, Griffin stresses that to accomplish this we need to "recover the analytic tools of formalist consideration and close reading too often missing from our contemporary criticism by showing their compatibility with—indeed, I would argue their necessity for—historical study."[28] Herbert Tucker similarly speaks of the need to bring out again "our disciplinary best": the tools of formal literary analysis.[29] In interrogating the narrative functions of financial transactions in nineteenth-century fiction, this literary history of financial plots is firmly situated within this current redirection of Victorian studies.[30]

Narrating Financial and Emotional Instabilities

What stands out among the versatile functions of financial plots as they developed over the course of the nineteenth century is that the individual's vulnerability newly came to the fore once the financial machinery was seen to engulf speculators as mere cogs. Misrepresentation as well as deliberate fraud entailed the exploitation of the naïve, easily misguided amateur speculator. On one level, this necessarily generated a need to render the economic system familiar, to make information about its processes more accessible. Cautionary instructions embedded in often thinly fictionalized accounts of failed enterprises amply fulfilled this function, while trading on this very need for reassurance as a business opening for the popular press. It therein perhaps most prominently contributed to the definition of the various instruments of a changing economic system (and their narratives). That stock-market speculation, more than any other monetary undertaking, came to constitute such a crucial focus for anxieties about instability had undoubtedly much to do with the fact that its definition had become posed against that of investment in economic theory and its popularization as a cultural fiction. This somewhat reductive differentiation was to prove extremely persistent. It informed figurative language, generating extended metaphors that structured financial plots. On a much more self-reflexive as well as creative level of engagement with economic discourse, speculation stood in as a synecdoche for an unstable financial system propelled by chance and, by extension, for speculative society at large. Critiques of the marriage market, for example, employed the fluctuating demarcations of investment and speculation in order to unpack new economic metaphors.

The distinction between speculation and investment, moreover, importantly involved a triangulation with a third form of pecuniary transactions: gambling. Within economic discourse and its absorption by popular culture, then and now, investment could operate as the term for a secure monetary transaction, whereas financial speculation constituted by definition a form of risk taking. Speculation's association with gambling made it possible for nineteenth-century economists to distinguish it from investment, with the latter embodying the professional, trustworthy, secure, and stable, whereas speculation became linked to the amateurish as well as the risky and ruthless. This placement of speculation and gambling in opposition to investment was meant to promise a purging process thought necessary for the legitimization of a capitalist economy. J. Jeffrey Franklin maintains that gambling functioned as "the necessary evil other" to facilitate the Stock Exchange's establishment as "a source of real value."[31] A dichotomy of trustworthy investors and speculating swindlers could provide manuals for responsible behavior in a rapidly evolving economy. Premised on the exclusion of gambling from strictly defined economic activities, this triangulation was to guarantee the acceptance of transactions at the stock market as a legally legitimized business.[32]

These lines of demarcation without doubt informed public perception, yet it would be too simple to suggest that even the novelists most invested in ideas of economic progress (tied up with virulently popularized self-help ideologies as they were) swallowed these explications wholeheartedly. The majority of writers remained suspicious of both the speculative economy and the economic theories supporting it. In a heightened self-reflexivity, awareness of the ongoing redefinitions of both investment and speculation in economic discourse created some of the most satirical exposures of risk management. Fiction debunked paradigms promoted in advice manuals.³³ The unpacking and literalization of rhetorical invocations of "papers" of various kinds formed a markedly explicit working out of a new fictional potential. It frequently became realized through anthropomorphism or object narratives, as well as the appropriation of specific paper fictions as clues, or false clues, in plots of detection. Similarly, it was in a self-consciously satirized fashion that novels wove deliberately excessive webs of alignments between speculations on the marriage, the book, and the stock market. The very excess of rhetorical figures allowed an unraveling of metaphors that often succeeded in enfolding a complex social critique in what may otherwise have been limited to a trite identification of mercenary marriages and chances at the Stock Exchange. At the same time, the association with chance ensured that the representation of business speculations continued to be fissured by the longer standing rhetoric of gambling.

Among the earliest occurrences of "speculation" in English literature to describe "a commercial venture or undertaking of an enterprising nature," and especially "one involving considerable financial risk on the chance of unusual profit," William Cobbett's *Rural Rides* (1830) already dismissed it as a form of "adventurous dealings, or rather commercial gamblings."³⁴ Mid-century novels regularly employed traditional anti-gambling rhetoric when referring to the stock market. Dinah Mulock Craik's *Olive* (1850) is one of numerous domestic novels that use a posthumously disclosed failed business venture as a device of plot and character. The titular heroine's father takes to drink and secret speculation, whereby the latter clearly stands in for gambling. The linkage is explicit: "Truly, there was coming upon him, with this mania of speculation, the same desperation which causes the gambler to clutch money from the starving hands of those who even yet are passionately dear."³⁵ Secrecy—the complete separation of the home and of business as his exciting world of speculation—symptomatically associates the failed speculator with dishonesty. His reputation, like his life, is overpowered by a proliferation of papers. A newspaper discloses sudden failure, exaggerating its extent; he suffers a seizure, leaving behind a mysterious piece of paper that fails to identify the man who has signed a bill of exchange on his behalf. It is the speechless speculator's futile attempt to communicate his fiscal responsibility, "in characters scarcely legible" (105). The business papers that intrude into the domestic plot—fatal newspaper reports, ironically "partly false, as afterwards appeared" (103), the mysterious paper as a legacy of guilt indicating debt, the bill of exchange that embodies it, and the harsh business letters it occasions—bear ominous meaning. They serve first and foremost as vehicles for plot developments and a means of characterization. Olive's fiscal obligations allow her to develop into a professional artist, and little is made of the mystery attached to the father's last paper as a possible plotline.[36]

Sensation novels of the 1860s, by contrast, capitalized on fiction's problematic relationship with such overpowering papers and their use as narrative devices in earlier fiction (including precisely this elision of a possible detective plot). As I shall show, the stock-market narratives created by popular writers of sensation fiction such as Mary Elizabeth Braddon, Wilkie Collins, Charles Reade, and Ellen (Mrs. Henry) Wood then became reworked, frequently with pointed self-irony, by such ambiguously antisensational novelists as Margaret Oliphant and Anthony Trollope. What is important to note here is that the association with gambling permeated Victorian popular fiction to the extent that Trollope's deliberately blatant juxtaposition of scenes at the card table and at board meetings in *The Way We Live Now* was poignantly satirical of what had been eagerly appropriated as a literary convention, albeit generally with a tongue-in-cheek bow to current discourses in finance journalism. It is such intertextual rewritings, including these satirical inversions, that structure literary texts, forcing us to realize that fiction never merely reflected public perception, even as it gleaned new topoi from shifting alignments.

Far from prizing apart investment and speculation, in fact, linkages to gambling served to express an encompassing sense of economic instability. Even when financial plots worked to occlude expellable disruptive elements, this narrativization was never simply about risk management. Victorian financial fiction was much more concerned with charting false fault lines. Not only did the spurious distinction between investment, speculation, and gambling feature as a symptom of the precarious boundaries of such attempts at containing perceived risk factors, as Mr. Pancks's self-conscious insistence on terming his failed speculations "investments" in *Little Dorrit* will illustrate (chapter 3). Misrepresentation and, by extension, representational issues at large came to be explored as inextricably bound up with the uncertainties associated with any gamble: with the instabilities of the market forces as much as with chances in the marriage market. In structural metaphors engendered by these interlinked anxieties about instability, various papers came to epitomize this power of representation. Since paper currencies were at the same time made of intrinsically fragile material (paper), they opened up a range of metaphorical and metonymical constructions for their exploration in an emergent narrative discourse of finance.

The majority of Victorians indisputably viewed the representational, or fictitious, value of paper currencies with both suspicion and a sense of enthrallment. They created and consolidated what were to become the prevailing moral accounts of capitalism's impact on literature.[37] An ongoing controversy on the commodification of popular fiction made sure that identifications of these different papers remained central even after paper money had long become part and parcel of everyday life. In his 1837 *The French Revolution,* Thomas Carlyle symptomatically coined the phrase "The Paper Age" to characterize an age in which both "bank-paper" and "book-paper" as rapidly succumbed to inflation as they were mass-produced. As a monetary metaphor, it registered the loss of substance, so that if "bank-paper" had no gold, "book-paper" had no thought.[38] Carlyle particularly referred to the mass circulation of ideas, papers (including the first mass-produced paper notes), and uncontrollable masses during the Revolution, but the paper society was there to stay; the conditions of mass print culture had revolutionized the idea of paper itself. In referencing counterfeit money, Carlyle's monetary metaphor moreover described something patently fake. As Kevin McLaughlin has suggested, "even before the disappearance of convertibility or of the gold standard [. . .], the power of paper money is virtual," and through Carlyle's memorable metaphors, this loss of substance became extended to mass-produced writing.[39] In the traditional metaphoric logic of monetary exchange, money is of course always at once ideal and real, substantial and virtual in representing something "real" or of substance. Paper money imbues this duality with an important difference in that it merely refers to metallic money, to something that is representational in itself.[40] In other words, paper money is by definition the representation of something that is already at once real and ideal.

In Victorian popular fiction, these alignments became converted into a source of metaphorical constructions of considerable complexity. That they were often loosely employed testifies to the confusion that the rapid changes in the economic system were seen to occasion. It was not merely that the role of art and literature became newly contested exactly at a time when they were conscripted by market forces to be rendered at once more widely available and more extensively determined by consumer demand. Since the novel as a major cultural expression of the time did more than simply participate in the formation of a speculative society, it transformed prevailing anxieties as well as the structures that were meant to deal with them into intriguing opportunities for the development of literary representation itself. It produced increasingly mass-marketed adjustments of the Paper Age's construction through narrative—in exchange for money that was issued primarily in paper form. These various exchanges of papers, in turn, foregrounded self-reflexive references within the narratives.

This adaptation of financial instability as a structural metaphor was two-pronged. The individual's experience of different forms of instability was both realized and occasioned by financial speculation, which consequently became a metonymy for the indeterminacies associated with the changing economic system. In "an economy that can swiftly move from boom to bust and then recycle," as Brooks puts it, money itself represents instability, encompassing "the fluidity and vaporousness of things" as well as "representation itself."[41] Since paper as a material is inherently fragile, and paper currencies are viewed with misgiving, they suitably embody such indeterminacy. Simultaneously, the expanding set of financial motif-structures becomes self-reflexively redeployed both to underscore the fictionality of papers as an overarching metaphor and to address the commodification of literature and art. *The Way We Live Now* illustrates the fortuitousness of fortune itself as an outmoded form of fiction within a novel that brings out the pervasiveness of speculation plots in a tongue-in-cheek manner. As Lady Carbury lives on the publication of fashionable novels with revealing titles such as *The Wheel of Fortune,* her novels join a mass of indeterminate paper fictions subject to the chances and risks that rule the market: "She had no particular fortune in her mind when she chose it, and no particular wheel [while] the very idea conveyed by the words gave her the plot which she wanted."[42] Despite the inherent suspiciousness and the resistance to such an absorption (Trollope, of course, is being ironic here), the circulation of such papers about papers that engaged, critically as well as defensively, with the conversion of book paper into bank paper and of popular fiction into paper money contributed to a standardization of both as definitive elements of a modernity determined by mass print culture and the credit economy.[43]

It may be tempting to see such standardization as part of a larger assertion of an evolving economic system, yet the most intriguing as well as memorable narratives of financial speculations cut through the advised paradigms of risk management. In adapting financial motifs, they refute any reduction to a policing function. The figure of the speculator as insider crystallizes anxieties that refuse to be easily assuaged. His dealings defy geographies of risk. Financial fraud or intentional misrepresentation, like speculation promoted as investment, consequently constitutes a major driving force of the Victorian novel's financial plots, demonstrating what may happen when identities shift, boundaries collapse, and safety as well as risk can be found in the wrong places. The most effective emplotment of pressing concerns utilizes the permeability of attempted containment. In interrogating the changing representation of financial speculation, I shall specifically take account of the anxieties (cultural, social, and emotional) that speculation is felt to generate.

What I seek to highlight is that Victorian fiction capitalizes on the subject of financial speculation as a plot device, grafting it on to other familiar plots such as, most pertinently, the inheritance plot. In exploring the making of financial fiction, I shall show that while the Victorians were engaging in financial speculation, fiction was investing in it as well. Its interest in finance was by no means monolithic and not necessarily economic. The following discussion entails much more than a reconsideration of the ways in which money was regarded or depicted. Above all, the novel's absorption of financial anxieties as well as of proposed solutions as plot-structures was always more than merely a contribution to cultural discourses on finance. The fluctuations on the stock market came to express a larger sense of instability that could yield a network of interconnected metaphorical and metonymical constructions. Novelists were keenly aware of new structuring devices offered by pressing cultural and social preoccupations. But while literary representations of the effect of supply and demand on the production, circulation, and consumption of literature and art have recently received more attention, a much needed reappraisal of the Victorians' fascination with financial speculation also calls for a close reading of the versatile ways in which the novel genre was remodeled by, and in turn redefined, attitudes to the various instruments of finance capitalism as they developed over the course of the century. Before I outline the present study in more detail, I shall therefore first critically review the disparate historical and literary elements that made it possible (and indeed inevitable) that the Victorians' own attempts to audit their financial history in fiction created some of the most self-conscious ways of plotting financial speculation.

Bubbles of the Past: The Stock Market's Literary History

"You have read of bubbles: the Mississippi Bubble and the South Sea Bubble. Well, in the year 1825, it was not one bubble but a thousand," writes Charles Reade in his tellingly titled sensation novel *Hard Cash* (1863) before contrasting the financial crises of the Regency period with the railway manias and their international repercussions in the 1840s.[44] The most imaginative narratives necessarily go beyond a detailing of specific financial crises, yet a look at their conspicuous presence in cultural discourses can help explain why financial speculation plots achieved unprecedented popularity in Victorian literature. In his discussion of the nineteenth-century "criminal upperworld," George Robb stresses that financial crime might be as old as capitalism itself, but that before the major railway manias of 1845–46, large-scale fraud had been sudden and infrequent.[45] The Industrial Revolution had greatly accelerated developments in banking, credit, and company formation, culminating in a second, more profound financial revolution in the mid-nineteenth century. The Partnership and the Limited Liability Acts of 1855, followed by the key Companies Acts of 1856 and 1862, further contributed to an atmosphere of great instability as well as of great opportunity. Limited liability especially appeared as the other side of the coin of personal accountability as it declared each shareholder liable only for a fixed amount, generally the amount of the shares subscribed for.[46] Novelists were not slow to suggest that this was instrumental in limiting fiscal responsibility. In the words of a bored clerk in Mary Braddon's sensational stock-market novel *Charlotte's Inheritance* (1868), the novel's murderous villain is "up to his eyebrows in companies, but I don't see how he's to make his fortune out of them, for limited liability now-a-days seems only another name for unlimited crash."[47]

Prefiguring this climate of rampant change, the financial revolution of the eighteenth century had crucially set the scene for the speculative economy of Victorian Britain. The repercussions of the first large-scale financial panics disclosed a general indeterminacy alongside international interconnectedness. Bubbles abroad affected the competition between the English, French, and Dutch East India companies, and wars in Europe spilled over into international economic activity. Financial interplay between the French Revolution and the British Industrial Revolution likewise underpinned cultural fictions of foreign finance that were to determine subsequent international transactions.[48] In the emergence of what we now term finance capitalism as a system of credit, economic concerns became transferred from household management—from the control of the house, the original meaning signified by Greek *oikonomia*—to the public sphere of the country's economy. This transfer had a decisive impact on the production of popular fiction, and not merely because, as Colin Nicholson has suggested, it was "seen as entailing the emergence of new types of personality, unprecedentedly dangerous and unstable" in a replacement of the "traditionally valorised landed gentleman."[49] Early literary engagements with the paper economy satirized the credit system, expressing a general unease with this instability, but it was not until the mid-nineteenth century that the cultural and emotional costs of financial crises were articulated as fully fledged stock-market novels.[50]

Speculators in Augustan satire were chiefly comical figures. In Thomas Shadwell's *The Volunteers; Or, The Stock-Jobbers* (1693), speaking names such as Nickum ("nick 'em") and satirical invocations of "the honest Vocation of Stock-jobbing" identify stock-market speculation as simply a new game for rogues: "Sharper! A pox on that new game, / The old one is Rogue and Cheat."[51] The schemes introduced in the play tellingly include a mouse-trap.[52] After the South Sea Bubble and, closer to home, the large-scale bank failures of the 1820s, literary representations of the promises and disillusionments that characterized the rise and fall of speculation manias began to address the issue of credit itself. The retrospective fictionalizations of the bubbles of the past not only made much of the benefit of hindsight, but placed particular emphasis on the fluctuations that denoted stock-market speculation as risky in the first place. Although the staginess of stock-jobbing rogues continued to mark them out as convenient embodiments of a specific fad, their representation became intrinsically concerned with financial temptation. Even the stock-market villains of sensation fiction were, at their most interesting, morally ambiguous characters. In the last third of the century, a project of recuperating, as it were, a profession that had quickly become a major source of fictional villains then prepared a welcome twist for financial fiction. The development of what had so quickly been taken up as a favorite stock character came full circle, and yet the lasting impression of the Victorian speculator remained that of a plotting villain associated with instability, indeterminacy, and a foreignness registered in class or ethnic terms that might perhaps all too easily suggest a desirable expulsion from domestic confines.

Since financial discourses continued to concentrate on the recurrence of manias and panics in order to indicate possible patterns that could be useful in dealing with and maybe even predicting future crises, novelists likewise turned such panics into narratives that promised resolution, although predominantly in order to undercut it. Conversely, the use of literary devices in nonfictional financial writing additionally fed into this manifold nexus of interchange between prevailing discourses across disciplines. Thus it was that D. Morier Evans, an economic writer who consciously played with the developing clichés of financial fiction, addressed a pressing issue when he attempted to reconsider the possible patterns of economic flows. His influential *History of the Commercial Crisis 1857–1858 and the Stock Exchange Panic of 1859* employed "a retrospective glance at the several similar 'dread visitations' which have occurred since the remarkable epoch of 1825 [. . .] to trace financial history for more than the last quarter of a century."⁵³ The regularity of panics may have appeared disconcerting, but their expectedness invited a kind of augury:

> Within the last sixty years, at comparatively short intervals, the commercial world has been disturbed by a succession of these terrible convulsions that are now but too familiar to every ear by the expressive name, "panic." Each separate panic has had its own distinctive features, but all have resembled each other in occurring immediately after a period of apparent prosperity, the hollowness of which it has exposed. So uniform is this sequence, that whenever we find ourselves under circumstances that enable the acquisition of rapid fortunes, otherwise than by the road of plodding industry, we may almost be justified in auguring that the time for panic is at hand. (1)

By the second half of the century, such discourses on financial panics had become a prominent narrative structure in fiction and nonfictional accounts alike. It changed language itself. "Panic," Walter Bagehot declared in 1864, had "become virtually an economic term."⁵⁴ Charles Mackay's *Memoirs of Extraordinary Popular Delusions and the Madness of Crowds*, first published in 1841 and repeatedly reissued over the following decades, popularized the history of bubbles by applying a proto-psychological interpretation. Mackay revaluated John Law's involvement in the Mississippi Scheme in the early eighteenth century from the vantage point of a society that had by then begun to accept the "philosophy and true principle of credit."⁵⁵ Historians might still have been "divided in opinion as to whether they should designate [Law] a knave or a madman," but this assessment needed to be reconsidered, Mackay stressed, given that the man who had conceptualized a national bank abroad (France) and issued paper currencies on a national scale "understood the monetary question better than any man of his day" (1–2). When Mackay turned to a reappraisal of the South Sea Bubble, he blamed the speculation mania on, in nineteenth-century parlance, a French "infection" and suggested that England had coped much better: "thanks to the energies and good sense of a constitutional government, [the bubble] was attended with results far less disastrous than those which were seen in France" (44). What had been underestimated in both cases (and this interested Mackay most) was the power of this "avaricious frenzy" itself, of the excess of confidence in speculation: Law simply "did not see that confidence, like mistrust, could be increased almost *ad infinitum*, and that hope was as extravagant as fear" (2). Mackay proceeded to portray mob behavior as the easily most dramatic aspect of speculation. This underlying melodrama yielded a narrative interest that lent itself to the production of new cultural fictions.[56] They could encompass proto-psychology as well as economic history and the familiar projection of the threateningly unstable onto a foreign "infection."

Although fictional representations of financial panics became a central participant in this interdisciplinary attempt to make sense of their recurrence, it never was only as a reflection on current events, or even as a way of trading on scandals. Undoubtedly, recognition of their sensational potential formed an important factor. Yet the role of such interchanges within an expanding network of influence and intertextuality was essentially twofold. D. Morier Evans's prolific output provides a particularly illustrative example. He consciously employed literary devices in finance journalism. The short pieces collected in his *Speculative Notes and Notes on Speculation, Ideal and Real* (1864) show this clearly. The first of these anecdotal accounts opens up with an emphatically literary, even poetic, invocation of "a beautiful afternoon in March, crisp, clear weather," with the sun "throw[ing] his bright rays over the façade of the Royal Exchange, the frontage of the Bank, and the surrounding buildings."[57] The bright sunshine is to bring to light the incongruities obscured by the demonstratively cheerful behavior of a seemingly successful businessman shortly before the exposure of extensive fraudulent activities. By the mid-1860s, assumed cheerfulness, even sunshine itself, had become part and parcel of a familiar introduction of the modern economy's new villains. Recalling the fascination with clever criminals in the sensational detective novels of the time, these "schemers [are] ready to take advantage of periods favourable to the floating of any nondescript project, the creation of a fertile brain or unscrupulous conscience" (51). Underscoring this association, Evans likens his reconnaissance, his search for "the special knowledge [he] wish[es] to secure," to detective work, while the presence of actual detectives lends additional interest to the description: "Like the detectives—some of whom actually cross my path, and in turn for a moment eye me suspiciously [...]—I am on the spot scanning particular styles and particular gaits" (2–3). This imbues his work (the discovery of relevant information that may attract a general reader) with a sensational element.

Accentuating this deployment of literary devices, narrative interest is not confined to the sensationalism inherent in crises and panics, although the paradigms of 1860s sensation fiction are at once Evans's target and the stock he deals in. Evans offers a guided tour that far exceeds, even sidesteps, the confines of the advice manual. He indulges in meticulous descriptions not only of the location and the weather, but also of architectural change, as he walks the reader through the streets of London's financial district:

> It requires no great stretch of imagination to lead us back to Lombard Street, or other precincts of the general banking community, to trace the difference in the style and manners of transacting the financial engagements of the day—for even, as Mr Ruskin would say, the very stones themselves speak and tell of the decided and important change that has come over the monetary world in this respect. (7–8)

Notice the invocation of architectural metaphors to depict changes in the City as solid and traceable. Beyond this literalization of the metaphorical or a transposition of familiar fiscal tropes (the "whirlpool" referring to the traffic in front of the Exchange is a favorite), Evans draws extensively on aesthetic terms. What singles out his writing as such a revealing assessment of financial fiction's literary value for nonfictional accounts is this conscious creation of fiscal metaphors, this pointed reuse of recognizable stock characters and motifs. He conjures up such well-known, hackneyed images as the "rotatory motion of Dame Fortune's wheel" (51) to adapt it specifically to stock-market speculation.[58] "Gaunt panic" becomes personified: it "stalks hurriedly through the land" with "uncertain gait and distorted visage," and "[t]he slightest blast from his lividly scorching breath remorselessly crumples up credit, and destroys" (36). This may not be figurative language at its most sophisticated or poetic, yet it illustrates the cultural pervasiveness of financial narratives and the literariness to which such nonliterary material could aspire as economic writing and the Victorian stock-market novel evolved side by side.

Many of the pieces proliferating in the periodical press without doubt remained first and foremost instructive manuals or thinly fictionalized cautionary tales. Popular discourse on financial speculation became both more pervasive and more invested in literary productions that could be seen to offer a distorted—satirized or vilified—picture of work at the stock market. As a result, there emerged more direct counterpoints, if not counterattacks, that sought to appropriate financial fiction's most popular clichés. Writers of mainly nonfiction began to work through parody themselves, capitalizing not merely on (partly parodied) literary devices, but on a self-reflexive interest in the power of paper fictions in which they rivaled its exploitation in sensation fiction. Laurence Oliphant's "Autobiography of a Joint-Stock Company (Limited)," published in *Blackwood's Magazine* in July 1876, warns of risky speculation, and yet it does so in a partly parodic reworking of various popular "papers" that include stock-market novels. Targeted at a potentially all-too-gullible public that needs to be warned, this short tale explains terminologies in simple, straightforward language. It exposes the bulk of the circulating prospectuses as fictitious by employing fictional devices to bring out the scam's predictability. The potentially patronizing advice is couched within the charmingly disarming autobiographical narrative of the anthropomorphized joint-stock company itself: "conceived in sin and shapen [sic] in iniquity," this eponymous first-person narrator tells how its "fraudulent career" derives "powerful support" especially from "the trusting contributions of confiding or speculative female investors."[59] What is repeatedly termed its "melancholy history," recounted in retrospect as the company scam lies reclining "in the arms of [its] official liquidator," is a "most timely and instructive warning" embedded in a "thrilling story" (96–97). The choice of narrative mode is premised on this projection of the fraudulent (and hence doubly fictitious) venture as outlined on paper. This parody of the sensationalized fictionalization of a predictable course of events allows additional explicitness:

> My melancholy history is now closed. If I have wearied you, my patient readers, and still more patient investors, my apology must be that it would have been quite impossible for you ever to have obtained the valuable information which has been disclosed in this veracious history, excepting through the medium of an abstract being like myself. (121)

Beyond the extra license, as it were, with which the "abstract being" can be invested, this peculiar narrative situation combines a first-person account of the innocuous object of speculation with an omniscient overview of its own typical "career." The entire plot stands exposed as the embodied scam observes from its "advantageous position in [its maker's] breast-pocket," catching his soliloquies (101). Once it is "printed in so many forms [that it fills] the pockets of all the syndicate members," it can overhear further plotting (110). In one sweep, this acknowledgment of the fraudulent prospectus's omnipresence in a speculative society accounts for the narrative structure, hints at the very proliferation of circulating papers, and continues with its description of how scams work.

Such fictionalized advice manuals policed public attitudes towards speculative operations by laying much of the blame on the ignorant amateur speculator in need of such warnings. Recourse to literary devices in part underscored their suitability for this project, preventing these articles from becoming either too dry or too patronizing, yet these devices also claimed to own the true story of speculation, of fraud, crashes, and scandals. Oliphant's writing straddled different modes, exemplifying the converging of fictional and economic discourses and the formative role of mutual parody in shaping both. His earlier, less pithy, but more elaborate, satirical novel, *Piccadilly* (1866), sketches a history of civilization "from a purely Piccadillean" point-of-view, to pivot on failed stock-market speculation.[60] It culminates in the hilariously bizarre parody of the first-person narrator's failed suicide attempt. Briefly, Lord Frank Vanecourt receives a telegram from his beloved's mother, hinting at a possibly fatal situation. The emergency boils down to old Lady Broadhem's losses in the stock market, and she attempts to blackmail Lord Frank into paying her debts if he does not want her daughter to be offered as part of "a very hazardous speculation" to a Mr. Chundango purposing to be "an affluent native of Bombay," but who turns out to be as fraudulent as his own speculations (87, 82). In an excess of metaphorical constructions revolving on finance, the narrator despairs not because "the Broadhem family [are] bankrupt in estate," but because he fears he is "to become bankrupt in mind" (90). Sensation fiction's suicidal speculators are grotesquely mimicked as he throws himself on Lady Broadhem's couch, lands on a vial labeled "POISON," and taking it as a sign, drinks it only to recognize its taste as that of a "pick-me-up" commonly used for "nervous depression" among the effete leisured classes (90–91). In this escapist self-poisoning, the satire of a risk-seeking society is twofold: "better far face the ills of life with the aid of stimulants, than fly for refuge in the agony of a financial crisis to the shop of an apothecary" (94). In another ironic twist, the draught gives him the upper hand as he takes over the speculations' management, although Oliphant's interest in proffering cautionary instructions soon adds an important proviso:

> I feel bound not to conceal from my readers that I have made it a rule through life to confine my knowledge of business strictly to theory, and though I am as thoroughly conversant with the terms of the Stock Exchange as with the language of the swell mob, I avoid, in ordinary life, making use of either of one or the other. (106)

Despite the moralizing warning, *Piccadilly* is a tour-de-force of familiar fictional clichés. Satirized speculations range from Chundango's "Back Bay shares, cotton, [and] the great Parsee house of Burstupjee Cockabhoy" (279), to "The Metropolitan Crossing-Sweeping Company," the "Seaside Bathing-Machine Company," "two Turkish baths, a monster hotel, and a music-hall" (95–96), as well as the Patent Lamp Company proposed by Mr. Wog, an American from "that magical city" Pithole (25). Avid readers of Victorian fiction will easily recognize parodied scenes taken from Dickens's *Martin Chuzzlewit*, Thackeray's *The Newcomes* (1855), and a plethora of "silver-fork" novels I shall examine in chapter 1.

While such parodic twists of popular plotlines testify to their pervasiveness and to the multidirectional influence between literary and nonliterary accounts of economic developments, they are of interest chiefly for the insight they provide into cultural formations. The adoption of literariness in economic history generated new frameworks for fiction as well as vice versa. Before exploring some of the Victorian novel's most complex engagements with these intersecting discourses, I shall proceed to juxtapose this conscious deployment of the literary (and its parodies) with two historical stock-market novels that straightforwardly reproduced what had quickly begun to be identified as the recurrent tale of stock-market crashes. William Harrison Ainsworth's *John Law; The Projector* (1864) and *The South Sea Bubble* (1871) directly translate specific financial crises into fiction, while contributing to the widespread endeavor to contain renewed manias and slumps by situating them within a history of crashes. Like retrospective analyses in economic journalism, historical stock-market fiction sought to guarantee that apocalyptic readings of seemingly sudden crashes could be absorbed as part of a tradition of speculative bubbles that dated back centuries. Ainsworth drew on stock-market crises of the past at a time when they had become regarded as staple food in the popular consumption of financial narratives. His contribution to this enterprise of writing up the instabilities of a speculative economy lays bare some of the most revealing intersections and interchanges between cultural discourses on economic change. A look at his fictionalization of well-known financial crises shows why some of the Victorian stock-market novel's exponents became more intricate than others.

John Law; The Projector is the fictional version of Mackay's widely popularized studies. As this mimetic representation of the crashes of the past seeks to follow historical accounts as accurately as possible, it captures what had become a cultural myth by the mid-nineteenth century. In the early 1700s, the Scotsman John Law saw his opportunity to prove a newly conceptualized banking system. In Ainsworth's often hyperbolic description, it was a "financial revolution [to be] accomplished in a wonderfully short space of time" in a debt-ridden France.[61] The arrangement was that Law would be given a bank to revive the economy by issuing paper money *en masse* to promote it as the only proper agent of circulation because, in a bow to current fears of paper money's indeterminacy, "it has no intrinsic value" (45). It was a successful scheme until a fever of speculation, combined with political intrigues, caused the system to crash. Not only did France become inundated with paper money fairly quickly once the issuing of notes was no longer based on any solid foundation, but depreciation was compounded by the Mississippi project, a speculative venture that took advantage of the exclusive trading privileges of the French East India Company in different parts of the world. To prevent a run on the bank,

Law attempted to police the possession of gold coin and quickly became one of the most unpopular men in the country. By the time Mackay, and later Ainsworth, wrote, Law had become a touchstone of the sheer scale to which financial speculation could be taken, just as the South Sea Bubble was identified with the dubiousness of overseas enterprises. In the mid-nineteenth century, recurrent railway crashes and bank failures, combined with legislation limiting liability, attracted renewed attention to an increasingly encompassing instability. The cycles of recurring crashes could present a much needed image of containment, and Ainsworth responded to this need both by sensationalizing parts of economic history that were well-known and by assembling a structure that could be seen to repeat itself in later bubbles.

Written at the tail end of the sensation craze, *The South Sea Bubble* bears out the increasing predictability of its interconnected plotlines within a complex awareness of their narrative potential. This partly evinces the impact of sensational writing on an intricate conversion of pressing cultural or social anxieties into plotlines and motif-structures. Ainsworth's novel can nevertheless most usefully be read as a manual for an effective, straightforwardly realized speculation plot. Its tellingly titled sections promise a customary projection of a stock-market graph: "The Blowing of the Bubble," "The Bubble Blown," and "The Bubble Burst." This tripartite structure is thinly clad in convoluted plots of inheritance, courtship, and sensationalized infant abduction. The prologue, set in 1710, juxtaposes the foundation of the South Sea Company with this domestic tragedy. The kidnapping of a child—a robbery that goes hand in hand with the vanishing of a pile of gold—thereby translates a redefined narrative of an orphan's fortuitous inheritance into a stock-market novel. The fortune is ultimately regained in a loophole for the traditional inheritance plot, a plot twist that sensational stock-market fiction of the 1860s, as I shall show in detail in chapter 2, had turned into a popular cliché. The bursting of the bubble, meanwhile, acts as a moral catalyst. As it metes out poetic justice, the moralized redistribution of wealth is almost too clear-cut. Speculators and kidnappers are punished; the victims regain their inheritance. Still, a curious nostalgia for ruined financial houses seeps into the retrospective account. The history of famous stock-market crashes is a cultural legacy, an inheritance itself:

> Such was the South-Sea House in 1720—the period of its greatest splendour. It is now a gloomy pile, and its courts are deserted. But it was then full of life and activity, resorted to by the wealthiest merchants and traders,

and its grand porticos and passages were thronged like the alleys of the Bank of England or those of the Royal Exchange.[62]

By indiscriminately lifting phrases from what had become the parlance of popularized economic writing (such as references to a currency's "intrinsic value"), Ainsworth inadvertently undermines the project of risk management. Instability emerges as simply ubiquitous rather than as part of an explicable and hence containable economic cycle. Still, his stock-market novels not only closely abide by the historical accounts given in popularized economic writing; they flout a satisfactory dénouement. It may operate through a reassertion of the traditional inheritance plot, so that the speculation plot of *The South Sea Bubble* achieves a somewhat forced closure that short-circuits its full narrative potential instead of arriving at full completion.[63] Yet through this close adherence to the mimetic representation of prevailing cultural fictions of finance, appropriations of financial crises can assist in illuminating how straightforward speculation plots were to become basic paradigms out of which some of the most often recurring narratives of the century were to emerge. What is particularly important to note is that it was not until well into the nineteenth century that novels engaged with past and present bubbles to the extent that they made them essential to their plot-structures. As their changing representation over the course of the century evinced growing interest in various retrospective accounts that attempted to make sense of stock-market frenzies, the initial detailing of bubbles as abnormal catastrophes became importantly redirected. At first, interest in recurrent, cyclic patterns of manias and crashes were shown to manifest themselves primarily in narratives that foregrounded the vulnerability of the individual in increasingly indecipherable and indeterminate systems. This formed the basis of a new focus on plotting characters that were shown to work, or work against, such systems. Ainsworth may have most directly turned economic history into fiction, but the most interesting literary representations of financial speculation articulated a widening variety of changing anxieties and agendas. They went beyond the confines of the bubble's tripartite life story, as captured by the structure of *The South Sea Bubble*, to explore speculation's fictional potential itself.

In drawing on contemporary theories of crowd behavior and historical accounts of financial crashes, Ainsworth's stock-market novels can be seen to eschew "thick description for the synoptic view."[64] They form the mirror image of Evans's conscription of literary devices for economic analysis. As James Phelan has pointed out in a recent article, we need to look at narratives of thick description and at those that "stand above the myriad details of experience, using the mode's finite means in the service of abstraction and simplification."[65] They form alternative, contesting ways of engaging with the same material, with the same story, reminding us that "[n]arrative is not just an object to be interpreted and evaluated but also a way of interpreting and evaluating."[66] To tell a story about an experience is always "to give that experience shape and meaning by setting it off from other experiences, placing it in the grooves of an intelligible plot, and judging its agents and events."[67] The changing economic system of the nineteenth century engendered a wealth of uncertainties that generated intricate clusters of motifs. Financial instability was a widespread experience and, in connecting personal losses to a broadening spectrum of interlinked economic struggles, a pervasive cultural preoccupation. Both Ainsworth and, from a remarkably similar vantage point, Evans responded to a growing need to retell, to try to account for the recurring crises it was causing. This narrativization mined the sensational potential inherent in financial crises—an accusation that can be leveled at an admittedly extensive number of the century's financial novels that reacted directly to specific panics or current scandals. The by far most significant and interesting development, however, is that this trading on the scandalous in print soon came to form a theme itself. In analyzing how narrative structures and motifs change as they are moved along competing literary trends, we can trace significant patterns in the novel genre's development through its relationship to historical events and economic conceptualizations. This is why it is essential to combine formal analysis with an inquiry into the Victorians' indisputably troubled attempts to "re-present" economic and social conditions.

Mapping Plots of Financial Speculation

Financial Speculation in Victorian Fiction: Plotting Money and the Novel Genre, 1815–1901 explores the ways in which financial speculation was imagined and turned into narratives in Victorian Britain. The first two chapters proceed chronologically in discussing the emergence of and intertextual interchanges between literary representations of financial transactions in the nineteenth century. The chapters that follow depart from this chronological approach by tracing specific motifs as they become transformed in the novel genre's development. In taking up contesting narratives of finance as both catalyst and tracking device for shifts in literary trends, these analyses work together to highlight how new thematic and formal arrangements shaped Victorian literature. While outlining a historical trajectory, the present study also seeks to stress that the changing representation of finance was not a simple chronological progression, but a complicated map of overlapping domains in which the divergent appropriations by diverse subgenres can be seen to intersect. These points of intersection, or areas of agreement, can best be imagined in a series of overlapping circles, in the form of Venn diagrams. The emplotment of financial speculation cuts through and, in the process, newly interconnects developments in genre that span narrative forms as different as the fashionable "silver-fork" fiction of the century's first half, the social-problems novel of the 1840s, the notoriously populist sensation fiction of the mid-century, including the earliest detective novels, as well as works that are traditionally considered part of the canon of Victorian realism. In variously intersecting circles, therefore, specific structures and motifs constitute the common domain, as financial speculation functions as an organizing principle of both well-known and still little read, noncanonical fiction. Picturing these subgenres as overlapping circles helps to clarify how they relate to each other. In order to accentuate the significance of these overlaps for a comprehensive analysis of the ways in which nineteenth-century writing on finance enriched literature, I shall juxtapose familiar novels with lesser-known works that engage with the same constellation of narrative elements, but in revealingly different forms.

The areas of multiple intersections generated by the figure of the stock-market speculator as a continuously modified stock character illustrate how these diagrams extend beyond simple symmetrical circles. The aptly named Flimflams or Doublepops of early-nineteenth-century writing develop into fully fledged characters, and yet the initial emphasis on satire continues to play a pivotal role. Parodic rewriting works in various ways, as Jane Austen's take on the more and more problematic typecasting and ambiguous defense of the speculator will show. In Austen's *Sanditon* (1817), Mr. Parker may be a more developed character than the said Flimflams of such cautionary tales as Thomas Surr's *The Magic of Wealth* (1815), but Austen's deluded amateur speculator is also part of a parody of just these proliferating narratives. In a similar vein, satirical elements continue to inform Catherine Gore's silver-fork novels. Intriguingly, this is both because of the self-reflexivity arising from the continuously reworked traditions of financial narratives and because of Gore's later foray into the emergent social-problems novel. A close reading of *The Banker's Wife; Or, Court and City* (1843) will explore the startling overlaps between two sets of popular subgenres that could at first sight perhaps not be any more different. Conversely, the persistent modes of fashionable fiction—what George Eliot was to term novels of "the mind-and-millinery species" in her notorious article on "Silly Novels by Lady Novelists"[68]—function as metonyms of a general shift in narrative interest in Elizabeth Gaskell's *North and South* (1855). Both Gore and Gaskell stage an ambiguous defense of their men of business as main protagonists that presage the villains of sensational stock-market novels through force of contrast: the respectable businessman's double becomes an established part of a sensational repertoire.

Chapter 1, "Silver-Fork Speculation and the Making of Financial Fiction," begins by mapping out the making of the stock-market speculator as a recognizable, recurring figure that forms a major source of intersection across evolving subgenres. Although "[i]nheritance, dispossession, and gambling were major interests of English fiction at least from Walter Scott's time," as John Reed has remarked, the Victorian speculator came to be "the most contemporary representative of Mammonism" and, as such, "was to serve as a topos for what many English people feared as the chief economic disease of their time."[69] This topos had a distinct literary history, in the course of which the cardboard characters of early-nineteenth-century accounts of financial transactions developed into psychologically complex victims of risk taking and sensationalized plotting villains before they became redeployed as stock characters in often newly defensive narrative structures. The speculator's most salient attributes take on a thematic significance that helps us to unpack fiscal metaphors. As it stood in for what had come to be regarded as an increasingly unstable financial (and, by extension, social) system and the transactions that were ruling it, financial speculation marked out attendant figures as part of structural metaphors revolving around the stock market. The figure of the speculator operated on a set of interconnected levels: first, as a double of the responsible businessman and hence of risk management at work; second, as an externalization of a fascination with risk; third, as a projection of various forms of indeterminacy (including the attraction of the exotic); fourth, in ever more pressing associations with suicide, as the embodiment of a speculative economy's inherent self-destructiveness. Finally, when speculative suitors turned out to be involved at the stock market, the self-consciously literalized metaphor of the mercenary marriage as a form of speculation perhaps most directly spelled out the conversion of traditional courtship and inheritance plots into a different kind of financial plot. In short, the business of speculation worked as a theme, a plot device, and a metonymic representation of an increasingly speculative economy and commercialized society. While the proliferation of lesser-known stock-market narratives alone already shows how widespread they really were, widely divergent novels can be linked together through their use of financial speculation to drive plots.

Within this complex set of overlaps, the 1860s emerge as a defining moment for the representation of financial speculation. As speculation plots occupy central areas of these overlaps, they simultaneously underscore and modify the sensation novel's cultural significance. Sensational writing can consequently be neither bracketed off as merely a curiosity appended to realist domestic fiction nor considered as the single most influential literary trend of the decade. Chapter 2, "The Sensational Stock-Market Novel," proceeds to explore the self-reflexive reworking of motifs that became very quickly associated with the sensationalized plot-structures of financial speculation. Yet while stressing the importance of sensationalism for stock-market narratives, this discussion also queries this association. It draws on various novels of the "sensational sixties" to emphasize not only the pervasiveness of the newly emergent financial plots, but also the interchanges between divergent popular subgenres. Juxtaposing Trollope's *Can You Forgive Her?* (1865) and *The Shadow of Ashlydyat* (1863) by the prolific sensation novelist Mrs. Henry (Ellen) Wood, the chapter's first section foregrounds the different ways in which they question the assumed origins of the white-collar offender as an intruder. In Mary Braddon's *Aurora Floyd* (1863), the chapter then shows, the "magic" of paper money propels the plot. While the tracing of banknotes perhaps most remarkably realizes interest in paper fictions, what is by far the most significant in the novel's mapping out of speculation's prevalence is the conceptualization of credit and creditworthiness at home as well as in the City. Such reversals form part of a creative breakdown of genres as well as a remaking of types. The literary history that results from a sustained attention to financial speculation indicates that sensational writing of the 1860s formed a watershed for the novel genre on interconnected levels.

Continuing the overall trajectory in this tracing of financial motifs and plotlines across literary history, but leaving strict chronology behind, chapter 3, "Speculators Abroad," focuses on the development of specific motifs. The treatment of connecting topoi in novels of the 1850s and the 1860s discloses neglected instances of intertextual influence, while highlighting interchanges between evolving subgenres as more than simply symptoms of shifts in literary taste or cultural preoccupations. The chapter compares the crucially indefinite uses of commerce in "the East" in novels of the 1850s with the ambiguous evocation of an almost celebratory triumph with which the indeterminacy of such foreign papers is presented in 1860s sensation fiction. Thackeray's *The Newcomes* (1855) and Dickens's *Little*

Dorrit (1857) critically tackle conceptualizations of fiscal responsibility as they revise stock characters such as the Anglo-Indian nabob or the guilt-stricken returnee from an essentially amorphous "East." They reference false clues within a self-conscious renegotiation of the typecasting attendant to public perception of foreign speculation. Dickens's novel thereby generates an incipient detective plot that is then aborted in a pointed anticipation of emergent narrative trends. Charles Reade's *Hard Cash* (1863) and Wilkie Collins's *The Moonstone* (1868), by contrast, exemplify sensational rewritings of geographical risk management. As they complicate the expected depictions of financial speculations in and on the British Empire, they capitalize on the multifaceted power of the papers that seek to contain the foreign.

Testifying to the shaping power of the novel genre's fictionalization of financial transactions, foreign speculation becomes a structural metaphor as well as a theme. The final chapter, chapter 4, "Speculators at Home," works in two sections that pair self-reflexive engagements with frequently interlinked speculation at home and abroad. Their use of projections ranges from the exploration of internal colonization mapped out in critiques of suburban building speculation to the inversion of prevailing modes of typecasting in late-nineteenth-century representations of the foreign businesswoman. Drawing on a number of texts that negotiate such variously appropriated topoi in distinctly different forms, the chapter begins by analyzing metaphors of imperialist expansion in the literary and journalistic investigation of Victorian suburbia's "colonization" of the countryside. Suburban Gothic, as it emerges at the mid-century, literalizes this incursion of the alien, or foreign. Charlotte Riddell's *The Uninhabited House* (1875) can be seen to rework concerns on which Trollope already elaborates in his early realist novel of commuting, speculating suburban clerks, *The Three Clerks* (1857). Both novels thematize the dual interrelationship between speculation and suburban developments: suburbia functions as the home of the frequently fraudulent speculator and is itself premised on building speculation as a form of colonization that brings business and business crime with it. In rendering these dual metaphorical constructions as spectral doubles, Riddell's ghost story demonstrates an awareness of the conventionality of the topoi it deliberately defamiliarizes.

The functions of financial speculation plots as a major conduit for the intersecting influences between sensationalism and domestic realism then offer a pointed conclusion to this discussion of speculation's "domestication." The role of business within the confines of the home and the marketing of domesticity as a sellable, sensationalized article form two sides of the same coin. The chapter's final part concentrates on intertextual interchanges written with the aim to present a specific reworking of earlier financial fiction and its association with particular narrative modes. *Hester* (1883), Margaret Oliphant's late engagement with the sensational stock-market plots she had already evoked in her fiction of the 1860s and 1870s, and *The Massarenes* (1897) by Ouida (Marie Louise de la Ramée), a novel structured on a reversal of Trollope's *The Way We Live Now,* can be seen to rewrite financial fiction as an established, recognizable category of nineteenth-century literature. Both feature foreign-born young women who successfully "domesticate" the business world, a management that is formally realized by the domestication of the stock market's sensational potential in popular women's writing. Such adaptations of financial speculation plots compel a new understanding of their influence on the form as well as the content of the Victorian novel. In interrogating and remaking a distinct grouping of specific, recurring elements, they engender a narrative discourse of financial speculation that significantly cuts across otherwise divergent literary developments. Since the overlaps, or interstices, between subgenres constitute narrated sites of conflict, this study also brings largely forgotten works back to critical attention, while placing the more canonical novels firmly within that tradition.

One

Silver-Fork Speculation and the Making of Financial Fiction

The silver-fork novel, or novel of fashionable highlife, played a much more influential role in the development of nineteenth-century literature than has commonly been acknowledged. Given its emphasis on the retrospective representation of the high society of the recent past, it is perhaps surprising that it became so fundamental to the formation of financial fiction. By registering an increase in socially mobile stock-market speculators among the nouveaux riches, however, it integrated concern with the ways in which speculation was seen to be reshaping the makeup of established elites within traditional courtship and inheritance plots. In addition, it built on and furthered the patterns of consumption of a society in which the retelling of past fashions could encompass both an aristocratic flair that had come to be considered outmoded and the social clashes of old and new financial considerations. Silver-fork writing, in short, was a speculative enterprise itself and, as it simultaneously channeled anxieties engendered by a rapidly changing socio-economic landscape into an ambiguous nostalgia for the Regency, this intrinsically malleable genre had an essentially twofold impact on the Victorian novel. The social differentiation signaled by old and new money rendered the representation of getting and spending central to the development of both character and plot as they began to reflect a shift in popular fiction's depiction of social milieus. As fashionable writing was investing in the changing fashions of new elites, it already guaranteed a level of self-reflexivity that became crucial in later adaptations of its literary legacies.

The market for silver-fork fiction was intensely promoted by Henry Colburn as a venture that was to make the pricey triple-decker fashionable. He counted both on the desire for social emulation among the rising "middling classes" and on impecunious aristocrats' need to write for money, seeking out titled writers to cater to a demand for insider accounts. He traded on an unstable economy determined by the struggles of cash-poor traditional elites and powerful parvenus, what Catherine Gore was to term, in her eponymous late silver-fork novel of 1857, the collision of "the two aristocracies" as the landed classes contracted "intermarriages with the shopocracy."[1] The rivalry between these two competing upper ranks and their gradual absorption of bourgeois domestic values was to become a recurring topos in nineteenth-century fiction, but Colburn's strategic exploitation of this redistribution of power and wealth as a publishing strategy made him notorious from the beginning. The temporary slump in the market caused by the financial panic of 1825 had enabled him to profit from the difficulties experienced by his more established competitors. In his seminal overview of the silver-fork genre, Matthew Rosa speaks of "a series of fortunate financial and literary speculations" that set up Colburn and, with him, the silver-fork novel as an immensely successful enterprise.[2] With his strategic "puffing" of popular fiction, he could be said to have inaugurated the modern publishing industry.

As early as 1825, Charles Molloy Westmacott provided a satirical sketch of such speculative strategies at the book market and specifically of the fashionable productions of what William Hazlitt was to term the "silver-fork" or "dandy school" in a likewise largley derisive article entitled "The Dandy School," published in the *Examiner* in November 1827.[3] Published under the pseudonym of Bernard Blackmantle, Westmacott's *The English Spy* is a compilation of sardonic anecdotes of fashionable Regency society. Illustrative of the inherently self-ironic mode of much silver-fork writing, it sums up some of the most central themes as well as recurring tropes, including the pastiche of the popular writer's own financial projects. It opens up with "Reflections, Addressed to those who can think," an "apologia for a preface" that presents the publishing process in emphatically pecuniary terms.[4] What Blackmantle bewails is not merely that he is compelled to write by acute want of money, while he is inhibited by "a formidable army of critics in pursuit of the bubble fame" (8), but that he is pushed by "the speculating tribe in paper and print" (10). A Mr. Index seeks out the debt-ridden aristocrat on purpose to commission a satire of high society. The fact that Blackmantle is said to have suffered much at the hands of the fashionable world singles him out as particularly suitable for the project. The publisher describes himself as "a man of business" engaged in "bookselling speculations" (9–10). His ideal author is to turn his personal experience into profit. The order is for an array of rehashed clichés. It is a synopsis of silver-fork fiction, sporting a moral ending to a titillating display of spendthrift excess. As Mr. Index suggests,

> [W]ho has suffered more by the fashionable world than yourself? Have you not dissipated a splendid patrimony in a series of the most liberal entertainments? [. . .] And have you not since felt the most cruel neglect from these your early associates, and much obliged friends, with no crime but poverty [. . .]? And can you hesitate to avail yourself of the noble revenge in your power, when it combines the advantages of being morally profitable both to yourself and society? (11–12)

The woes of aristocrats suffering from the repercussions of financial crises sold well. The popularity of narratives of declining highlife was unsurprisingly heightened by the growing market forces boasted by the "shopocracy." The Regency period became repackaged for a readership that in many ways felt ambiguous about the values of the recent past. In a brief aside in Catherine Gore's *The Banker's Wife* (1843), a novel I shall discuss as a representative silver-fork text that exemplifies these shifts, fashionable novels are mocked as consumer products catering to a "financial aristocracy, a nobility of the counter."[5] But it is a Mr. Flimflam, a minor prop at dinner parties, who rails most against "those dreadful, flimsy, flashy, unwholesome tissues of false sentiment and flippancy, called fashionable novels [. . .] composed for the delight of the bankers' wives" (3:165–66), while he himself lives on the circulation of scandal. What I chiefly wish to explore in this chapter, in fact, is the changing representation of financial speculation from its first extensive uses as a plot-structure to such increasingly self-reflexive references at the mid-century. The development of financial plots in nineteenth-century fiction describes a literary history that can best be understood as a complex map of overlapping domains where subgenres intersect and inflect each other. The series of representative texts that most effectively illustrate the overlaps between emergent fictional categories will be taken from the, roughly, four decades stretching from Jane Austen's unfinished last novel, *Sanditon* (1817), to embedded silver-fork elements in fiction of the 1840s and 1850s. Fashionable women novelists saw themselves in the tradition of Austen, while they also reacted critically to fiction of the (predominantly male) "dandy school" that had become popular from the mid-1820s onwards.[6] Late exponents of these fashionable novels in turn intersected with social-problems novels to form an alternative society fiction. A departure from Austen's earlier novels, *Sanditon*'s integration of speculation into her property plots forms a particularly revealing point of entry as it touches upon a number of elements and modes that are located precisely at these intersections.

Silver-Fork Enterprise

Puffed up from "a quiet Village of no pretensions" into a rising center of fashion premised on the mere "probability of its' [sic] becoming a profitable Speculation," the projected development of the fictitious seaside resort Sanditon in the eponymous fragment shows land proffered as market collateral.[7] Left unfinished at her death in 1817 and published only in 1925 as *Sanditon: Fragment of a Novel*, edited by R. W. Chapman, Austen's last work of fiction is a symptomatically fragmentary adaptation of property plots. According to family tradition, Austen had first intended to call it "The Brothers."[8] The resort's suggestive cognomen, however, powerfully brings out the instability of a socially and geographically mobile society. Everyone and everything is on the move. Land is turned into a commodity; a family estate exchanged for fashionable constructions; inheritance subjected to the processes of both building and stock-market speculation. In her creation of Mr. Parker, moreover, Austen generates the first fully fledged characterization of a financial speculator in nineteenth-century fiction. Developed in reaction to the proverbial "Flimflams" of often cursorily fictionalized economic writing, he anticipates the stock-market villains of Victorian fiction. Yet in contrast to their carefully planned, often deviously laid schemes, the hastily erected realizations of his elaborate castles in the air are a foible rather than a serious threat. Mr. Parker is "an Enthusiast;—on the subject of Sanditon, a complete Enthusiast.—Sanditon,—the success of Sanditon as a small, fashionable Bathing Place was the object, for which he seemed to live" (1502).[9] He does not attempt to cheat anyone for pecuniary gain and hence is—at least as far as the fragment indicates—the chief victim of his own enterprises.

Symptomatic of the replacement of landed property by cash flow in the ways in which social position was being evaluated, Mr. Parker's own ancestral home has been exchanged for a vague investment in a futurity. It is a fashionable creation that seeks to move with the times, striving for a mobility that remains elusive: "Trafalgar House—which by the bye, [he] almost wish[es] [he] had not named Trafalgar—for Waterloo is more the thing now"—is physically and, by design, removed from the inherited family home, a "snug-looking place" reminiscent of the "comforts" of Willingden

(1507), the village the Parkers reach only by mistake. A touchstone of rural stability, it is left behind fairly quickly in the narrative and then remains securely offstage. The desertion of such spaces of the past is a literalized re-placement that has rendered Mr. Parker theoretically, if not practically, homeless. Land has made way for circulating papers as it is turned into mere raw material (a mine) and a risky gamble (a lottery): "[Sanditon] had indeed the highest claims;—not only those of Birthplace, Property, and Home,—it was his Mine, his Lottery, his Speculation and his Hobby Horse; his Occupation, his Hope & his Futurity" (1502–3). This displacement of a place traditionally defined by associations with the past (place of birth, of belonging, and nostalgic returns) is not matched by a similar obfuscation in the text itself, however. Landed interest and speculative projects coexist, and the juncture at which they meet articulates larger concerns with economic instability. Speculation, the novel illustrates, does not so much replace property plots as it makes them part of new narratives

Although Austen has metonymically been associated, as Clara Tuite has argued in her recent study of "the Romantic Austen," with "green England," ever since the first studies of Austen's life and work in the late nineteenth century and likewise, in an exceptionally persistent "*mis*understanding or misprision" of her class location, with the aristocracy, her novels register a growing pervasiveness of economic and social instabilities.[10] As Raymond Williams has already pointed out, Austen's fictional communities were by no means feudal and ossified, but scenes of constant flux. Far from forming a "single, settled society," they were determined by "an active, complicated, sharply speculative process."[11] Jane Stabler has gone further to suggest that "[o]ne of the great themes of Austen's fiction is moving house."[12] Loss of property and the potential homelessness of the impoverished single woman hang over Austen's heroines. The Bennet sisters in *Pride and Prejudice* (1813) live under the constant threat of being turned out of a house entailed away from "a family of five daughters, in favour of a man whom nobody cared anything about" (271). Elizabeth Bennet's love interest finds a boost in her apparently belated surmises on what it might have been like to live on the desirable estate of the man she has recently rejected. In one of the novel's most memorable scenes, a touring of Darcy's estate induces her to rethink her decision, for "to be mistress of Pemberley might be something" (382). Alistair Duckworth speaks of Elizabeth's "spatial recapitulation of her association with Darcy."[13] It may be linked to a form of speculation that revolves on the pecuniary advantages of marriage, anticipating what became a recurrent metaphor in fashionable silver-fork fiction throughout the following decades, yet inheritance and marriage remain the uncontested primary cause of the acquisition of estates. Only willfully ignorant Mrs. Bennet, nearly driven to distraction by the responsibility of having to marry off five daughters, can reasonably believe that "nothing can clear Mr Collins from the guilt of inheriting Longbourn [her husband's estate]" (271).

Despite a growing preoccupation with mobility, Austen's fiction primarily retained its focus on the landed classes and those attached to them.[14] As it drew on the effects her brother's financial failure had on the extended Austen family, *Sanditon* formed a departure. In founding Austen, Maunde, and Tilson of Covent Garden, probably sometime between 1804 and 1806, Henry Austen had taken up a questionably genteel profession. In the course of the economic slump following Waterloo in 1815, provincial bank closures badly affected his venture, ultimately causing his bankruptcy. Both his brother Edward and his uncle, Mr. Leigh-Perrot, had sunk their savings into the enterprise, much as the protagonists of *Sanditon* are encouraged to pull their resources together for the benefit of Mr. Parker's castles in the air. Although traditional gentry society endorsed the country Tory ideology that posited landed property alone as proffering real and stable value instead of a fictitious and mobile one, in the early nineteenth century their lives became ruptured by modern finance capitalism to an unprecedented extent. Austen's last piece of writing tapped into the consequent obfuscation of the exclusive values of property and property holders.[15]

Austen's Business: Sensibility and the City

Sanditon is structured on a tripartite play with a misreading of positions: (1) Lady Denham assumes the unofficially acknowledged rights of the resident aristocrat despite her somewhat dubious class background; (2) Mr. Parker's creation of a fashionable estate is removed from the inherited family home; (3) the village of Willingden is literally discovered in the wrong location. The rushed speculator's nearly calamitous reliance on a misread paper sets the plot in motion. The explicit use, literalization even, of structural metaphors verges on parody. Having lit upon an advertisement at the last minute, Mr. Parker simply assumes it refers to a place that is conveniently on his route. He proceeds to the wrong Willingden, where he naturally cannot find what he wants (a surgeon to boost the resort's value), and when the roads turn out to be much steeper than expected, his carriage overturns. In other words, he nearly comes to grief in a business rush. It is a literalized crash of the building projector's project in pursuit of an agricultural village that keeps eluding him. The Parkers have been "induced by Business to quit the high road," to toil up a "long ascent half rock, half sand" (1498). This sandy foundation literalizes the rising seaside resort's instability. At the same time, the crash reconfigures the trope of the young lady's false step that brings about her "fall." Society, like circulating capital, "must now 'move in a Circle,'—to the prevalence of which rototory Motion, is perhaps to be attributed the Giddiness & false steps of many" (1534). It is just such giddiness—giddiness not induced by sexual desire or calculated schemes to entrap eligible young bachelors into matrimony, but instead by a rush into business—that overturns the Parkers:

> All done in a moment;—the advertisements did not catch my eye till the last half hour of our being in Town;—when everything was in the hurry & confusion which always attend a short stay there—One is never able to complete anything in the way of Business you know till the Carriage is at the door. (1499)

This crash is located in an agricultural village that represents "green England." The Parkers are retrieved by the aptly named Mr. Heywood, who emerges from the haystacks. A gentleman farmer of small property in Willingden, with a proliferation of children, and no inclination to fly about for business, Heywood embodies rural stability and agricultural interests. He stands in as a personification of an older economic system that is about to be replaced by the Mr. Parkers produced, or taken up, by a speculative economy. In a key scene, Heywood asserts that his knowledge of his birthplace is unshaken by the authority of the London papers, or any papers the speculator may swear by: "if you were to shew me all the Newspapers that are printed in one week throughout the Kingdom, you would not persuade me of there being a Surgeon in Willingden,—for having lived here ever since I was born" (1498). By comparison, belief in paper of any kind is strong in Mr. Parker. His Sanditon is constructed by advertisements, prospectuses, and circulated plans.

In one of the narrative's main ironies, the projected influx of health tourists on whom his speculations are based turns out to be largely a paper fiction itself, the product of all too enthusiastically written letters. Parker's eldest sister symptomatically matches her brother in zealous projections. They may usually be confined to a similarly speculative approach to possible diseases, injuries, and especially hypochondria as a "luxury" illness of the leisured classes. The alignment is stated with poignant irony in the narrative itself, yet this is only the beginning of an insightful paralleling that plays with the associations between a speculative fever and imagined illnesses: "The Parkers, were no doubt a family of Imagination and quick feelings—and while the eldest Brother found vent for his superfluity of sensation as a Projector, the Sisters were perhaps driven to dissipate theirs in the invention of odd complaints" (1528). Having written, copied, and circulated letter after letter, Miss Parker arrives in Sanditon despite a compilation of illnesses in the family (their own pet projects) to take houses in the unconfirmed names of projected visitors. To Heywood's sensible daughter Charlotte, the Parkers' down-to-earth guest, this is simply "Activity run mad!" (1526). When the carriages of these projected consumers arrive they are a sight "full of speculation" (1529). In a self-conscious conflation of projections on buildings and their potential tenants with a general busybody's idle curiosity, financial speculation is identified with a form of gossip. In other words, the scheme to populate the resort with health tourists so far only existent on paper promises another crash. As this bubble bursts, two expected sets shrink down to a group of four women; advertised and circulated under different descriptions. Yet Miss Parker is only temporarily taken aback: "There were so many to share in the shame & the blame, that probably when she had divided out their proper portions [...], there might be a mere trifle of reproach remaining for herself" (1533). Just as in speculations on a larger scale, responsibility for this particular blunder is cashed out like devalued shares.

As Sanditon itself is replete with commercial undertakings that do not promise well, real estate speculation becomes an overarching metaphor for an encompassing capitalization on projections. Who is going to buy the blue shoes provocatively displayed in the shop windows to Mr. Parker's delight as he reads them as a sign of the fishing village's commercialization? Not the young women of the ladies' seminary. They have come to Sanditon to recuperate or retrench, having run into extravagant expenses elsewhere. Neither is the chilly half-mulatto heiress at all interested in profiting from the donkeys Lady Denham keeps on speculation. Symptomatic of the general pervasiveness of commercialization and commodification, their milk is refused "in favour of some Tonic Pills, which a Cousin [of the lady who keeps the ladies' seminary] had a Property in" (1534). Much has been written on the text's identification of invalid and consumer culture and what is diagnosed as a speculation on the body that parallels, even supplements, speculation on building projects. John Wiltshire speaks of "physical speculation,"[16] and Tony Tanner has entitled the chapter on *Sanditon* in his seminal study of Austen "The Disease of Activity" to highlight the "cognitive dissonance generated by the infiltration, if not invasion and colonisation, of the signs of a new consumer culture and fashion and leisure industry, into an older rural economy."[17] The function of commodification, however, extends beyond that of the sick (or hypochondriac) body that at once is passive and demands attention.[18] The seaside resort is largely erected on a financial speculation on failing physical health that feeds into leisured consumption.

A site of building and real estate speculation named "Sand–i–ton" leaves very little to the imagination as far as its future as a venture is concerned. It is not just that the resort is metaphorically and literally built on sand. Fashionable fiction forms part of the consumer culture it seeks to promote, and the dissection of imaginative projections comprises an exploration of reader expectations. When the Parkers accompany their own (unpaying) guest to the underused, overstocked circulating library, they find the librarian "sitting in her inner room, reading one of her own Novels, for want of Employment" (1523). A random volume of Burney's *Camilla* (1796) reminds Charlotte Heywood of the titular heroine's financial distress, a distress caused by irresponsible spending. While it is true that Charlotte is able to extract useful information by touching a familiar book, the library foremost works as yet another example of commodities purchased on vague calculations both on the book market and on the resort's expansion for which the institution of the library is meant to be read as a sign. As in the importation of the blue shoes, it has been prematurely erected, built on speculation. Such excess fosters a speculative attitude to Sanditon's potential at large, and in this, the text refers at once to the resort's potential to grow, to attract customers (and readers), and to provide a site for plot development. Upon leaving the library, even sensible Charlotte expects the place to boast a suitable heroine for the traditional narratives that dominate the library's stock. Lady Denham's household, when viewed through the lens of the avid reader of circulating fiction, promises an exploration of female financial dependence. A needy relative immediately strikes Charlotte as "the most perfect representation of whatever Heroine [in] all the numerous volumes: they had left behind them [in the library]" (1515).[13] Although *Sanditon* stands in a tradition of self-defensive fiction, the irony with which this projection is treated becomes interlinked with a predominantly parodic negotiation of myriad speculative ventures, promising a successful integration of financial plots into domestic fiction.[20]

The Business of Silver-Fork Upstarts

Brian Southam was the first to suggest that Thomas Surr's *The Magic of Wealth* (1815) might have been an inspiration for Austen's *Sanditon*.[21] The parallels between their representations of the seaside resort as a speculation certainly are striking, yet while Austen's fragment is most important for its absorption of a new cultural as well as economic preoccupation into traditional courtship plots, Surr's panoramic depictions of Regency society present an array of bankers and merchants in order to differentiate between opposing applications of wealth in general. This evaluation of money's uses in and effects on society explicitly eschews a straightforward rehearsal of the "simple truism that money is the root of evil."[22] The novel's main plot exposes the upstart banker Flimflam, buoyed up by "this new wheel of fortune" and ranking "among the worst symptoms of the present times," as is his chief speculation, Flimflamton, "a new and rising watering place, created, as it were, by magic, out of a few fishing huts, by the power and wealth of a certain rich banker."[23] Money itself, however, is endorsed exactly because it presumably has no intrinsic moral value. Its "magic" can work either way: it is "the magic power of wealth in effecting good, or perpetrating evil" (1:232). The redemptive figure sent to avert the evil wrought by such magic is an enigmatic newcomer who seems to have (magically) dropped from the moon:

> You will feel in a moment, that if such magic opulence be not subservient and conducive to your [Flimflam's] circulation and credit, it must be the destroyer of it;—and that such a man should drop from the moon, in the very neighbourhood of your NEW TOWN, and at the very moment in which you have converted your last Exchequer bill into bricks and mortar, is the very climax of ill luck. (1:272)

The reiteration of "magic" establishes a duality that undercuts the novel's commitment to mimetic, realist description. Resolution is achieved when the speculator's "black-magic" is counteracted by identical means. Far from condemning monetary enterprises, Surr stresses how important it is that good businessmen take over the field. An astonishingly versatile writer, he had been publishing widely on banking and commerce from the beginning of the nineteenth century onwards. His *Refutation of Certain Misrepresentations Relative to the Nature and Influence of Bank Notes* (1801) already evinced his dedication to the analysis of popular misconceptions about paper currencies as a suspicious source of money's magic. After the financial crisis of 1825, he followed up with a study of *The Present Critical State of the Country Developed; Or, An Exhibition of the True Causes of the Calamitous Derangement of the Banking and Commercial System at the Present Alarming Crisis* (1826). Nor was *The Magic of Wealth* his only or even first work of fiction. Preceding his financial advice manuals, his novels had achieved some degree of popularity from the 1790s onwards. They included *George Barnwell* (1798), based on George Lillo's play *The*

London Merchant; Or, The History of George Barnwell (1731), *Splendid Misery* (1801–2) a Gothic tale sporting mysterious orphans, castles, and abductions, and *A Winter in London; Or, Sketches of Fashion* (1806). True to its title, *Splendid Misery* ends with the violent deaths of the main protagonists and a bishop extolling the preeminence of virtue, while "the possession of boundless wealth, unrivalled talents, and even health itself, would only serve to teach us, that all these acquisitions will not exempt the heart from Misery."[24] That money alone cannot make you happy may be the moral of this Gothic tale. By contrast, as Surr's most explicit fictionalization of controversies on paper money, *The Magic of Wealth* ironically inverts this admonition altogether:

> Wealth, you well know, has the power of magic; I have a purse ample as your benevolence can wish; and I am confident that in investing you therewith, form a *good* Magician.—Let us combat these Clintons and Flimflams, with their own weapons, and they shall find that, however powerful the magic of which they are the masters, the spirit of benevolence shall encounter it with success. (1:225)

The magicality with which speculative enterprises become invested simultaneously accounts for much of the novel's narrative interest, endorsing a fascination with the very intangibility of paper money. It is not simply that the upstart and the returnee are paired off as equally mysterious foils. "*Flimflam's local notes*" have made Flimflam, his bank, and the town named after him: "and it was no one's business to enquire, by what magic the purchase money was created" (3:28–29). But money itself can successfully counteract the most detrimental effects. An enigmatic stranger of "endless *alias's* [*sic*] of name" and nationalities (1:121) arrives with "a general design of playing the MAGICIAN by the means of WEALTH" (3:221). He sets about on his charitable work with an unquestionably businesslike air: "So—So—Here is work for me! With wealth, that gives me over millions of my fellow-creatures the powers of the genii of romance, I am here in England, where poverty and riches are terms almost synonymous with vice and virtue" (1:39). It is at once a social critique of money-mindedness and a vindication of money itself. In scattering coins among the deserving poor, rescuing the shabby-genteel from the workhouse, and exposing a web of crimes with the help of the social influence that money brings, the redemptive stranger reverses the "magic" of speculation wielded by the likes of Flimflam.

At first, such cardboard characters promoting financial speculation undoubtedly remained Flimflams, Doublepops, or Hazards, personifications that could suitably articulate cautionary advice that indicated affinities between early financial novels and economic journalism. Thomas Holcroft's *Bryan Perdue* (1805) describes "gambling transactions in the Stock Exchange" undertaken by a Mr. Hazard who considers a demolished church "a good speculation" in building materials and "should like to undertake the rebuilding of London-bridge, on a plan of [his] own."[25] Henry Siddons's *Virtuous Poverty* (1804) similarly defends the thoughtlessly enthusiastic "projector" Doublepop. His proposed patent for an engine is the main source of "air-bred bubbles," yet he means no harm: "I caused your ruin—but I did not *mean* it!—I have ruined a great many others, but I did not *mean* it!—that's my comfort I say!—I did not *mean* it!"[26] The novel, moreover, introduces perhaps the earliest suicidal speculator of the English novel. A fashionable young man, having wasted his fortune, pays "all his worldly debts" by shooting himself, leaving one of the most sardonic suicide notes of nineteenth-century fiction: "To my creditors I bequeath my body. [. . .] To Tibullus Melford I leave my bill at the tavern" (1:264, 266–67). The said Tibullus may contemplate "a desperate *imitation* of the last most dreadful action of his life," but is snatched back from the brink of a river by a merchant who delivers a "trite" sermon and a more welcome stack of banknotes (2:14, 20). Tibullus ultimately profits from a fortuitously realized inheritance, and it is instead his disinherited brother who jumps out of the window over the complications of a love affair. Despite this quick shift onto romance and inheritance plots as necessary for this early narrative's closure, the speculator's suicide as a metaphor for financial speculation's self-destructiveness was to recur as an immensely popular motif.

Surr's most fully fledged dandy novel, *Russell; Or, The Reign of Fashion*, published by Colburn and Bentley in 1830, completes and already parodies fashionable fiction's endorsement of speculation plots by linking this self-destructiveness to the bubbles of popular literary productions. As it is pointedly put in a chapter entitled "Paper Against Gold," this novel about "the reign of fashion" is chiefly about the making of a paper nobility, of "that speculating class," "the new nobility, which paper had created."[27] Within this interrogation of identities and social structures constructed out of paper, popular writing as a potentially libelous paper fiction becomes paramount. By referring to both Theodore Hook's and Surr's own earlier fiction (1:77–78), a reporter for fashionable newspapers mocks the clichés he deals in. In yet another of the satirical stabs at Colburn that had already become a common strategy in silver-fork writing, a publisher is said to be "considered, in certain circles, as having a little degraded the dignity of the press; inasmuch as he is favourite pander to the public appetite" (1:80).

The fluctuating fashions of print culture are pastiched within a convoluted plot that involves a "foundling of fortune" who turns into a speculator. He is imbued with all the attributes that become this figure's most recognizable features. Gregory has arrived at the top of "that speculating class" (2:304) through a series of machinations in an intrinsically shady business (involving food adulteration) as well as on the marriage market and the Stock Exchange until he becomes outdone by his double, M'Gregor. In a split of the speculator's expected ends (suicide and emigration), this more successful stock-market villain realizes "a well-planned scheme of flying to America" (3:293), leaving the displaced *doppelganger* to shoot himself. This pairing of suicide and emigration, we shall see, keeps recurring throughout the financial plots that begin to permeate a range of different subgenres.

The End of the Speculator's Defense

Silver-fork fiction by women writers had a complex relationship with Austen's fiction as well as with dandy novels. In the preface to *Pin Money* (1831), Catherine Gore significantly promised her readers that she would "transfer the familiar narrative of Miss Austin [sic] to a higher sphere of society."[28] Yet what Gore is now usually remembered for is her rewriting of male dandy fiction in *Cecil; Or, The Adventures of a Coxcomb* and its sequel, *Cecil, The Peer* (both 1841). Matthew Rosa has suggested that in these novels, Gore "summed up all she had to say about her favourite era—1800 to the Reform Act, the period which saw the virtual rise and fall of the phenomena known as Dandyism and Byronism; saw the last flourish of English Aristocracy, slowly collapsing before the rise of the middle class."[29] This could be said of much of silver-fork fiction. Considering Gore's representative status in discussions of the genre, it is therefore vital to note that her work is particularly versatile, and her representation of the fusion of "the two aristocracies" often peculiarly complex.[30] Norman Russell even maintains that "[n]o Victorian novelist more closely explored, or more thoroughly understood, the clash of old and new, of squirearchy and City magnate, than did Mrs Gore."[31] More recently, Lyn Pykett has gone further to propose a direct linkage between different forms of "society fiction": Gore's preoccupation with the changing social climate after the 1832 Reform Bill promoted a fusion of silver-fork fiction and the other "women's genre of the early decades of this period," the social-problems novel.[32] April Kendra has similarly drawn up a useful distinction between male and female fashionable novels: the "dandy novel" (mostly by men) and the "society novel" (mostly by women).[33] In that Gore's prolific output spanned from the early-1830s into the mid-1850s, her novels can be seen to invest in a combination of components taken from distinct, albeit related, modes and their newly intersecting developments.

Gore's earliest fictional works primarily set out to expose a "profitable matrimonial market" in which impecunious aristocrats "forward [their] speculations, at any cost," as it is put in *Mothers and Daughters* (1831).[34] With telling titles or subtitles, *Stokeshill Place; Or, The Man of Business* (1837), *The Moneylender* (1843), *The Banker's Wife; Or, Court and City* (1843), and *Men of Capital* (1846) engage with the world of business more explicitly, although the most intricate adoption of new financial concerns can nevertheless be found in the metaphorical usage of interlinked "markets" to critique mercenary marriage.[35] The cross-class alliance is necessarily a definitional theme in fashionable fiction. Gore's later novels explore the various effects of the expanding social power of industrialists and financiers with a growing ambiguity. The class that "has ripened in a night," in "a sudden outbreak of national gambling," as it is put in *Peers and Parvenus* (1846), becomes an object of complex inquiry, not satire alone.[36] *The Two Aristocracies*, published as late as 1857, symptomatically concludes with a somewhat haphazardly accomplished union between established and rising elites that is premised on a dubious supposition: "Better suppose the whole world to be as happy and contented as the united representatives of—THE TWO ARISTOCRACIES" (3:230). In *The Banker's Wife*, it is similarly suggested that "the aristocracy of wealth is beginning to be nicely balanced against that of descent; and a few generations may give it the ascendancy" (3:199). At the same time, class anxiety is shown to have become more pronounced as the result of social mobility: "pride of birth was never more influential in England than at this moment. [. . .] The increasing fusion, or confusion, of classes necessitates a sort of fanaticism in the order whose privileges are invaded, just as religious persecutions beget religious enthusiasm" (2:16). Such "exclusivism" constitutes a defining theme in silver-fork fiction so much so, in fact, that it has been termed the "ruling principle" of Regency society.[37] In bridging different forms of society fiction, Gore carefully probes the all too easily streamlined dichotomies of old and new money. What is more, as such female society fiction begins to absorb the newly dominating modes of domestic realism, these clashes between shifting classes are primarily acted out at home.

The banker's growing emotional, moral, as well as financial instability in *The Banker's Wife* forms the novel's most important contribution to the development of the stock-market villain as a literary figure. It is a turning point in the genre's fictionalization of financial issues. Drawing attention to the importance of character study beyond the satirical display of types that occupies an admittedly extensive part of early fashionable fiction, his collapse is carefully prepared for. Hamlyn is "a cold, methodical, prudent man," "the far-sighted financier of Lombard Street" (1:5–6, 38). He may well be "cut out for a man of business," but this does not prevent him from suffering from the strain of "gold-spinning,—all the wear and tear of filthy lucre,—all the care and anxiety of money-making,—all the yellow leprosy" (1:91, 87–88). In an intriguing slippage within the moral economies that denounce money-mindedness as an infectious disease, it is the demands of work that wear out the banker. The morality of his undertakings is not an issue to him, or even to the text itself at this point. Hamlyn is a hard-working man of business whose physical and mental distress becomes an expression of the financial and social turbulences of the time. He at once acts as an epitome of larger developments in society and becomes, in a forgetting of the novel's initial focus on his suppressed wife, the main protagonist.

Alternately evoked and undercut, the reader's sympathy itself can be seen to fluctuate. At first, it is the banker's wife, the titular character, who is shown to suffer under the "evidence in private life of the irritating stress of an anxious vocation" (1:40). By the middle of the first volume, however, the effects of this ongoing anxiety on the banker himself become pivotal. Increasingly, pity becomes mingled with a touch of *Schadenfreude* that suggests that it is a form of poetic justice that this cause of so much general affliction is afflicted himself: "No rest that night for the throbbing head of Hamlyn the banker!—" (2:163). That his sons object to the profession puts an additional strain on him. What Gore does here, in fact, is pairing familiar, easily recognizable types of fashionable fiction in order to group them around her study of the speculator. As he emerges from this grouping as the central character it is important to summarize briefly the main plotlines' intersections. Having "contracted aristocratic tastes," Walter, "his fashionable son," becomes a spendthrift soldier (1:127, 138). The younger, Henry, excels as a scholar at Cambridge and falls in love with a young widow, who is right to marry him only provided he refuses to "involve [him]self in the hateful speculations which have so hardened the heart and dried up the very nature of [his] father" (2:216). As Colonel Hamilton, a good-natured nabob, who acts as the speculating banker's double (the similarity of their names underscoring this doubling), pithily puts it, "[n]either of my friend the banker's sons seems to inherit much taste for the shop" (2:23). In addition, Hamlyn is hounded by his confidential clerk, Spilsby, who has his own suspicions of certain "peculiarities" in his employer's accounts (2:276). This is the first explicit mention that Hamlyn is not simply overworked.

After the novel has gone to great lengths to create compassion for the harassed banker, in short, it swerves away from his defense. Instead, it clarifies his swindling practices. His breakdown is sympathetically detailed, and yet the amount of hypocrisy necessary to carry on the façade only the more emphatically underscores his facility to keep up the deception. After a climactic collapse, his son may well wonder "how much of his father's habitual serenity might be a matter of hypocrisy," although this display of distress also lays bare "the real character of Hamlyn, the banker" (1:296). Hamlyn's son Walter at first dismisses this breakdown as a sign of "mental infirmity" and "morbid emotions" (1:292), but it certainly secures the banker from any allegations of insensibility despite his avowed aversion "to all display of sensibility" (1:35) early on in the narrative. His "mental uneasiness" is not merely relegated to his son, but as the climax of the first volume, it shifts sympathies once more:

> Walter was undergoing severe mental uneasiness; because witnessing, for the first time, inconsistency and incoherency on the part of one whom he had hitherto regarded as utterly passionless,—utterly immovable,—ruthless as destiny, but steady as time. And to behold the man of stone thus passion-stricken,—the man of business thus lost to all considerations of prudence,—filled him with alarm. (1:295)

Patrick Brantlinger has suggested that "Gore treats the profession of banking as more respectable than either stockbroking or manufacturing,"[38] yet it is vital to take into account that the seemingly respectable banker turns out to be a swindling speculator. It is therefore also peculiarly ironic that Gore had dedicated the novel to her own banker before then falling victim to a bank scandal in 1855. Matthew Rosa speaks of "a remarkable coincidence": "What actually happened to Mrs Gore twelve years later is so close to the novel in general outline that if the chronology were reversed, the commentator would be forced to believe that the novel was founded on fact."[39] When Gore reprinted the novel in 1858, she removed the dedication and added a preface. This testifies to the ambiguities inherent in nineteenth-century attitudes to banking and bankers as they are fascinatingly encapsulated by repeated shifts in the text.

What emerges as the most striking adaptation of financial speculation as a plotline is the curiously twisted exploitation of inheritance motifs. In contradistinction to the sons of failed businessmen in subsequent stock-market novels, including Gaskell's *North and South* or Dickens's *Little Dorrit,* Hamlyn considers his own legacy of debt and guilt simply a justification for embarking on even more dubious business transactions. He attempts "to cut through the knot of his difficulties by mad and unjustifiable speculations" because he has inherited a ruined business from his father (3:284). In addition, *The Banker's Wife* swerves back to aristocratic values of lineage, patronage, and dueling as a way to reestablish honor. Even at his deathbed, Hamlyn holds on to his belief that he has acted to preserve his father's memory (3:297). This is compounded by the fact that, being killed in a duel, Hamlyn is rewarded with a death that is marked as "fashionable" and "aristocratic." He may be wrong in believing he can dispatch this business of a duel "as coolly, methodically, and triumphantly, as his business on the Stock Exchange" (3:234), but the allegations of stock-market suicide is sheer libel in this case.

This is vital in the novel's construction of the banker as its central character. A rumor circulates "connecting the event with the fatal word SUICIDE! It was reported on Change that the unfortunate banker had perished by his own hand [and] in the city, one only cause suggests itself to sicken a man of life—*viz.* a scarcity of money" (3:255). Loss of public confidence is more likely to be fatal to the business than a fatality itself. In this instance, it is a fabrication, a financial fiction that vilifies the speculating banker. As a result, he figures as the victim of an already standardized stock-market narrative. Despite the list of the crash's ramifications across society (a standard topos as well), the failed banker is presented as a casualty himself. There is even "something almost fiendish" in the "malignant care" with which every "private paper" is converted into an "advertisement on all the walls and palings of the metropolis, to augment the sale of the Sunday papers" (3:310). This obscures the fact that a crucial part of this denunciation is by no means a misrepresentation. Instead, praise is extended to those members of the aristocracy who support the bankrupt's family. Although "hundreds of Flimflams vibrating about in London clubs and London society" do their best to keep "the flash notes [of scandal] in general circulation" (3:306) in a mockery of the shares circulated by the banker, a young marquis has fallen in love with Hamlyn's daughter. His gratefully received patronage reasserts the power of wealth to do good in the right hands: those of the generous aristocrat. And yet Hamlyn is accorded an honorable death (honorable in a silver-fork world), and his children are matched with wealthy partners. If the stock-market villain has become the main protagonist in a marked leaving behind of the Flimflams of early-nineteenth-century financial narratives, of whom Austen's Mr. Parker forms a parody despite the fact that he is the far more fully fledged character, it is yet important to note that the dénouement circles back to a fashionable, aristocratic world that has been diagnosed as fading. The cross-class marriage that ends the narrative encapsulates a forced completion as it derails the incipient engagement with social-problems fiction.

In the Great Scheme of Commerce

Given the extent of the interpenetration of social-problems and silver-fork fiction, it is hardly surprising that they formed competing narrative modes in otherwise very different novels of the time. As Louis Cazamian has already shown in his study of "social fiction," the "novel-with-a-purpose" and the silver-fork novel helped to create each other by sheer force of contrast, whereby original overlaps were continuously negotiated. Works of the "silver-fork school," Cazamian maintains, provoked "by their utter insipidity a public reaction in favour of realism."[40] Since a number of silver-fork novels interacted with this new kind of society fiction, this reaction was more subtle than Cazamian implies. Its full title encompassing this interchange of genre paradigms, Catherine Sinclair's *Sir Edward Graham; Or, Railway Speculators* (1849) mines the railways' incursion into the aristocratic boudoir in the form of financial speculation adapted as a fashionable pastime. Her idea for the novel preceded the exposure of the major railway swindles so that the "allusions to railway speculation were made long before the recent disclosures, which betrayed that some have been doing on a larger scale only what others were doing on a smaller."[41] In the aftermath of the Railway Manias of the 1840s, fashionable novels significantly began to issue explicit warnings against such enterprises, but discourses on railways and railway speculations in the fiction of the time were simply ubiquitous.[42] Sinclair explored their presence in fashionable highlife through a reworking of silver-fork fiction, while carefully assessing its most attractive components. The resulting dissection of society remains, as it does in Gore's works, concentrated on clashes between contesting elites, but in Sinclair's contribution to this cross-fertilization between subgenres, the revamping of silver-fork elements is realized through intersecting layers of intertextuality. The reuse of these outmoded paradigms as a framework of new narrative interests brings out a working together of divergent ways of representing a rapidly changing society. These competing narrative strands increasingly locate their negotiation of traditional courtship and inheritance plots in "the great scheme of commerce," as it is put in Gaskell's *North and South* (1855).[43] As the following analysis of these two paralleled texts (a belated silver-fork novel and a canonical social-problems novel) demonstrates, mid-century fiction interwove topical issues with some of the most enduring fashionable formulae ultimately to erase them within a new form of society fiction.

Fur Railway Cloaks and the Engine in the Boudoir

Sinclair's belated contribution to the silver-fork genre originated as a sequel to a series of tales for children. The debut of the "noisy, frolicsome, mischievous children" of *Holiday House* (1839) in fashionable highlife at first threatens to turn them into types.[44] Harry Graham is a "juvenile *debutant*" of "general popularity"; his sister Laura hardly more than "a mere lovely vision of muslin lace, ringlets, and blue ribbons" (1:2, 35). The novel, however, leaves both its textual origins (as a sequel and a silver-fork novel) behind fairly quickly to make the most of the collision of the emergent speculative economy and what is described as a stagnating aristocracy. This integration of different narrative modes and interests becomes reflected in its representation of both readers and writers of popular fiction. For one, the stepmother is a dedicated consumer of the genre. Formerly Emily Percival, a figure of fun in *Holiday House*, Sir Edward Graham's bride-elect is the product of fashionable fiction in more than one sense. She can be summed up by the millinery that envelops her: "[s]o vulgarly a slave to fashion, too [...] that if one or two duchesses wore their gloves with six fingers she would copy them" (1:185). It is in the same vein that she takes up speculation: "My friend Lady Glentilt is wearing every day what she calls her railway cloak, lined with sable fur, which cost 100l., entirely made by a little amateur speculation of her own in the Great Northerns!" (1:253). While this appropriation of speculation as a leisure activity is satirized, the production of fiction as a commercial enterprise that equally trades on the boredom of the Lady Grahams of the world is defended by the introduction of a successful novelist.

This revaluation operates through a self-conscious reference to a necessary updating of society fiction. One of the mysteries hinted at throughout the novel is the authorship of a popular novel. Charlotte Grey's *Fortitude and Heroism* adapts a style of writing her notoriously witty brother Peter ridicules as set "in very high life" and "full of silver-fork-isms" (2:221). But if this revamping of an outmoded genre is accomplished through a new interest in moral economies, in fortitude rather than levity, the incursion of railway stock into the homes of the elite features as the other side of the coin in an infiltration of essentially bourgeois values that include self-help ideologies. The consequent displacement of the fashionable characters' social debut by plots involving upstart speculators registers the novel's not always smooth management of the transitions between the genres it attempts to negotiate. In an at first cursorily introduced subplot that begins to take over the narrative, Lady Graham's cousin, Sir Fitzroy Perceval, has set up an old nurse's "young rascal of a nephew" as a railway stock-jobber (1:140). The careful differentiation between the likes of Fitzroy and of his agent, Tom Thornton, bespeaks the prevailing unease at the foregrounding of the rising middle classes. Gore may retain a satirical mode when delineating shifts in social strata, yet her representation of ultimately fatal speculations in *The Banker's Wife* at the same time proffers a carefully detailed fictional analysis of distress as well as of temptation. For Sinclair, the bourgeois speculator first and foremost has the making of a good stock-market villain. Prefiguring the more mysterious speculators of sensationalized financial fiction, Thornton circulates a "choice of stories" in order "to throw an air of dignified mystery over the whole subject" of his origins (1:152). Since he remains an embodiment of vulgarity, this deliberate obfuscation is mocked. His "large vulgar-looking umbrella" alone already announces the penetration of aristocratic space by such a telltale indicator of vulgarity (1:257).

In presenting infiltration, the novel proceeds to reiterate the identification of the stock market as an unintelligible sphere that intrudes into domestic space. Initiated by Fitzroy, who makes her a present of two dogs with the "singularly mercantile names" Ditto and Scrip (1:252), Lady Graham becomes altogether unintelligible to old-fashioned Sir Edward, who embodies all that is worthy of preservation in an admittedly outmoded social strata. He retains "an odd, whimsical, inconvenient fancy for acting honourably," and that "[n]o matter how many duchesses [his wife] can quote as stock-jobbers" (1:254, 264). Her talk of shares is "a chaos of unintelligibility," all part of "that railway jargon" (1:261, 313). Interest in railways, including paper shares in them, is associated with the suicidal and nightmarish:

> One might really fancy that I had married a stock-broker! All you say is an unknown tongue to me! I know nothing, and desire to know nothing, of railways except the price of my first-class ticket to London. In fact, Lady Graham, I would almost as soon stand on the rails and face the engine at speed as buy a single share, for in my opinion a railway speculator can scarcely be an honest man. (1:262)

This is the extent to which gentlefolk ought to be familiar with railways: "as I have said that no gentlemen can be a gentleman who *finesses* in railways, still less could any lady be a lady" (1:264). It is the beginning and end of interest in the railways according to Sir Edward. At the level of plot-structure, however, the detailing of his fading world soon becomes displaced by plotlines in which these new interests become invaluable. Sinclair's intriguing mélange of competing modes rechannels a fascinating inclusion of mystery elements that prefigures detective fiction. Proof of what is perceived as the criminality of such a finessing, Lady Graham becomes "an actual thief" when she clandestinely uses her husband's check (2:170). In anticipation of what was to become one of the favorite motifs of the sensational detective novel of the 1860s, the "conspiracy" Peter Grey lays bare as he traces the check includes the incarceration of a reticent lord as insane. Lord Edenthorpe's persecution is a scheme realized through a fiction, a manipulated paper signed by Thornton as his man of business, the Percevals as his nearest relatives, and a corrupt physician. Unlike in later sensationalized versions, his liberation is not the end, or even the turning point, of the novel, however. Nor is the collapse of Fitzroy's projects, even as they are exposed as bursting bubbles: "inflated like a gas-ball" until they "have shrivelled up now to nothing in his grasp" (3:256). The narrative's closure is admittedly somewhat forced, undercutting the completion of all its strands. The general meting out of poetic justice, in fact, stops short of the upstart stock-market villain. Fostered by irresponsible patronage, Thornton has offended the most by intruding himself into the home of his betters. His dubious "escape" is therefore appropriate to this social crime, and yet he is absent from the meticulously detailed dénouement.[45] He makes "his escape, however from justice," and furthermore intends to capitalize on both ends of the failed speculator, suicide and emigration: he "is now supposed to be in the diggings at California, having made a last attempt to extract some farther advances from his respectable aunt, by threatening to commit suicide over Westminster Bridge" (3:368). The easy invocation of these two plotlines as the speculator's expected ends shows the extent to which this literary figure had become a recognizable type at least by the late-1840s. In his usefulness as the embodiment of a social development, Thornton encapsulates the cultural significance and narrative potential of this figure, while he also provides a negative model for the reconsideration of new businessmen in the shape of his namesake in Gaskell's *North and South*.

Capitalizing on "Millinery Fiction"

Gaskell's fiction offers promisingly complex material for such a comparative approach precisely because her writing has been assessed first and foremost for its seminal contribution to the "Condition-of-England" novel. She experimented with a range of literary trends. Their adaptation could work through parody or pastiche without necessarily forfeiting their inherent narrative thrust (such as in transposed courtship plots, for example). Anticipating the symptomatic use of millinery metaphors within new financial fiction in *North and South*, even *Cranford* (1851–53), Gaskell's most rural and domestic of works, introduces a speculation plot to achieve a minute gradation of character. The mock-pastoral becomes ruptured by a bank failure that teaches a naïve spinster the instability of paper currencies once she realizes that notes on a joint-stock bank are worthless after its collapse. I shall return to the financial and likewise intriguingly interwoven colonial subtexts of *Cranford* when I discuss the changing representation of foreign speculations (chapter 3). What I seek to highlight in the remainder of this chapter is that the areas of agreement we have remarked among the overlapping subgenres of nineteenth-century popular fiction can be found among the work of a single writer, and even one who has been identified with industrial fiction.[46]

Opening up with a decking out of the heroine in Indian shawls, Gaskell's *North and South* employs parameters of fashionable fiction in order to discard them in the course of the novel. In the midst of preparations for Edith Shaw's marriage, women are enveloped by millinery and its attendant narrative structures.[47] They are "in the depth of business—ladies' business" (10). It is the happy end of a smoothly realized courtship plot set in fashionable society; with a young heiress reclining "on the sofa in the back drawing-room in Harley Street, looking very lovely in her white muslin and blue ribbons" (5). She is a ball of millinery, pretty, soft, passive: "Edith had rolled herself up into a soft ball of muslin and ribbon, and silken curls, and gone off into a peaceful little after-dinner nap" (5). Contrasting cousins or sisters of course form an established narrative device, and Margaret Hale as the heiress's companion is literally on display as a substitute and point of comparison: "Her aunt asked her to stand as a sort of lay figure on which to display them [. . .], a sort of block for the shawls" (9). But just as Edith is subsumed by clothes just as pretty as herself, Margaret stands out. The "long beautiful folds of the gorgeous shawls that would have half-smothered Edith" only set off Margaret's presence, her "tall, finely made figure" in a black dress (9). It is a distinction that prefigures her emergence from just such packaging. As the two cousins go their different ways, their separate worlds parallel the divergence of narrative forms. The periodically resurfacing silver-fork clichés map out the expanding interest in more widely defined sections of society.

The duality established in the novel's title is partly misleading, unless we are reminded that London (and London highlife) really is the center of southern England, the "Home Counties," in the majority of novels at the time. Helstone, the hamlet Margaret Hale idealizes with such tellingly vague nostalgia, only comes to stand in for "the South" after her latest removal in a series of movements within geographical and socio-economic shifts. The opening chapter emblematically foreshadows an intricate displacement of narrative modes and the central themes associated with their competing claims. When Margaret's father is driven by religious doubts to give up his position as vicar of Helstone, he leaves for "the North," the manufacturing town of Milton in Darkshire, modeled on Manchester, to work as a tutor to wealthy manufacturers. This happens so shortly after Margaret's relocation to her parents' house from her aunt's in London that Helstone remains the country home of early childhood memories and holidays. London is where Margaret has been raised, where her other suitor, the ambitious young lawyer Mr. Lennox, rival to the "New Man" Mr. Thornton, is based, and where Edith eventually sets up a fashionable establishment after her return from her sojourn in Corfu. The divergence of the two cousins' lives could not be any more pronounced. Margaret is well aware of the contrast between her new home in an industrial town and "the gay new life opening upon [Edith]" (66). Lest this parallelism should seem nothing out of the way of fashionable fiction, the new extremes are highlighted through comparison with their mothers' parallel histories. Theirs is a more conventional dichotomy. Almost cursorily summed up, it centers on aristocratic highlife and pivots on the choice between marriage for love or convenience. It is this marriage market that, in the context of silver-fork narratives, justifies the common prejudices Mr. Thornton's mother voices: "but this Miss Hale comes out of the aristocratic counties, where, if all tales be true, rich husbands are reckoned prizes" (77). Little has so far been made of the preconceived ideas of "the South" that need to be written out as well in the course of the novel, while the new ideas and practices of "the North" are being revised.

The embedded silver-fork history presents an important key to this twofold revaluation. Fashionable Regency ladies, Margaret's mother and aunt enter high society as the desirable Miss Berefords. One sister marries an elderly, wealthy general; the other a vicar. The success of their respective matches is defined by access to fashionable finery. Aunt Shaw repeatedly references "the beautiful Indian shawls and scarfs [sic] the General gave to [her]" (7) as one of his main (or sole) assets, whereas Mrs. Hale is unable to attend her niece's wedding because she cannot afford new clothes, a problem her sister simply cannot imagine anymore. She had "really forgotten" the possible existence of such a dilemma: "it was nearly twenty years since

Mrs Shaw had been the poor, pretty Miss Beresford, and she had really forgotten all grievances except that of the unhappiness arising from disparity of age in married life, on which she could descant by the half-hour" (15). All that remains of this narrative structure after the opening chapters is the dubious idealization of aristocratic lifestyles of the past exhibited by proxy by Mrs. Hale's maid, Dixon. With some resentment, Dixon recalls how she was "engaged by Lady Beresford as ladies' maid to Sir John's wards, the pretty Miss Beresfords, the belles of Rutlandshire" (21). That she remains attached to the family throughout their misfortunes indicates that the traditional, feudal ways of former elites are by no means condemned in their entirety. In a novel so centrally concerned with tolerance and the integration of different modes of life, there is space for fondly, if critically, presented remnants of the silver-fork world of the recent past. Yet its narratives are ultimately cast aside, like the excesses of millinery that would smother conventional heroines. Instead, they become the frame-story of one of the most influential social-problems novels of the decade.

Considering to what extent the novel's opening is embedded in London society, the marginalization of Edith's life thereafter is no less than astonishing when reviewed in the context of the still predominating fashionable fiction at the time. As London disappears in a new dichotomy of industrial North and agricultural South, Edith's letters are reduced to an incursion, even a parody, of fashionable fiction within the industrial novel. At first, it is the contrast of the cousins' fates that strikes Margaret most forcefully, and in this her musings replicate her mother's remarks on Aunt Shaw's marriage into highlife. But it is not merely that the ribbons and shawls of the first chapter are displaced by carts of cotton obstructing the streets in a world of "[c]otton, and speculations, and smoke" (352), where "the hands" (the workers) freely finger the clothes of passers-by to comment on the material in a world altogether more determined by the production than the consumption of clothing. On the rare occasion that Margaret is asked to a formal dinner, she notices an incongruity that marks out a change in herself as well as in her circumstances:

> Margaret could not help comparing this strange dressing of hers, to go where she did not care to be—her heart heavy with various anxieties—with the old, merry, girlish toilettes that she and Edith had performed scarcely more than a year ago. Her only pleasure now in decking herself out was in thinking that her mother would take delight in seeing her dressed. (159)

It may be a development that moves predictably from childlike lightheartedness through wholesome depression to maturity, but as it encompasses the heroine's moral growth, or *Bildung*, it hinges as much on a changing conceptualization of society as on personal suffering. The basic structure of the traditional *bildungsroman* is integrated into a social critique, and it is so by ejecting the elements of the lingering mode of what George Eliot was to condemn as novels of "the mind-and-millinery species." This "composite order of feminine fatuity," Eliot remarked, only drew on social panorama to outline the impossibly perfect heroine's desirability as "the ideal woman in feelings, faculties, and flounces [...] with perhaps a vicious baronet, an amiable duke, and an irresistible younger son of a marquis as lovers in the foreground, a clergyman and a poet sighing for her in the middle distance, and a crowd of undefined adorers dimly indicated beyond."[48] In Gaskell's transposition of a potential heroine of fashionable London life into an industrial novel, the shift from one genre to another becomes identified with (and articulated through) character development. Margaret here thinks principally of her mother's fatal illness, but she has also come to learn that Milton demands a larger conceptualization of social interdependence than she has experienced in her sheltered life in London drawing rooms or in a country vicarage. Fashionable society with a capital S has made way for class struggles between manufacturers and workers. Industrialization proffers more of social and narrative interest than ballrooms and boudoirs. The representation of the men of the North may at first remain centered on the redefinition of the gentleman, which becomes so explicitly articulated in the discussion of the "true man" between Margaret and Mr. Thornton, but it is with reference to the manufacturer's responsibility towards his workers that the novel most emphatically departs from fashionable society fiction.

Redressing Mr. Thornton

Sinclair's Thornton clearly is one of the most stereotyped parvenus who introduce stock-market speculation into high society by tempting the weak aristocrat. When Gaskell's Thornton scorns to pass judgment "on another's gentlemanliness," his understanding of "the true man" (164) forms an extension of silver-fork concerns with the making, or make-over, of the gentleman. *North and South* thematizes upward mobility as an ideal that was to be influentially promulgated in Samuel Smiles's *Self-Help* (1859) and *Lives of the Engineers* (1861–62), seminal case studies that defined the man of industry against earlier conceptualizations of the born gentleman.[49] But while Thornton's claim to (gentle)manliness is acknowledged by Margaret (and the novel) fairly quickly, his role as a master who needs to unite fiscal and social responsibility becomes central to the transformation that smoothes the progress of Margaret's recognition of his qualities. At first consciously "choos[ing] to be the unquestioned and *irresponsible* [italics added] master of [his] hands, during the hours that they labour for [him]" (124), he needs to accept the fact that masters and men depend on each other. Ironically, he trades on this dependence itself as a business opening: "the opportunity of cultivating some intercourse with the hands beyond the mere 'cash nexus'" (431). Shared meals at once save money and build up a better working relationship (which saves trouble and hence more money). And yet it is a striking out of a balance, and as such, part of a desired containment of risk taking.

North and South defends investment by defining it against high-risk speculation. This distinction admittedly forms one of the most straightforward realizations of the eminently useful split between investment and speculation, and it even triangulates it with gambling as a common projection. As a crucial part of her revaluated prejudices against the industrial North, Margaret needs to abandon her biased denunciation of "the gambling spirit of trade" (81). At first sight, this revision may appear almost embarrassingly clear-cut, yet in that the novel introduces a series of intriguing twists within the overall acceptance of such dichotomies, it shows that such a convenient explanation cannot simply be translated into the complexities of social interaction or its literary representation. If the New Man can be set up as doubly safe—impervious to the allure of speculative manias and resistant to the emotional as well as physical effects of pecuniary losses—this requires more than an expulsion of risk. It is not merely that Thornton has to reject the gambling spirit with which his fellow industrialists, including his sister's husband, enter into high-risk ventures. He achieves this partly by profiting from a stock-market plot that has ended badly in his father's case. The most common narrative of speculation is—like the millinery fiction of the opening chapters—contained in a narrative of the past. In a quick rehearsal of a clichéd death by speculation, Thornton experiences the despair that is said to have driven his father to suicide. Unlike the majority of fictional speculators, when promised a share in an exciting new venture, Thornton is an image not of excitement or exultation, but of physical depression: "his arms thrown half across [the table], his head bent face downwards" and "[s]uch a strange, pallid look of gloom" on his face that seems "the forerunner of death" (425). What is more, whereas the father's suicide can act as a warning, the circular nature of the Thorntons' fortunes complicates the novel's presentation of the new businessman. Throwing Thornton junior's fiscal responsibility into sharp relief, the father's fate is also a testimony to the predictability of economic cycles:

> His father speculated wildly, failed, and then killed himself, because he could not bear the disgrace. All his former friends shrunk from the disclosures that had to be made of his dishonest gambling—wild, hopeless struggles, made with other people's money, to regain his own moderate portion of wealth. (87)

This background story has significantly interconnected functions, some of which inadvertently push aside the self-made man's promotion to a possible fictional hero. The moral and financial bankruptcy at once accounts for the Thorntons' position and yields additional proof of the New Man's sense of responsibility. That the son has had to make up for the father's defalcation is an acknowledgment of moral economies beyond legal obligations: "long after the creditors had given up hope of any payment [. . .]—it was done very silently and quietly, but all was paid at last" (87). This fiscal responsibility does much to set up Thornton's credibility in business, yet it needs to be complemented by a connection that is about more than an exchange of labor and capital. Instead, in the present-day social-problems plot, the speculator's potential self-destruction is upstaged by the gruesome suicide of a laid-off rioter found face down in a brook that is not even deep enough to drown a man unless he displays unusual determination: "He was a determined chap. He lay with his face downwards. He was sick enough o'living, choose what cause he had for it" (294). It is a final expression of willpower in a mockery of self-help gone awry.

This is not the only complication in Gaskell's version of the self-help man as a responsible character. The father's suicide invests the family with a history of financial loss as well as of scandal. Their former relative prosperity is why Thornton junior has a dimly remembered familiarity with the classics, and even more symptomatically, Mrs. Hale's millinery-driven prejudices are alleviated by Mrs. Thornton's old lace: "It must have been an heir-loom, and shows that she had ancestors" (96). So if they are not really parvenus at all, this questions the novel's representation of the New Man, threatening to undermine its interrogation of social prejudice. Such incongruities formed a common problem in Victorian social-problems fiction. Reviews of Dinah Mulock Craik's *John Halifax, Gentleman* (1856), for example, vehemently criticized the fact that a connection to gentle blood spoils the presentation of self-made men, that John Halifax's "antecedent gentle birth undermines the validity of Craik's idea of self-help."[50] Halifax's heritage is written on his face, spelling out his "right" to social status even more clearly than the inscription of his father's name as that of "a gentleman" in a book he has left his son: "Ragged, muddy, and miserable as he was, the poor boy looked anything but a 'vagabond.'"[51] Gaskell's novel tackles the problem of inheritance in a more complex and self-reflexive way by, first, engaging centrally with a legacy of wrong that compels fiscal responsibility beyond legal requirements: a negative inheritance, as it were, that becomes the premise of new moral economies. Second, since an almost cursorily reintroduced inheritance motif assists in the novel's resolution, it constitutes not so much a counterpoint to the main speculation plot's climax, but becomes itself contained in a narrative that needs to move beyond the achievement (or reassertion) of social status and financial security through a *deus-ex-machina* legacy.

It is in this final integration of competing inheritance and speculation plots that the need for revised financial narratives is dramatized. The temptation of risky speculation constitutes a key episode that may seem at first submerged in the novel's rapidly approaching dénouement as the courtship plot involving Margaret, Thornton, and Lennox briefly achieves precedence until it becomes engulfed by this renegotiation of narrative modes. The incorporation of inheritance by a carefully redefined idea of investment is the neglected turning point of the novel's reclamation of a self-made industrialist as a new gentleman. Familiar plotlines become rechanneled into a new narrative of progress in which their most popular paradigms (including the successfully resolved courtship plot) continue to gleam through the interstices. The much flaunted speculation that reminds Thornton so painfully of his father's last desperate actions is "full of risk," but would save his endangered textile mill (423). Thornton's musing on this business opportunity succinctly sums up and then rejects the sophistry of the Victorian stock-market villain. Instead of embarking on "so desperate a speculation" (424), Thornton lives up to his reputation as "safe," that he is "so prudent with all his daring!" (418–19). In short, Thornton manages risk by heeding the warning proffered by his father's suicide. What brings out the full meaning of this decision, however, is that the speculators Thornton refuses to join are rewarded financially, while Thornton has to face his impending bankruptcy. In a deeply ironic distortion of a rhetoric of prudent investment, his brother-in-law is admired as far-seeing: "It was a nine days' wonder. Success brought with it its worldly consequence of extreme admiration. No one was considered so wise and far-seeing as Mr. Watson" (426). Thornton emerges from his difficulties financially impoverished, but morally and emotionally enriched. He is rewarded with the desired marital contract that helps him to reestablish his business.

Far from suggesting a disjunction in the novel's negotiation of competing narrative modes, traditional marital and inheritance plots are pressed into the service of business transactions. Unexpectedly made an heiress by her godfather, Margaret has the opportunity to offer the failing manufacturer the use of her money, which is "lying just at this moment unused in the bank, and bringing [her] in only two and a half per cent" (435). After her formative stay in the North, she considers this as tantamount to stagnation. Margaret's "proposal" simultaneously shows her awareness of the need for money's circulation and sees her taking the lead in her future relations with her husband and business partner.[52] In his discussion of Victorian writers' standard denunciation of commercial marriages, John Reed has already noted that *North and South* presents an important exception.[53] We have seen the rich texture of financial metaphors that fashionable fiction gleaned from a more and more pervasive rhetoric of speculation with the purpose to satirize mercenary marriages. It became a motif that could easily be evoked in stock-market novels of the forties and fifties as the fictionalization of the railway manias dovetailed neatly with the continued exposure of commercial marriages. By contrast, the ending of *North and South* proves that "[m]oney could work positively as well," so that when Margaret offers her inheritance to boost Thornton's business, it clearly "serves as a declaration of love which Thornton instantly recognises."[54] Cedric Watts has questioned the uniqueness of this resolution, identifying it as the "plot-device of the providential bequest" that imbues a needy heroine with the financial independence that renders her marriage possible.[55] Pearl Brown has similarly suggested that "Gaskell might also have intended irony by employing the narrative strategies conventionally used to settle the future of the heroine in a romantic plot—the legacy and marriage."[56] Yet there are additional twists in Gaskell's novel in that this "double partnership" also allows the inherited money to return home, as Watts puts it: the bequest comes from Mr. Bell, Mr. Hale's old friend and Margaret's godfather, an Oxford don who seems to embody the values of the quiet, more sophisticated South, and yet his wealth comes from properties in Thornton's hometown.[57]

This reworked marriage ending through the reestablishment of his business with her inherited money and on principles that go, like their "partnership," beyond the cash nexus, completes the novel's conversion of the paradigms of fashionable fiction into a social-problems novel. Bell's money combines with Thornton's second offer of marriage to enable Margaret to make a business proposal that is prompted by love, not level-headed calculation. Although it has been suggested that this results in a form of dependence instead of allowing her independently to formulate plans for her future,[58] this reading of marriage and inheritance as a form of restitution is present in the narrative itself. It is confined to Mrs. Hale's ladies' maid, Dixon, whose "memory had an aristocratic bias" (402). To Dixon, the godfather's legacy means a triumph of fortuitous inheritance over financial speculation. It should counteract, she reasons, Margaret's interest in the industrial town: "Dixon was not over-fond of the subject [the industrial town], rather wishing to leave that part of her life in shadow. She liked much more to dwell upon speeches of Mr Bell's, which had suggested an idea to her of what was really his intention—making Margaret his heiress" (403). It is the structure preferred by an outmoded maid, enveloped in carefully preserved hand-me-downs of a more fashionable past. This counternarrative becomes successfully absorbed into the novel's promotion of the New Man's business. By the time Margaret is ready to sink her money into Thornton's enterprises, the point of real interest is the best way to invest her inheritance for the benefit of masters and workers. It is to the exclusion of the fashionable world as embodied by outdated maids. While it may be startling how much a novel about millinery as well as mills *North and South* really is when it comes to its reworking of expected narratives, its plot literalizes the shift from traditional property plots to a new narrative interest in investment and its double, speculation.

Two

The Sensational Stock-Market Novel

Containing the first fictional ghost shackled by chains made of "cash-boxes, keys, padlocks, ledgers, deeds, and heavy purses wrought in steel," Charles Dickens's *A Christmas Carol* (1843) opens up with a declaration of Scrooge's reputation in the City. His "name was good upon 'Change for anything he chose to put his hand to."[1] In all his proclaimed misanthropy, Scrooge makes "a point always of standing well in [businessmen's] esteem: in a business point of view, that is; strictly in a business point of view" (60). There is provocatively little change in this as his transformation is curiously effected less through conversion than through a form of augmentation or extension. Scrooge becomes doubly beneficial to the city and the financial world of the City, London's financial heart: "He became as good a friend, as good a master, and as good a man, as the good old city knew" (76). Audrey Jaffe has succinctly summarized this paradox: "the story of a Victorian businessman's interpellation as the subject of phantasmatic commodity culture in which laissez-faire economics is happily wedded to natural benevolence."[2] Such a happy union becomes increasingly improbable in Dickens's later works, as he focuses more on the ruthless strategies of "men who have helped themselves," as he pointedly puts it in an article on "Convict Capitalists," published in *All the Year Round* in June 1860. In a stab at Samuel Smiles's seminal self-help manual, *Self-Help,* Dickens lists the most notorious swindlers of the age:

the "purest examples of 'men who have helped themselves' [were] born with no directorial silver spoon in their mouths [and] almost ended by becoming convict millionaires."³ Published when the sensation novel was achieving the height of its popularity, *Our Mutual Friend* (1865) contains a brief, yet incisive, mock-eulogy on "Mighty Shares" that evokes a different spectrality by pivoting on the proliferation of largely fraudulent "papers" that include such self-help fictions.⁴ The socially obscure and morally suspect merge with vaguely foreign business to declare indeterminacy a speculative society's apt output:

> As is well known to the wise in their generation, traffic in Shares is the one thing to have to do with in this world. Have no antecedents, no established character, no cultivation, no ideas, no manners; have Shares. Have Shares enough to be on Boards of Direction in capital letters, oscillate on mysterious business between London and Paris, and be great. Where does he come from? Shares. Where is he going to? Shares. What are his tastes? Shares. Has he any principles? Shares. [. . .] Sufficient answer to all; Shares. O mighty Shares!⁵

By the mid-sixties, shares had clearly acquired a specific, easily recognizable function in fiction. The capitalized "Shares" create a social speculator whose whole reputation is based on the fact that "[h]e goes, in a condescending amateurish way, into the City [and] has to do with traffic in Shares" (114). Whereas the metaphorical connection between such trafficking and human birds of prey is spelled out the more insistently in Braddon's tellingly titled *Birds of Prey* (1867), a dust contractor's legacy, "a hilly country entirely composed of Dust" (13), in Dickens's novel plays with "filthy lucre" to be comically evoked in *Can You Forgive Her?* (1865), the first of Trollope's political novels. In a subplot, a merry widow can afford to please herself when choosing a spendthrift lover over a solid suitor who boasts of his dung-hills, but she nevertheless urges her niece not to be financially squeamish: "Kate shouldn't give herself airs. Money's never dirty, you know."⁶ Of course it often is in Victorian novels, but if the memorable dust mounds of *Our Mutual Friend* or the guano in which the commodity trader Ferdinand Lopez speculates in Trollope's later *The Prime Minister* (1876) are both once again explicitly linked to excrement, their reduction to mere paper fictions (untrustworthy shares and disputed wills) only makes them more suspect, not cleaner to handle. Symptomatically, after satirizing Dickens's pivotal dust mounds, the main plot of *Can You Forgive Her?* moves away even from the substantiality of marginalized dunghills to concentrate instead on circulating paper.⁷ Analogously, its stock-market villain is falsely regarded as "safe" in business because he is the squire's grandson and probable heir. Risk management simply cannot be that easily effected. Instead, the main interest of the fully fledged stock-market novel as it emerged in the 1860s rested precisely in the fissures of such attempts to manage speculation and sensation crazes.

The Plagiarisms of Commerce: Rewriting the Figure of the Speculator

If the 1860s formed a watershed in the making of Victorian stock-market villains, it was precisely because moral economies were being questioned and their indeterminacies made the subject of fiction. Interested in opportunities for and definitions of crime, sensation novels were instrumental in creating the concept of the clever villain, and memorable perpetrators of white-collar crime in Victorian literature were among the most impressive exponents.[8] They had to be in order to navigate believably a progressively complex financial system. As a result, they disclosed the villainy this system could produce. As sensation novelists wrote against what had come to be seen—with a quickness that testified to the sheer urgency of reactions to the increasingly pervasive bubble economy—as the typical stock-market narratives, they could do so only because they drew on plotlines that had become established as early as the 1830s and been central to the reformulation of financial accountability from the 1840s onwards. By mid-century, fictional responses were being worked into more and more self-conscious reflections on the definition of fiscal responsibility. Sensational stock-market novels hijacked such moral economies with striking effect. When a realist writer like Trollope critically engaged with the sensation genre's attractions, he likewise addressed the imaginative appeal, the versatility, and above all, the controversial literary value of financial plots. Anticipating the ambiguity of Melmotte's reception in *The Way We Live Now*, speculators in Trollope's novels of the 1860s served to question the presumed origins of the stock-market villain as a sensational intruder.

Popular fiction of the "sensational sixties" without doubt most compellingly testified to the growing attraction of speculating villains. The decade formed a multiply transitional phase for the Victorian novel, as scholars of sensation fiction have argued. Reassessments of its variety and cultural impact have done much to recuperate some of this subgenre's most virulent opponents as well. The importance of satirical components within domestic realism's incorporation of the most successful sensational formulae additionally directs attention to the contribution of self-reflexive parody, beyond straightforwardly anti-sensational rewriting, to the shaping of the novel genre. Patrick Brantlinger has suggested that the "inscription of anti-novel attitudes within novels is so common that it can be understood as a defining feature of the genre" so that novels "are always anti-novels," prefigurations of the *contre roman*.[9] It could even be said that "any fictional narrative which does not somehow criticise, parody, belittle, or otherwise deconstruct itself is probably not a novel."[10] Nevertheless, the sensation phenomena of the mid-century generated a new urgency that, in turn, helped to produce some of the most self-critical references to fiction within fiction. Since the sheer range of sensation novels prompted their frequently ambiguous exploitation in domestic realism, this also highlights the impasses of any simplifying delimitations of emergent subgenres.

As fully fledged sensational stock-market novels capitalized on the potential of paper's intrinsic fragility to link social instability and fluctuations in the book market and the stock market, they accentuated an inviting parallelism between the interconnected manifestation of paperwork (from checks and shares to popular novels) and what Braddon termed "the plagiarisms of commerce" (52) in *Charlotte's Inheritance* (1868). Picturing the hack writer Valentine Hawkehurst hunched over stacks of papers, like the credit economy's new miser, with his literary output literally converging with banknotes on his desk, this sequel to *Birds of Prey* perhaps most emphatically substantiates the metaphorical identification of the forging of imaginative fictions of disputed literary value and the circulation of paper currencies: "How he gloated over the deposit receipts in the stillness of the night, when he added a fresh one to his store [. . .] and he looked at them, as if the poor little bits of printed paper had been specimens of virgin ore from some gold mine newly discovered by Mr Hawkehurst" (81). Not only is he aware of the "effervescence" (81) of his productions, as of the papers for which he exchanges them, but his progress through the mines of literature is embedded in a stock-market plot. Valentine's hack jobs, though not strictly reputable, are nothing, it is pointed out with an emphatic vindication of the professional writer, compared to the much more damaging fictions produced at the Stock Exchange: "the plagiarisms of commerce are infinitely more audacious than the small larcenies of literature" (52). Commercial fraud, Braddon's sensational stock-market novels suggest, is both more audacious and more damnable than the liberties taken by popular writers, even should they resort to plagiarism.

Discussions of plagiarism and copyright reform played a central role in debates on white-collar crime as well as on intellectual property rights as they were being defined at the time. Since it was difficult to claim intellectual property, novelists frequently turned to the shared rhetoric surrounding the construction of the inventor within these emergent discourses.[11] Clare Pettitt has recently argued that copyrights and patents may eventually have allowed writers and inventors to "gamble" on future returns of their work so that it became "a peculiarly modern form of 'stake-holding property,'"[12] but on the whole, fiction remained mainly concerned with the intangibility of papers, including the effervescence of mass literature. Even as the sensation novel was accused of cashing in on what one of Braddon's severest critics in the *Athenaeum* termed a "manufacture of novels," it posited a "magical" attractiveness of papers while playing with conceptualizations of their fictitiousness.[13] The debate sparked off by the *Athenaeum* was taken up by the *Pall Mall Gazette* in anonymous articles entitled "Not At All A New Novel" and "Our Naughty Novelist." They arraigned the "rapidity with which certain novelists produce what are called their 'works'": the suspiciously massive output supplied by "the facility of a Braddon or the fertility of a Wood."[14] But when novelists defended the popularity of the novel genre, (hack) writers against accusations of plagiarism, and the translation of commercial pressures into often self-ironic critiques of society's growing obsession with papers (including the popular press) in general, fictitiousness itself served to testify to the writer's imagination, to the ability to create a "phantasmal universe," as it is put in Braddon's most extensive defense of popular fiction, *The Doctor's Wife* (1864).[15] Nevertheless, the hack's depiction chiefly expressed anxieties generated by a growing sense of social and economic instability. Hence the usefulness of narratives of the stock market to illuminate controversies about popular fiction as well as, vice versa, of self-reflexive explorations of any paper fictions to argue out discourses on financial speculation.

The narrative discourse generated by the new sensational speculation plots is intrinsically self-reflexive in a frequent play on the power as well as the exchangeability of various forms of paper. It is therefore in a twofold reworking of the popular writer as an emblematic figure in fiction that Valentine Hawkehurst, as a stockbroker-turned-hack, first appears as a minor character in Braddon's suggestively titled *Birds of Prey* to be redeemed in the sequel, *Charlotte's Inheritance*. Both novels feature Braddon's most villainous speculator, the dentist-*cum*-stockbroker Philip Sheldon. This fraudulent and ultimately murderous upstart trades on his stepdaughter's doubtful inheritance just as he does on railways or company schemes, on a steady demand in false teeth as well as on his best friend's death and the insurance money that should be forthcoming after yet another murder. It is in an excess of markedly exploitative ventures that are very different, but are all premised on diverse human weaknesses. Given the significance of manipulative reading as well as writing, exposure is appropriately precipitated by a much-fingered page in a medical journal on untraceable poisons. At a crucial turning point in *Charlotte's Inheritance*, a page that falls open by itself has the murderer's intent inscribed on it by "faint indications of a pencil, which had underscored certain lines, and the marks of which had been as far as possible erased" (231). With even more barbed irony, Sheldon's most daring speculation is foiled by a *deus-ex-machina* will that reestablishes order. Legacy hunters are foiled as the disputed inheritance revolves back to a presumably lost branch of an aristocratic family.[16] As in a growing number of sensation novels, paper's power works in more than one direction.

Disappointed expectations of inheritance of course form a standard motif of Victorian literature, but it is in their sensational realization that comparisons with business in the City feature the most prominently. Society, it is suggested, has become an array of speculators. Legacy hunters look out for the unpredictability, even unlikelihood, of an inheritance. Such speculations are not simply premised on falsely raised hopes (such as Miss Havisham's deliberately misleading hints to Pip in Dickens's *Great Expectations* or Uncle Featherstone's taunts of Fred Vincy in George Eliot's *Middlemarch*); they are dubious calculations on remote contingencies. The "idea of all this speculation as to who shall stand in a dead man's shoes," as it is put in Braddon's *Eleanor's Victory* (1863),[17] echoes through the sensational adaptation of inheritance plots as they become absorbed into newly surfacing plotlines. In the same vein, in Ellen Wood's *Lord Oakburn's Daughters* (1864), the upstart surgeon Carlton is marked out as a villain, capable of any crime, as soon as he voices his opinion that it must be everyone's desire to "be speculating upon reaching [the British peerage]"—something the future Lord Oakburn himself dismisses as "looking after young man's shoes."[18] Carlton's calculations on his future father-in-law's fortune become foiled by the lord's remarriage (and the consequent birth of an heir) as much as by the exposure of Carlton's murder of his first wife. Such a linkage between schemes to attain an elusive inheritance and speculation on the stock market becomes a standard device.[19] The spirit of speculation can be said to haunt aristocratic estates in 1860s sensation fiction.

In *Can You Forgive Her?* (1865), written at the height of the sensation genre's popularity, George Vavasor may be marred by an eerily communicative cicatrix, yet he is regarded as "safe" in business simply because he is the squire's grandson and probable heir. Once he runs into financial problems, the extent of his roguery becomes subject to self-reflexive questioning. As the narrator declares, Vavasor "should have been more of a rascal or less. Seeing how very much of a rascal he was already, I think it would have been better that he should have been more" (2:59). Trollope's novel creates in the squire's stockbroking grandson a murderous blackguard who shares a large number of characteristics with sensational stock-market villains, but who fails to exhibit any charm whatsoever. In undercutting all mysteries and exhibiting the speculator as at once cowardly and brutal, it ridicules the idea of an attractive "wild man" of modern civilization. While the source of Vavasor's villainy is attributed to his desire "for money till the Devil has hardened his heart" (2:244), and this connection with devilry literally suits him, "making the hole in his face gape" (1:41), the risk factor he embodies is obscured by his insider status.[20] In Ellen Wood's *The Shadow of Ashlydyat* (1863), handsome George Godolphin, descendant of an ancient family and partner in "an old-established and most respected firm, sound and wealthy," similarly fails in his speculations and resorts to fraud, "plung[ing] into shoals and quicksands" of dubious financial gambles.[21] His double life inverts the rapidly stereotyped characteristics of the fictional speculator. As these exposures of an internalized stock-market villain open up new vistas (or abysses) of the credit economy's instability, they reveal attitudes to speculation to be much more complex than they seem when personified by upstarts or foreign intruders.

Speculation's Curse:
The Fall of the House of Ashlydyat

Instead of focusing, as many of Wood's novels do, on social upstarts who speculate on a sudden inheritance,[22] *The Shadow of Ashlydyat* shows the aristocracy craving a piece of the City's cake. As it details the fall of a great house family turned bankers, the novel not only sees a family curse worked out in the banking business, but this unusual arrangement is capped by the antihero's twofold social camouflage. He is doubly sheltered by reverence for the resident squires and respect for "an old-established and most respected firm, sound and wealthy" (9). With his "gentlemanly figure," this "most attractive banker" excels in high society as well as at the bank:

> Look at him as he rides through the town, Charlotte by his side, and the two grooms behind them! Look at his fine bay horse, his gentlemanly figure!—look at his laughing blue eyes, his wavy golden hair, at the gay smiles on his lips as he turns to Charlotte! Can you fancy care an inmate of that man's breast? Prior's Ash did not. They were only content to admire and to envy their handsome and most attractive banker, George Godolphin. (241)

In a seeming absorption of the best of competing spheres of life, we are led to believe that feudal allegiance matches bourgeois enterprise: "The Godolphins could trace back to the ages of the monks [...]. [T]o be lords of Ashlydyat was an honour they would not have bartered for a dukedom. They held by Ashlydyat. It was their pride, their stronghold, their boast" (102). The heir, Thomas Godolphin, may be a dull squire whom "a casual observer might have pronounced [...] 'insignificant,' and never have cast on him a second glance" (3). His attractive younger brother George, by contrast, is a charming man of pleasure. Still, before stock-market speculation tempts him, even he is "buried five fathoms deep in business; though he would have preferred to be five fathoms deep in pleasure" (40). At first sight this balance of the hard-working aristocrat and the charming banker seems to reconcile old and new ideals of gentlemanliness, but the mismatched sides ultimately work the family's downfall. As the resident banker, newly married, with a growing family, ready to settle down to bourgeois domesticity, George Godolphin might dutifully follow a recommendation that "business men be at their place of business" (67), yet easy accessibility to the bank's safe tempts him to remove title deeds at night. The presumably safest space to keep savings is invaded by the squire's son who plays "pranks with the Bank's money" (311); the man of fashion led astray by the presence of tempting papers. But his social position prevents him from being regarded as the chief suspect. The ultimate exposure of this camouflage articulates growing anxieties about financial speculation's sway over seemingly stable settings.

George Godolphin's emotional and moral vacillations mimic the uncertainties of finance capitalism. They are symptomatic of a sense of instability in a society in which bank failures recur with an oxymoronically regular irregularity. Just as the stock-market graph comes to embody the ups and downs of the speculator's moods, his body articulates the self-destructiveness of speculation, illustrating what Audrey Jaffe has called "the idea of the stock market as an emotional projection" in Victorian fiction.[23] Godolphin's good qualities, like his hopes and fears, alternately surface and are submerged by his moral vacillation. Like Vavasor in *Can You Forgive Her?*, he is aware of his rising share of roguery, but while Trollope's villain endeavors to trace the flows of his increasingly murderous calculations with the sensationalized criminal's admiration of his own daring, Godolphin is wrecked by his oscillation between guilt, self-deception, and self-pity. The failure to realize his accountability marks out such a lack of a fiscal responsibility towards society as a moral failing. This becomes especially apparent when one of the bank's junior clerks is wrongly suspected of having taken the title deeds that Godolphin has misappropriated for his speculations. This exploration of moral economies, however, is quickly abandoned for a consideration of false clues.

The clerk's main function in the novel is to underline the perfection of Godolphin's social camouflage. This brief episode at the same time bespeaks an enmeshing of distinct narrative modes. Mr. Layton is an upstart dandy, introduced through a satirized rendering of silver-fork fiction. He becomes a suspect in a likewise partly parodied detective plot that is as quickly short-circuited. His seemingly spendthrift behavior is a false lead that induces an old clerk, loyal to the point of feudal obeisance, to play amateur detective as he registers the "display of glass" and the "sight of the silver forks" in the young man's house as evidence of his guilt: "Wine, and wax candles, and silver forks, and supper, and visitors!—who but Layton could have taken the deeds?" (280). It is revealed very quickly that an uncle of Layton's wife allows them an addition to their income. This subplot is chiefly comical, yet it foregrounds the tragedy of Ashlydyat's fall—a fall linked to slumps in the stock market. The misleading clue does not so much enhance any mystery as confirm the unlikelihood that a Godolphin could possibly be suspected by anyone who may feel any residue of feudal allegiance to the family.

In a doubling common in nineteenth-century domestic Gothic, Godolphin's original tempter, Verrall alias Rustin, serves as the vacillating stock-market antihero's *doppelganger*. He operates as an externalization of the double life in that he renders it literal. Called Rustin in town, Verrall in the country, and at the center of "the great bill-discounting firm, Trueworthy and Co" (202), to which he goes "*incog.*" (43), he is a characterless "gentleman from London" of whom nothing is known "except that he was fond of field sports, and appeared to be a man of money" (17). It is an essential feature of the firm's "internal economy" that "no client ever got to see Mr Trueworthy" (202). An appropriate embodiment of the intangibility associated with financial speculation, he is "invariably invisible" (202). He is an alien entity with no traceable origins: "Who is he? Where did he come from? Did he drop from the moon?" (74). Yet precisely because the double himself deploys a fictitious *doppelganger,* any easy projection as an expulsion of risk is cut short. Verrall invokes Rustin as an elusive, tight-fisted partner against whom he pretends to defend Godolphin. It is through the splitting and hence the further obfuscation of these unstable identities that the speculator manages to infiltrate aristocratic strongholds.

But in a sensation novel in which supernatural premonition breaks through domestic realism, the specter of speculation altogether engenders a different spookiness that brings out fear of a wider instability, while relocating domestic Gothic once again in redefined aristocratic spaces.

Chapter Two

The squire's son is led to destroy the family, ironically by setting loose an ancestral legacy. As his financial irresponsibility brings down the House of Ashlydyat, it realizes its famed curse and consequently does away with its inherited mystery: an "old tradition in our family—a superstition I suppose you will call it" (15). This tradition foretells that when the Godolphins leave Ashlydyat, their ruin is at hand. It is prefigured by the mysterious apparition of a dark "shadow" lying over a plain on the estate. This preternatural occurrence is never disproved in the novel. Instead, "the Shadow" duly disappears once the prophecy has been fulfilled. An appropriately intangible heirloom, it embodies a guilty inheritance and, with a barbed hint at George Godolphin's addiction to speculation, a hereditary strain of wickedness that manifests itself in a proclivity towards gambling. Family history recounts that a "wicked Godolphin (by which complimentary appellation his descendants distinguish him) had cut off the entail, and gambled the estate away" (10). In this "updating" of the wicked Godolphin in the guise of a stock-market speculator, the family curse is worked out by the banking business:

> You are aware that Ashlydyat is not entailed. It is bequeathed from father to son; and to the bequest in each will, so far as I have cognizance of the past wills, there has always been appended a clause—a request—I should best say an injunction—never to quit Ashlydyat. "When once you shall come into possession of Ashlydyat, guard it as your stronghold: resign it neither to your heir nor to a stranger: remain in it until death shall take you." (16)

Eventually, this stronghold circulates as a commodity: George Godolphin "had sent that fair and proud inheritance of the Godolphins, Ashlydyat, into the market; and had hastened the passage of his brother to the grave" (412). Verrall, it is true, exploits a weakness traditionally associated with the aristocracy when he lures Godolphin into casinos abroad and strategically deploys carelessly frivolous Charlotte Pain, the fashionable sister of Verrall's wife, as the chief charm of his own company. But both aristocratic *fracas* and gambling for pleasure really work as a Trojan horse to initiate Godolphin into the high-risk games of finance capitalism. Verrall tempts him with paper money's misleading tangibility. The sensational language invests this transaction with an ominous magicality:

> He held out a heavy roll of notes to George. The latter's eager fingers clutched them: [. . .] Mr Verrall could not have taken a more efficient way of inducing him to play again, than to affect this easy indifference, and to

leave the money under his eyes, touching his fingers, fevering his brain. George took up the notes. (161)

It is important to keep in mind that Victorian moral discourses on speculation regularly denounced it as a form of gambling, often to distinguish it from investment. Stock-market speculation is described in terms of addiction. Tricked into this game, George Godolphin leads a hypocrite's double life: "Never a man more free from care (if appearances might be trusted)" (225). At the domestic breakfast table, he splits into two men: "There must have been two George Godolphins surely at this moment! The outer, presented to the world, gay, smiling, and careless; the inner, kept for his own private and especial delectation, grim, dark, and ghastly" (251). Part of him still believes that he has "a good deal of paper in the market" (288) in more senses than one. Most stock-market villains abscond or just as effectively disappear by committing suicide. But Godolphin is unable to pay his debts precisely because of his disarming generosity, and the result catches him by surprise. What is at the root of his irresponsibility is, in fact, innocence in financial matters. It is without doubt a somewhat forced excuse, considering that he has been trained as a banker. Nonetheless, his generosity redeems him: "The money in George's pockets amounted—*I am telling you truth*—to three and sixpence. With all his faults, he was open-hearted, open-handed" (305). When he commits fraud, he does it out of desperation, and his financial hypocrisy is preferable to the deception practiced by Verrall.

This is of course not to say that being hypocritical is a redeeming quality. On the contrary, Godolphin's hypocrisy is a form of social fraud that leads to forgery. It appropriately strips off his identity as Ashlydyat's heir. His questionable escape cannot even act as an exorcism, as exile or suicide does in so many subsequent stock-market novels. His wife and brother die of the worry he has caused; his child is practically orphaned; both the estate and the bank are ruined: "It was even so. The Bank had stopped. The good old firm of Godolphin, Crosse, and Godolphin had—GONE!" (294). Instead, George Godolphin's exportation to India suggests that the speculating gentleman's apposite punishment is a loss of status. The appointment is "[n]othing so grand" as a civil service position, but "only mercantile. The situation is at an indigo merchant's, or planter's" (412). Godolphin has lost his estate, reputation, and even his cultural capital in the shape of the cherished tradition of the family curse. In reversing the speculator's favored fiction that money can buy entry into aristocratic estate, Wood's novel posits speculation not only as the invading force of upstarts, but also as the aristocracy's self-destructive interest in bourgeois business openings.

When Trollope works middle-class morality into aristocratic plots, financial hypocrisy similarly proffers new enterprises to stock-market villains. However, while charming Godolphin is among the most self-tortured of sensation fiction's speculators, Vavasor is Trollope's most brilliantly calculative and most sensationalized villain.

The Cost of Hypocrisy: The Insider's Export

Ironically, if George Vavasor had been more of a hypocrite, he would not have been disinherited, and his speculation on his grandfather's estate would have paid off. He would not have felt pressed to rely on his cousin's money and her jittering (rising and falling) love interest in him, and the full extent of his villainy would never have been exposed. Like many presumptive heirs to estates, from the Blifils in *Tom Jones* to Mr. Elliot in *Persuasion*, Vavasor starts out by speculating on his inheritance. But while these earlier hypocrites are ultimately deposed of in triumph by truthful, open characters—Mr. Elliot's main flaw is indeed that he is "rational, discreet, polished" but "not open" (1318)—in an important move away from early-eighteenth-century concepts of politeness,[24] Vavasor finds in commercial enterprises and their increasing accessibility a new venture for hypocrisy as well as for financial speculation. His attempts to play the lover in order to have a rightful hold over his cousin's resources, his dabbling in politics as a mercenary scheme, and, in addition, his involvement in Alice's self-deceit add to a peculiarly financial hypocrisy: a mixture of self-deceiving insincerity and deliberate misrepresentations of his pecuniary obligations. He regards all contracts, including his engagement to Alice, in a monetary light. This is also why he attempts murder: he resents secret money transactions made behind his back as a personal insult. In the same vein, what sets his involvement in the stock market in motion is tellingly a quarrel with Old Vavasor about raising money on the estate to invest it in a "trade [that] might be extended indefinitely by the use of a few thousand pounds at moderate interest. Old Mr Vavasor was furious. No documents and no assurances could make him lay aside a belief that the wine merchants, and the business, and his grandson were all ruined and ruinous together. No one but a ruined man would attempt to raise money on the family estate!"(1:36–37). His position as presumptive heir roots Vavasor firmly in traditional inheritance plots, yet only in order to underscore his insider status. Like Wood's Godolphin, he poses a threat from within that fails to stand out clearly because it is endemic to society. Both novels suggest that a stock-market villain is as likely to be a seemingly safe squire as to shelter social obscurity behind bourgeois façades. Yet George Vavasor looks the villain. The seeming indeterminacy of the danger he poses is spelled out with ironic emphasis rather than exposed with a sensational flourish. His excitement about indefinitely extending businesses, moreover, finds its match in prejudice against turning landed wealth into circulating paper. In his quarrel with the old squire, the emergent speculator looks "like the devil himself" (1:41). Vavasor's scarred visage may align him with Byronic villains, yet this is in the very face of his own dismissal of romance as "all very well" for bedtime reading, "but when it comes to be mixed up with one's business it plays the devil" (1:398). If chapter 4, "George Vavasor, the Wild Man," introduces him as a "wild man," it posits a wildness of quite a different order: "It will no doubt be understood that George Vavasor did not roam about in the woods unshorn, or wear leathern trappings and sandals, like Robinson Crusoe, instead of coats and trousers. His wildness was of another kind" (1:34). This "wildness" and a reputation in the City reinforce each other: "In fact, he stood well on 'Change. [. . .] He was a stockbroker, a thorough-going Radical, and yet he was the heir to a fine estate, which had come down from father to son for four hundred years! There was something captivating about his history and adventures" (1:37–38). In an "established firm" of wine merchants, he symptomatically "scared his partners by the boldness and extent of his views," and when the quarrel with the squire puts a stop to his projected investments, he turns to more amenable ventures that require no capital: "After that George Vavasor had become a stockbroker, and a stockbroker he was now" (1:36–37). It is a suitable occupation, but it is considered "captivating" that he is at the same time heir to a "fine estate."

His hypocrisy is realized the most effectively as he capitalizes on the love interest that is perhaps all too generously expressed by his cousin Alice Vavasor. Increasingly, it is not only that their peculiarly pecuniary engagement is shown to lead to violent crime. The exposure of his calculations is complemented by the more traditional condemnation of a gambler and womanizer, as if to emphasize that it is really no great loss when Alice chooses her more colorless suitor, the financially and emotionally stable Mr. Grey after all. With the quick introduction of an abandoned woman as the undesirable output of another failed venture, or gamble, the wild man is additionally painted black: "You and I, Jane, have not played our cards very well" (2:325). All his gambles and gambols only underscore his calculations on the stock-market, his fiancée's (financial) reliability, and his grandfather's will—calculations that ironically fail precisely because he has left the instability he embodies out of the equation. Still, what condemns him most is the circulation of his fiancée's name on bills the City takes up "first horizontally, and then, with a twist of its hand, perpendicularly [. . .], as though it were not esteemed a good name on Change" (2:209), in a chapter tellingly titled "Alice Vavasor's Name gets into the Money Market."

While tapping into the already familiar pairing of landed solidity and unstable paper currencies, this association of the insider with the notorious indeterminacy of the money market doubles as the narrative node of the novel's loosely dovetailed plotlines. George Vavasor's calculated speculations in the fields of politics, marriage, and the stock market put him in sharp contrast to the unlucky gambler Burgo Fitzgerald, Plantagenet Palliser's rival for Lady Glencora's affections in the second main plot. While Vavasor's parliamentary career poses him against Palliser, "a steady, practical man of business, [. . .] with a deal of work in him, belonging to the race from which English ministers ought, in [the Duke's] opinion, to be taken" (1:194–195), and with no interest in risky speculation of any kind, Burgo's function as a traditional "wild man" highlights the extent, or kind, of Vavasor's villainy. Parliament means an expensive gamble for this "type of commercial politician" without private means, a "would-be political type most abhorrent to Trollope," as John Halperin has pointed out.[25] Politics is a wild speculation in itself, but the disappointments it entails also drive Vavasor wild. For him, it is an "immoralising process" that is helped by that part of his greed that is "indigenous" to his aspirations, yet which sets him onto a career path to become what Halperin terms "a real criminal" when the speculator attempts murder.[26] This additionally illuminates Palliser's old-fashioned code of honor, yet it does so by detracting from the Pallisers' centrality in the novel.

Despite its origins in Trollope's 1850 play *The Noble Jilt, Can You Forgive Her?* has been read chiefly for its introduction of the Pallisers. Juliet McMaster has already cautioned that this makes it "tempting to concentrate on the Glencora subplot [. . .] at the expense of the main plot, that which concerns Alice Vavasor," although the novel's three plots are also constructed as a set of parallels: it "shows a girl, a wife and a widow each hesitating between two suitors—'the worthy man and the wild man.'"[27] Introduced as "the speculating lover" interested in Glencora's fortune as much as in her love (1:2), Burgo fails to calculate the odds accurately, and precisely this failure distinguishes him from the novel's stockbroking villain. The third plot offers a comical counterpoint: Mr. Cheesacre of Oileymead attempts to outdo impecunious Captain Bellfield with his "solid attractions" that include "the fat cattle which he sends to market" and the "heaps of manure raised like the streets of a little city [which are] all paid for" (1:139–40). While Vavasor passes around his fiancée's name on paper,

Cheesacre boasts too much of earthy substantiality: "There ain't any of my paper flying about, Mrs Greenow. I'm Samuel Cheesacre of Oileymead, and it's all my own" (1:96). Yet he shares this preference for money talk with Vavasor, not Grey, and in the end spoils his proposal because he really should talk "a little more about [his] passion and a little less about [his] purse" (1:423). This fusion of marriage and business proposals underlines the critique of domestic politics as a mirror image of political corruption. Cheesacre may accuse Bellfield of forgery, but the latter is "simply an idle scamp" (2:260). He is a relatively safe undertaking the widow Greenow can afford, while she recommends Cheesacre to her penniless niece. Bellfield is a void investment, but not a risky venture:

> Indeed, for a woman wanting a husband of that sort, Captain Bellfield was a safer venture than would be a man of higher standing among his creditors. It is true Bellfield might have been a forger, or a thief, or a returned convict,—but then his debts could not be large. Let him have done his best, he could not have obtained credit for a thousand pounds; whereas, no one could tell the liabilities of a gentleman of high standing. Burgo Fitzgerald was a gentleman of high standing, and his creditors would have swallowed up every shilling that Mrs Greenow possessed; but with Captain Bellfield she was comparatively safe. (2:259–60)

Low credit makes Bellfield a safer version of "poor Burgo," a luxury commodity that can be kept within bounds. Both are mercenary as well as extravagant, yet there is sympathy for both. The fraudulent captain sees a secure livelihood in the widow; Burgo perceives Glencora's love as "a great chance," but "[w]ho can say, too, that his only regret was for the money?" (1:187–88). Just as a reckless plunge gruesomely puts his horse's "career" at an end (1:186), Burgo rides over those willing to support him, whether financially or emotionally, without intending to inflict pain. The same can certainly not be said for Vavasor: "George Vavasor would have ground his victims up to powder if he knew how; but Burgo Fitzgerald desired to hurt no one" (2:264). A spoiled beauty, Burgo ends up living on Palliser's assistance. Vavasor's wild allure is more ominous, manifest in a cowing cicatrix and eyes of "forbidding brilliance" (1:364). Burgo certainly resents his financial dependence, but Grey's transactions to prevent Alice's exploitation nearly get him killed. The attraction of wildness as such serves as a red herring when it comes to the juxtaposition of the novel's three "wild men."

There is considerable irony in the novel's inversion of any straightforward moral statement on prudence. To be "over-prudent" may generate a prevarication that follows the fluctuations of stock-market graphs in the same vein as risk taking does. Alice vacillates between suitors because she is "over-prudent in calculating the chances of her happiness and of his" (1:112). This complicates the restructuring of prudence and prevarication. McMaster has importantly dismissed interpretations of Vavasor as a libidinal figure and of Alice's predicament as "the familiar conflict of passion with duty" by reminding us that Grey is physically attractive. Alice's love for him is both sexual and combined with esteem, while she regards Vavasor with a mixture of political interest and physical revulsion.[28] In "Passion versus Prudence," Alice realizes with a sudden shock that her wish to support Vavasor's ambitions financially has committed her to a much more personal contract that she finds repulsive: "Of what marriage had she thought when she was writing that letter back to George Vavasor?" (1:383). Glencora's decision, by contrast, is clear: giving in to Burgo would mean adultery and financial ruin caused by "a man infinitely less worthy than her husband [. . .], a spendthrift, idle, given to bad courses" (2:182). Mrs. Greenow similarly knows what she is doing when she calculates the cost of maintaining, and keeping under control, her less extravagant spendthrift. But Alice's feelings follow the peaks and slumps of stock-market graphs. She starts out by speaking up for financial prudence: "It seems to me, papa, that there is a great deal of false feeling about this matter of money in marriage,—or rather, perhaps, a great deal of pretended feeling" (1:354). If she thereby rejects pretended feeling, she indulges a twofold self-deception when she persuades herself that she chooses passion, or that a reengagement to Vavasor is prudent because she supports his political career. Her self-deception is the converse of this rogue's losing struggle with his hypocrisy. Vavasor soon finds living on other people's money "a comfortless unsatisfying trade" and hence persuades himself that taking the money of a woman who loves him makes him less of a scoundrel instead of more:

> We all of us know that swindlers and rogues do very dirty tricks, and we are apt to picture to ourselves a certain amount of gusto and delight on the part of the swindlers in the doing of them. In this, I think we are wrong. [. . .] To get his half-sovereign with scorn is painful. To get it with apparent confidence in his honour is almost more painful. "D—it," he says to himself on such rare occasions, "I will pay that fellow;" and yet, as he says it, he knows that he never will pay even that fellow. It is a comfortless unsatisfying trade, that of living upon other people's money. (1:389)

The 1860s famously saw a fascination with rascals relishing their own rascality. With his flashing eyes and gaping scar, Vavasor exhibits affinities with such sensational villains, but any fascination with his schemes as a form of plotting is derailed. His degeneration maps the stock-market villain's progression as his "career" takes him from a failed proposition, based on an assumed inheritance, to wasting money in politics to resenting a rival's interference in his finances until he ultimately collapses, with a terrible feeling of relief, into "Bold Speculations on Murder." The novel illustrates this graphically: Vavasor's plots expand proportionally as his financial hypocrisy escalates. From vague imaginings of "some accident" and "some secret satisfaction in allowing his mind to dwell upon the subject, and in making those calculations [. . .] those little calculations of which I have spoken," they swell into a whole river of poison: "George Vavasor cursed the City, and made his calculation about murdering it. Might not a river of strychnine be turned on round the Exchange about luncheon time?" (2:111, 208, 209). He makes similar calculations on suicide as the "necessary termination of his career" (2:8), but estimates that it would be better to shoot someone else first (2:320, 326–27).

In its rupture of expected sensational speculation plots, the novel invites us to track the stock-market villain's moral as well as financial demise. At the end of the first volume, the new wild man is "not, at any rate as yet, an altogether heartless swindler. He could not take his cousin's money without meaning,—without thinking that he meant, to repay her in full all that he took" (1:367). The luxury of love shrinks to become reduced to the flipside of the coin of the "combined advantage" he seeks (1:363). He wants to have the woman as well as the money because possession of its owner would make her finances rightfully his. Of course, he tells himself, he could simply obtain money on "a mere visit of business" by calling on his affianced bride "as he might call on his banker," yet he realizes that he can no longer deceive himself: "and he told himself that he was a rascal" (1:389–391). When Grey, his rival in love, as in politics, interferes in his financial affairs as well (by transferring his own money, instead of Alice's, into Vavasor's account), he finally gives up on the self-deception and tries to shoot Grey. This venture, like all others, having failed, the last papers Vavasor takes up appropriately are "the programmes of different companies" offering emigration, and with that he "vanishes from our pages, and will be heard of no more" (2:327, 335).

Although this does not immediately bring Alice's vacillations to a safe conclusion, it rids society of one of its most villainous insiders more effectively than Godolphin's shamefaced departure to Calcutta does at the end of Wood's novel. Among Trollope's later speculators, Melmotte takes poison and Lopez throws himself in front of a train and, as Halperin has suggested, exile to America and suicide are "punishments almost equivalent for a Trollope character."²⁹ In their escapes abroad, both Vavasor and Godolphin foreshadow the often all too easy exorcism of bad speculators in later novels, yet their "export" does not change the stock-market villain's identity as a homebred inside speculator. When they depart for the geographical margins of domestic narratives to seek their fortunes in more congenial places, they leave behind home spaces turned upside down. This is particularly glaring at the end of *The Shadow of Ashlydyat*. It sees all the wrong people triumph, and the morally righteous resignedly pick up the pieces. Once Godolphin has disappeared, there is not even much sympathy for the crash's victims: "Time elapsed. [. . .] The great crash, which so upset the equanimity of Prior's Ash, was beginning to be forgotten as a thing of the past. The bankruptcy was at an end. [. . .] Compassion for those who had been injured by the calamity was dying out" (394). The effects of the heir's speculations, however, are to stay; the wicked Godolphin's curse has been fulfilled by the stock market.

When *Can You Forgive Her?* stages a more efficient expulsion of the squire's disinherited grandson, it works towards a projection that is responsible for the most insistent stereotyping of the foreign in nineteenth-century financial novels. Both novels, however, firmly locate stock-market villains at home amidst traditional elites. Before exploring the functions of foreign speculation as a prominent mode of projection that becomes increasingly queried and carefully dissected, I shall conclude this discussion of financial speculation plots in the "sensational sixties" with an analysis of the narrative uses of paper fictions at a retired banker's estate in Braddon's *Aurora Floyd* (1863). The Stock Exchange may feature only marginally as a former place of work, but this only the more emphatically evinces the sheer pervasiveness of a widening array of financial plots at the time. Surely nothing could better illustrate the ambiguous fascination with which the Victorians regarded the magicality of paper money than novels that remain firmly located on landed property, and yet are determined by the circulation of various paper fictions.

The Miser's New Notes:
Plotting the Magic of Paper Money

What makes the murderous miser in *Aurora Floyd* is "a roll of crisp notes: so crisp, so white and new, that, in their unsullied freshness, they looked more like notes on the Bank of Elegance than the circulating medium of this busy, money-making nation."³⁰ It is not simply money that makes him kill, not its exchange value, not even the allure of glittering gold. Instead, it is wads of paper. Their magic, at least in the eyes of an imbecile stableboy who, in his youth, fell on his head, transforms them into something of such importance that they make him commit murder. Money may not be intrinsically dirty and may start out in a neat, crisp, unsullied freshness that is corrupted only when handled, but if this coins a startling innocuousness, it also trades on paper money's lack of any intrinsic value. Not all that glitters may be gold, but hoarding banknotes can only be, Braddon's novel makes abundantly clear, the desire of a madman or an imbecile. This condemnation of miserliness abides by Victorian moral economies so closely as to recycle a much circulated theme, yet the banknotes figure in a peculiarly fascinating way that first invests in and ultimately deflates an expected narrative structure. Only if they reenter the market can the notes be traced, their numbers mapping out the novel's detective plot. The fruits of laborious extortion, they kill in more than one way and, more significantly still, do away with this spuriously evoked inheritance plot in a truly striking manner. A banker's meticulousness catches a thief (and a murderer) in a new twist of mid-century cultural myths of money that redirects Victorian representations of bankers and banknotes. Objects of desire, intrinsically innocuous, and clues to a sensation novel's mysteries—the notes become *Aurora Floyd*'s plot. In the process, the novel develops new benchmarks for moral economies. It shows this perhaps most compellingly when it dismisses a bystander's gloomy philosophizing on "unlucky speculators" as "dreary platitudes and worn-out sentimentalities" (151) that have become so tired that those who fail in their enterprises are met with less and less sympathy. *Aurora Floyd*, I wish to argue, converts established financial plots into a sensational detective story in which a murderous miser realizes for the first time the importance and ultimately also the traceability of paper money. His initial obsession with the tangibility of his valuables has become outmoded, yet his new interest in brittle papers shows them to be a much more reliable, because traceable, fiction.

The miser's new notes rechannel the fascination with the much bemoaned indeterminacy of paper currencies. All the papers circulating in the novel—distorted newspaper reports, anonymous letters, a marriage certificate, "that miserable scrap of paper which was the legal evidence of [Aurora's] folly" (329), stacks of money as brittle as a "little bundle of tissue-paper" (230)—are not only a form of currency that can be abused in an exchange economy run havoc among villains well-versed in finance. In its juxtaposition of the banker and the miser, the novel at the same time revaluates business ethics and their impact at home. It capitalizes on the opportunities created by financial fiction, including the languages of finance. That one of Aurora's suitors is, despite his "sordid riches," a spendthrift in quite a different "species of coin" bodes ill for his future share in the story: Talbot Bulstrode has "run through all the wealth of life's excitements and amusements, [...] a penniless spendthrift in this species of coin, though well enough off for mere sordid riches" (30). Among the three contestants to Aurora's hand and fortune, the changing parameters that constitute true worth are, as a result, disseminated as a twofold issue. Not only does her value seem to depreciate with her circulation in the marriage market, where she has passed through the hands of unknown possessors, very much like once crisp banknotes, but trust acquires additional significance as she is revaluated on the basis of circulating fictions.

Paper Fictions: "A New Species of Coin"

Since paper currencies are necessarily a matter of trust, they spell out the need for trustworthiness as the basis of the credit economy. As Herbert Spencer put it in 1851, "[a]mongst a people altogether dishonest, every mercantile transaction must be effected in coin or goods [...]. Conversely, amongst perfectly honest people paper alone will form the circulating medium."[31] Monetary contracts depend on morality, and if everyone can be trusted, "metallic money" is needless.[32] Yet Spencer also suggested that the gold standard guaranteed this trust.[33] It is therefore not all that surprising that the conversion of gold can effect Silas Marner's transformation in George Eliot's 1861 novel: glittering gold coins are redeemed for a child's golden curls. This marks the end of mid-century conversion narratives (from Scrooge to Silas Marner).[34] They are reworked in the sixties, starting with *Aurora Floyd* and culminating in the circulation of misers' tales in Dickens's *Our Mutual Friend*. As George Robb has convincingly argued in his study of business morality, trust is "that evanescent quality without which the operations of modern business would be impossible. Trust enables people to turn over their hard-earned savings to banks or stockbrokers rather than burying it in basements or stuffing it in mattresses."[35] This made its breach such a heinous crime in Victorian fiction, while an ability to trust without committing indiscretions needed to be revaluated, and creditworthiness alone could no longer be equated all that easily with the functioning moral economy that is still reinstated at the end of *A Christmas Carol*. Victorian sensation fiction built on precisely this collapse.

In *Aurora Floyd*, paper proliferates, and gold is reduced to a metonymy (for solid virtues), while the threat posed by the "gilt" exhibits the need for a measure of distrust in an assessment of creditworthiness. A display of "that gilt gingerbread of generosity which so often passes current for sterling gold" (185), the worthless, while legally validated, husband is posed against Aurora's "dearest and truest" (198), a husband declared not valid, but always a "lover; generous, pure, and true" (345). To be trustworthy and to have the ability to trust are both part of creditworthiness, but in business, as in marriage, it is just as important not to give credit for mere appearances, to "give him credit for thoughts to match with his dark, violet-hued eyes" (181) as the only yardstick of a partner's worth: "He was a prince in disguise, of course; he was a gentleman's son [. . .]. Why should I disbelieve him? I had lived all my life in an atmosphere of truth" (353). Aurora's realization of her first husband's true value has cost her dearly. It is one of the many clues to her "secret" that cluster the narrative as if to draw attention to the very transparency of this elaborate reconstruction of plots.

In a break with common narrative structures, the novel's opening sums up traditional narrative conclusions that reward work with an embowered estate. What becomes the banker's business after his retirement is ironically his daughter's circulation through a disconcerting proliferation of contractual arrangements. Since he has successfully reinvented himself as a landowner to obscure his origins in a "City banking-house" (6), she is enabled to enter the upscale marriage market. Yet instead, the "banker's daughter," as Aurora is repeatedly called, entrusts herself to her father's groom, James Conyers, who considers her a gamble "for a high stake" (354). She returns, like a bad coin, to the elderly banker. Believing Conyers killed in a steeplechase, Aurora becomes engaged to Talbot Bulstrode, heir to an ancient estate. But those that "mak[e] a market of any past events," a "business [to] trade upon" (83–84), alert Talbot to the existence of a secret, and unable to trust her, he breaks off the engagement. What condemns Conyers is not so much his seduction of the banker's daughter as his careful calculations. He is a speculator, a swindler, and a blackmailer. In short, the seductive groom is recast as a white-collar criminal. When the report of his death turns out to be only one of the many false or falsified accounts that circulate in the novel, Aurora bribes him with two thousand pounds to emigrate. But as soon as he receives the money, he is shot by the stableboy, "the Softy," a particularly revolting species of villain who reshapes the stock character of the miser, even as his miserliness externalizes the former groom's counterfeit value. Blackmail, bribery, and extortion become enterprises that are clandestinely conducted on the grounds of the retired banker's estate. They are significantly contrasted with the trust embodied by "truest" (198) John Mellish, Aurora's third suitor, whose financial innocuousness becomes the redeeming force in the novel.

Carefully evaluated trust in (business) partners is invaluable to any kind of business in an economy based on credit. With this much rehearsed proposition, the novel newly interrogates business morality. The City may largely remain offstage, but it not only supplies the "solid cash" (206) that finances the banker's estate and, for better or worse, his daughter's development (and hence the plot), but it figures as the benchmark for domestic moral economies.[36] Trust may invite exploitation of gullibility, but without it, there is complete stagnation. This is where *Aurora Floyd* swerves away from a rehearsal of moral discourses, of those "dreary platitudes and worn-out sentimentalities" (151). On the contrary, in a proliferation of monetary metaphors that Garrett Stewart has termed the Victorian novel's project of laying bare contractual economies of narrative fascination at the level of single phrasings in a "flood of metaphoric exaggeration,"[37] trust in a reliable creditworthiness is promoted in pointed contrast to miserly hoarding. Some ventures may be worth a risk. Simple Mellish, Aurora's deserving "dearest," "as unsuspicious as a child, who believes that the fairies in a pantomime are fairies for ever and ever" (59), builds his domestic happiness entirely on trust, outstripping his rival in the marriage negotiations: "How should I have acted, Aurora? I should have trusted you" (125). As proof of his trust and his trustworthiness, Mellish takes all his wife's debts on himself without question or investigation. Again, in a projection of ideal business relationships onto the economies of domesticity, this refers to pecuniary debts and, by metaphorical extension, to anything else Aurora may owe: "He freely took upon his shoulders every debt that she owed, whether of love or of hate; and he was ready to pay either species of account to the utmost farthing, and with no mean interest upon the sum total" (309–310). In an additional twist of this pervading debt-credit metaphor in the novel, Aurora's love for Mellish is a debt: "How could she be for ever his creditor for such a boundless debt?" (141). Ironically, he can invest in the worthwhile risk because he takes everything at face value: "Talbot drove himself half mad with imagining what *might be;* John saw what *was* [. . .]. He had his reward. He had his reward in her frank womanly affection" (142). The repayment is mutual trust.

If this aligns an avoidance of risk taking, whether in business or at home, with distrust, Aurora's blind belief in a pretty-faced scoundrel is a risky venture. It leads to blackmail, bribery, and ultimately murder aptly acted out by an imbecile miser. Dressed up in pseudogentility, Conyers glitters misleadingly, a counterfeit coin, wrapped in paper fictions, the novels Aurora has read: "Heaven help the woman who sells her heart for a handsome face, and awakes, when the bargain has been struck, to discover the foolishness of such an exchange!" (181). Evoking George Eliot,

Braddon makes the most of this narrative's reworking: "With what wonderful wisdom has George Eliot told us that people are not any better because they have long eyelashes!" (181). It is not only that Conyers "looked, in short, like anything but what he was" (190). He trades on his beauty, as on the heiress's interest in horses and on a marriage certificate sewn into his clothes, a part of himself that he likewise strives to exchange for a different species of coin: "Conyers's handsome face was a capital with which that gentleman knew very well how to trade, and he took the full amount of interest that was to be got for it" (184–185). Yet his worthless existence is of little consequence; what interests Braddon is that his capital acquires value only when we give him credit for it:

> You give him credit for thoughts to match with his dark, violet-hued eyes, and the exquisite modelling of his mouth and chin; you give him a mind as aesthetically perfect as his face and figure, and you recoil on discovering what a vulgar, every-day sword may lurk under that beautiful scabbard. Mr James Conyers is, perhaps no worse than other men of his station; but he is decidedly no better. He is only very much handsomer. (181)

The novel's main strength is that these very plots yield a proliferation of false leads. Mellish may build his hopes on a common story of pecuniary indiscretion, ready to sacrifice "poor Archibald Floyd's commercial integrity" as long as Aurora's secret can be confined to the banker's business: "Her secret! her father's secret, more likely. What secret could she have had, that a groom was likely to discover? It may have been some mercantile business, some commercial transaction" (315–16). In this, Archibald Floyd would merely join a list of cheating bankers in Victorian fiction, from Dickens's ostensibly self-made Bounderby in *Hard Times* to the monomaniac of Reade's *Hard Cash* and the hypocritical banker in Eliot's *Middlemarch*. Just as Conyers's eyelashes link him to Eliot's child-murderess in *Adam Bede*, and the casting of the miser as villain inverts the revaluation of pecuniary and sentimental exchanges in *Silas Marner*, Talbot Bulstrode prefigures the banker Bulstrode, a self-deceiving believer in Providence's interest in his finances in *Middlemarch*.[38] Talbot's belief in clear-cut moral issues (Aurora is either unblemished or corrupted) and faith in providential intervention are expelled from the moral economies of a new form of creditworthiness. In a restructuring of intersecting issues of inheritance, the novel works in concerns with business, and the business it has at home, even on landed estates, remote from the banking house from which the money springs. The banker's only indiscretion is his choice of a groom "on account of his good looks" (22). While this remains a "folly," financial speculation is a more risky game altogether. As Conyers puts it when coldly calculating the odds of Floyd's death and hence Aurora's inheritance (her husband's property): "I've risked my money on a worse chance before to-night" (206). The object of bets himself, the former jockey aptly succumbs to his final, fatal speculation on extorted banknotes.[39]

If the main plot is strikingly simple and cashes in the two central secrets—what happened during Aurora's missing year, and who shot James Conyers?—all too quickly, the novel recycles literary expectations to capitalize on the sensation reader's demand for narrative speculation. The banker, the booby squire, the adventuress, as literary stock figures, and further, the groom setting himself up as a lord in disguise, even the bigamist heroine with a secret, all function as so many red herrings, as false clues in a detective plot that is more about discovering a workable system of extending credit than about solving a mystery.[40] Most prominently perhaps, *Aurora Floyd* reverses the plot of Braddon's own most successful novel, *Lady Audley's Secret* (1862). While the novels share the ambiguous presentation of the heroine's secret,[41] Aurora is an inversion of Lady Audley. Sympathetically portrayed in all her tomboyish interests in dogs and horses (and unfortunately also the groom), Aurora contrasts with this former governess. When it comes to the cover-up of her bigamy, the latter is a fabricator of just such a "shallow fiction invented to deceive" (197) that Aurora refuses to devise. If she only "looked a childish, helpless, babyfied little creature," fraudulent Lucy Audley may be partly redeemed in the character of Aurora's cousin, truly angel-like Lucy Floyd, who makes Talbot a good, yielding wife.[42] But she is also projected onto that monster of marketable ladylikeness, Mrs. Powell, Aurora's governess and paid companion, with her "stereotyped civilities and sympathetic simperings" (325). A suggestively vague "story" of a foiled inheritance of "some enormous property, the particulars of which were never rightly understood" having set her up "in life as a disappointed woman" (51), this dependent hates Aurora "for the very benefits she received, or rather because she, Aurora, had power to bestow such benefits" (133). Mrs. Powell spies and plots, "in a lady-like way of course" (342), and ultimately resorts to the writing of anonymous letters, a particularly cowardly misuse of paper.

Given that her "precise" and "ladylike" demeanor, her wizened figure, and her hypocritical scheming are juxtaposed with Aurora's frank, somewhat wild, behavior and the looks of an "imperious creature, [a] Cleopatra in crinoline" (33), like "an Eastern empress" (41), it should not surprise us that discussions of the novel have chiefly focused on the heroine's masculine characteristics or the orientalist descriptions of her allure.[43] But this is really just another red herring, as are interlocked calculations on the legacy of her mother's acting career: that "the spangles and the sawdust were breaking out, and Aurora was, as they had always said, her mother's own daughter" (127). All she inherits from her mother is her beauty, her frankness, and an equally frank seafaring relation (her mother's brother), who features marginally in the plot. This refusal to trace her runaway match to her "low" origins as the daughter of an actress, a "successful adventuress," as "many a waning beauty [. . .] speculat[ing] upon the banker's income" terms her (8–9), sits oddly with the novel's recycling of inheritance and speculation plots. It is one more of the well-worn paper fictions it takes up, rides, and ultimately drops. In the remainder of this chapter, I seek to show how the reconfiguration of the miser and the banker brings out the magic of paper money as an effective, and affective, sensational plot.

The Miser, the Banker, and "a Little Bundle of Tissue-Paper"

The miser, like the cash he covets, and the banker, with the notes he disperses after meticulously numbering them, both have a central function in the novel's representation of paper money. In a twist of traditional inheritance plots and emergent speculation plots, the banker doubles as the circulating heiress's venerable old father. Ponderously cashing out the "crisp notes" as the "little bundle of tissue-paper," he counts them carefully, notes down the numbers, and locks the list in his drawer before handing them to his daughter: "There is always occasion to be business-like [. . .]. I learnt to be business-like when I was very young [and] I have never been able to forget my old habits" (230–31). Aurora might dismiss his professional training as the eccentricities of "dear methodical papa" (231), hardly befitting a country gentleman, but it is only because her father has retained his professional approach to financial transactions of any kind that the banknotes (and with them, Conyers's murderer) can be identified, thereby lifting suspicion from Aurora. This reemploys the banker's original value, just as it turns the banknotes into the plot. The miser's crime is, with a similar twist, not so much his overblown evaluation of paper, but the miserliness that keeps it out of circulation. What is targeted here is not the paper, innocent in itself, or its dispenser. The miser succumbs to paper money's magicality to the extent that he obstructs exchange, reminding us that Marx diagnosed a miser as "a capitalist gone mad."[44]

That such papers nevertheless need to reemerge from this audit as trustworthy is ironically for the same reason that mid-century realist fiction expressed deep distrust of the credit economy. Sensation novels engaged with the narrative potential generated by credit capitalism in peculiarly creative ways, and discussions that concentrate chiefly on realist fiction often discount this. Increasing demand for new villains ensured their delivery in unexpected places, specifically in the confines of what studies of the sensation genre have established as its domestic Gothic, yet also in the equally mundane spaces of the City. Aurora has symptomatically "two enemies, one without and one within her pleasant home" (141): the dependent companion and a coolly speculating, murderous miser. Interestingly, this pairing of villains leaves out Conyers. Guilty of extortion, he is absorbed by a proliferation of those who circulate some "wretched scrap of circumstantial evidence" (390). The account of a murderous bigamist is, like the suspicions of the banker's "commercial integrity" (315–16), a false clue. Neither the bigamist nor the banker is the culprit. What is more, if this venerable squire, sporting perhaps some added value in his professional training, is the most positively presented City man in sensation fiction, the miser comes out all the more stunningly as the double of both the good banker (Floyd) and the mean gambler (Conyers).

The Softy is one of the most overtly repulsive villains of nineteenth-century literature. He is "the sort of man who is generally called *repulsive*,—a man from whom you recoil with a feeling of instinctive dislike, which is, no doubt, both wicked and unjust" (134). It is a warning that seems to run counter to the novel's interest in misleading appearances. Yet, not only does his shambling gait, with its "resemblance to that of the lower reptiles" (248), underscore his linkage to limping Conyers, but his very imbecility is the most vital false clue. He is a "double-dyed villain" (457), "a precious deep one for all they call him soft" (437), who may contrive "to give 'em all the slip" (442). A professional detective lumps him together with the most typical of cunning criminals: "these fellows always go one way. It seems as if the minute a man has taken another man's life, or forged his name, or embezzled his money, his ideas get fixed in one groove, and never can go beyond Liverpool and the American packet" (442). In this case, the detective has partly jumped to the wrong conclusion. The villain is still within dangerous proximity.

What turns a "softy" from a hanger-on groping in the dust for shiny coins (140) and hoarding "sundry rubbish in the way of odd spurs and ship-handles, scraps of broken harness, ends of rope, and such other scrapings as only a miser loves to accumulate" (434), into a cold-blooded killer is paper money. At first, he fails to grasp its representative value: "he had wondered how it was that money could be represented by those pitiful bits of paper. 'I'd rayther hav't i' goold,' he thought" (262). Indeed, we could say that he starts out as one of the relatively harmless misers of Victorian fiction, much like Barkis in Dickens's *David Copperfield*, whose treasures comprise a "tobacco-stopper, in the form of a leg; an imitation lemon, full of minute cups and saucers, which I have some idea Mr Barkis must have purchased to present to me when I [David Copperfield] was a child, and afterwards found himself unable to part with" as well as guineas, "perfectly clean Bank notes, certain receipts for Bank of England stock," and a bad shilling (435). In a reversal of conversion narratives, an imaginary of stacked paper becomes the miser's vision. From wondering whether "the brass" Conyers extorts from Aurora "would be a great bulk of money [. . .] in a chest or a bundle," the Softy moves to a conjuring with figures: "'Two thousand pound! Twenty hundred pound! Forty times fifty pound!' with an unctuous chuckle after the enunciation of each figure, as if it was some privilege even to be able to talk of such vast sums of money. So might some doting lover, in the absence of his idol, murmur the beloved name" (249–50). Excited by mere figures, he soon ceases to doubt that two thousand pounds can fit into an envelope: "He had seen cheques sometimes, and banknotes, [. . .] and he had wondered how it was that money could be represented by those pitiful bits of paper" (262). Even solid cash need no longer be "a mountain of glittering coin" (262). The Softy quickly accepts the system of credit and debt, discovers a new form of "gloating upon [Aurora's] misery" as a way "to pay off them kind of debts" (330), and ultimately commits "a most cold-blooded assassination, perpetrated by a wretch whose sole motive was gain" (458).

The Softy's transformation into a hardened criminal embodies the transformation of hard cash into paper, compellingly encapsulating what formed an imaginative thrust in the 1860s. As I shall show in the next chapter, Reade's 1863 *Hard Cash*, first serialized in *All the Year Round* under the title of *Very Hard Cash*, similarly revolves on paper money's fragility as it tells the story of the Hard Cash's travels, in a captain's pocket, from an Indian bank across the South Seas, to be nearly lost in a provincial bank. It is called back by its receipt, "the soul of the lost Cash" (455), rendered tangible as a replica within the novel. Like *Aurora Floyd*, Reade's novel depicts those in the thrall of paper money as mad. There is no redemption for hoarders of banknotes, for those cooing calculations. In Dickens's *Our Mutual Friend*, misers' tales themselves proliferate, side by side with shares, famously revolving on Mr. Boffin's stunning misreading of avariciousness in order to redirect a money-minded girl's lack of emotional investments. The gold standard of Eliot's *Silas Marner* clearly becomes something quite out of the ordinary, as novels instead realize new paper fictions. Trollope's *Can You Forgive Her?* has a sensationalized speculator circulate his cousin's name on bills, while *The Last Chronicle of Barset* (1867), the final novel in Trollope's Barsetshire series, illustrates how the loss of a piece of paper can have far-reaching consequences if it happens to be a check. A number of protagonists learn that it is wrong to assume that "cheques were like any other money," but it is now those who fail to appreciate the magic that transforms paper into money who are accused of imbecility or insanity: "In all that he [an old-fashioned, scholarly curate accused of having stolen a check] said he was terribly confused, contradictory, unintelligible—speaking almost as a madman might speak."[45] As *Aurora Floyd* restages the miser and the banker, it works through current anxieties and literary traditions to question the value of trust, of giving credit where it can be most securely believed due. The startling double interest the novel takes in banknotes as the driving force of the plot and a measure for the intangibility of credit and creditworthiness makes it particularly compelling as an example of the Victorian novel's growing investment in financial speculation. Fascination with paper money prevails, and in dismissing conventional "sentimentalities," while proposing a workable business morality at home, it sustains an ambiguity that creates a sensational plot with marked new twists, a crisp paper fiction about money.

Three

Speculators Abroad

The functions of foreign financial speculations in the Victorian novel are indisputably among its most sensitive and complex issues. The central irony of Charles Reade's *Hard Cash* (1863) is that the eponymous cash is not safe in a country bank after this stack of money has been reclaimed from an Indian agency-house and likewise restored from the dangers it faces from pirates at sea. The titular diamond of Wilkie Collins's *The Moonstone* (1868) is similarly turned into a slip of paper that needs to be traced from a London bank into Victorian suburbia before it can be reconverted into a religious icon and returned to India. These sensational narratives of intersecting forms of speculation not only mine, but complicate, earlier fictional uses of dubious financial transactions. In that they render this redeployment a driving force of their detective plots, they invert the narrative trajectories of financial arrangements in domestic realist fiction of the previous decade. It is in order to accentuate the indeterminacy of financial speculation at home as well as abroad that Dickens's *Little Dorrit* (1855-57) evokes a legacy of colonial guilt in what is, however, an aborted narrative of detection. Thackeray's *The Newcomes*, likewise serialized in the mid-fifties, features an intricately ambiguous revision of stock characters that exposes mercenary society in the metropolis through its twofold projection of domestic micropolitics onto (financial) empire building. In taking a close look at the changing fictionalization of this wider cultural preoccupation with commercial ventures into foreign spaces, the following sections seek to reach beyond the Victorian novel's most glaringly—and stereotypically—orientalist engagements with imperialism and its hold on popular culture. If the fragility of paper currencies and the elusiveness of traffic in shares underpinned the prevailing fascination with the potential and the problems of finance capitalism, then representations of international commerce provided a particularly suitable vehicle for the fictional exploration of various forms of instability. Although popular fiction traded on stereotypes of the foreign, this was significantly more than simply a projection of undesirable business onto a convenient "other." At its most constructive, it instead generated a dual critique of imperialist commercialism.

Like the British Empire itself, its changing representation operated largely through a negotiation of financial transactions. At the same time, it struggled with the realignment of social classes that success abroad often meant at home. Some of the most memorable stock-market villains of Victorian fiction are implicated in a corruption of society: they are contaminants and hence part of a foreign "infection." They share their suspicious allure with other promiscuous exotica in the literature of the time, from the swamped enterprises in Dickens's *Martin Chuzzlewit* to the looted diamond in Collins's *The Moonstone*. Misappropriated religious icon and a failed investment in land (misappropriated, too, marked by the very absence of native Americans), these forays into colonized sources of sudden riches are inextricably bound up with business at home. *Martin Chuzzlewit* juggles fraudulent financial fictions, including an insurance scam instigated by a homemade upstart, on both sides of the Atlantic,[1] and it is in the same vein that the real villain of *The Moonstone* turns out to be an armchair philanthropist. And still, the lasting image of Dickens's "American novel" remains that of the promised city of Eden that turns out to be an undeveloped swamp. The projections as well as linkages that denote large-scale businesses in Victorian fiction become central to a questioning of familiar types and predictable outcomes.

Dead ends and red herrings of course suggest an inviting source of detective plots, but as the short-circuiting of risk management in realist fiction of the 1850s shows, this is not their only or even their most prominent function. It is when the preoccupation with the speculator's indeterminacy is turned around in an interrogation of anxieties about economic practices more generally that their narrativization can issue a significant reversal. It probes the connections between home and colony that Raymond Williams has influentially diagnosed as the narrative linkage between the fantasies of colonialists in tropical or arid places abroad and the idealization of "home" through the acquisition of embowered estates financed by work elsewhere—a linkage Edward Said has similarly described as the construction of "the East" as part of an essentialist dichotomy.[2] Franco Moretti has importantly cautioned that the main function of sites abroad in British domestic fiction is sometimes only the convenience that they are offstage.[3] The conversion of an inheritance of colonial guilt, of raided diamonds, or of a much traveled gold watch into paper arrests an inherently unstable attempt at risk management. These fictional explorations of new imaginary geographies dissect cultural anxieties about the most glaringly facetious projections themselves to find the most indeterminate components of financial speculation at home after all.

Such transpositions articulate the need to manage a disturbing recognition of a sameness that has been occasioned by an expansion of imperialist branches of what Dickens memorably terms the Circumlocution Office. It is the result of an exported institutionalization of "how not to do it." As it is put in *Little Dorrit,* as soon as any "intrepid navigator could plant a flagstaff upon any spot of earth," the Circumlocution Office dispatches one of the aptly named Barnacles, representatives of red tape encompassing the globe: "the Barnacles were all over the world, in every direction—despatch-boxing the compass."[4] This identification of paperwork here and there, at home and abroad, disrupts projections between the foreign and the familiar, to delay or prevent containment, and altogether to render risk management ever more difficult. Representations of foreign trade bring home the ubiquity of commercial imperialism and its costs. When a tellingly tentative association with the opium trade is traced to a much more encompassing muddle that reinstates the value of a revised moral economy of exchange in *Little Dorrit,* any legacies of guilt need to be reassessed at home. Thackeray's *The Newcomes* similarly defends the miscalculating colonial financier by posing a self-conscious redefinition of the stock figure of the Anglo-Indian nabob against a more extensively evoked, yet also more ambiguous, orientalist treatment of Indian bank swindles. Even a subplot in Gaskell's mock-pastoral *Cranford* teases out the significance both of colonial space and of imported products for the revaluation of financial concerns (and financial plots) at home. By contrast, when sensation novels like *Hard Cash* or *The Moonstone* rewrite the cultural fictions of foreign commerce that these narratives help to form, they do not merely accentuate the instability of moral economies and their expected conversion into monetary reward. Rather, they draw on the inversions prepared by earlier novels to make the most of dubious financial transactions in usefully mysterious, foreign spaces. A domestic work of fiction of the early fifties, *Cranford* can already be seen to trace this progressively complex narrative interest in the Empire.

The Conversion of Colonial Legacies

Serialized in *Household Words* in 1851–53, Gaskell's *Cranford* is an episodic novella in which narrative strands converge in financial plots. Colonial wealth constitutes a source of restitution, but in specific opposition to the effects of newly introduced financial instruments at home. At a crucial turning point in the narrative, the failure of the seemingly reputable Town and County Bank forces innocuous Miss Matty Jenkyns to sell tea to make up for her losses as a shareholder. Tea is, ironically, a cultural icon as much of colonial commerce as of Englishness. Most strikingly, however, Matty is rescued by the return of a successful colonizer in the shape of her long-missing brother. His return from India, laden with presents, saves a proudly perpetuated "elegant economy" of genteel poverty.[5] The materiality of the foreign treasure in the form of gifts successfully makes up for Matty's willing forfeiture of her last "hard cash" when she hands over her saved sovereigns to a farmer whose paper money is rejected because it is, as a shopkeeper tries to explain to the puzzled would-be consumers, not really "a forged note [and] a true note of its kind; but you see, ma'am, it is a Joint Stock Bank, and there are reports out that it is likely to break" (123). Matty's touchingly naïve interpretation of fiscal responsibility is rewarded by the *deus-ex-machina* device of imported colonial riches. It may be exactly this replenishing of domestic finances through the colonial fantasy of embowered estates as the returnee's reward that cannot be sustained in the sensational stock-market novel of the sixties. This appropriation of imperialist narratives for domestic realism is intriguingly multifaceted. It weaves together different narratives of the foreign as they are produced and circulated in a largely self-enclosed provincial town.

It is in a tongue-in-cheek juxtaposition with the Cranford ladies' largely unrealized desire for commodities of a heavily orientalist fashion such as the "great Saracen's head turban" (81) coveted by Miss Matty that colonized territories are claimed in a curious domestication of imperialist narratives. Given the conventional contrast of the colonial and the domestic in nineteenth-century literature, India provocatively serves as a remarkably familial space. Commenting on the absence of racism and the importance of the belief in a common humanity within an embedded narrative set in India, Raphael Samuel has cited *Cranford* as an example of as "provincial a novel as it would be possible to imagine" on which India is all the same "quite an insistent pressure."[6] With a melodramatic twist of a presumably (and this is of course problematic) universal sentimentalization of children, the wife of a former sergeant in the East India Company army relates how she walked to Calcutta with her one surviving child, along the way gratefully receiving the assistance of sympathetic Indians. It remains as much a tale of the colonialist's resilience as of the obliging behavior of the colonized. Nevertheless, what it does bring out is that imperialism's "insistent pressure" surpasses the importation of narratives, tea, or turbans to nourish an appetite for orientalist consumption.

The connection between these variegated narratives of the imported exotic is forged by financial plots. While they revolve on a bank failure, they also link together diverse forms of consumerism, elegant household economy, and the question of "genteel" employment. The consumption of foreign, or seemingly foreign, products therein plays a fluctuating role. It manifests itself not merely in embarrassing lapses in taste (the turban as exotic accessory), but also in xenophobic reactions that turn out to be misdirected as they are unduly applied to the amorphously, even fraudulently, "other." As a result, the exotic as a commodity that is enticingly difficult to slot away safely is by no means restricted to references to South Asia, nor is it entirely displaced by the imported story of human affection across cultures. Such a revaluation of commonalities does not prevent the town's ridiculed suspicion of the conjurer Signor Brunoni, "a magnificent gentleman in [...] Turkish costume" (86), who turns out to be plain Samuel Brown. He is engaged in a business venture that trades on the exotic, on orientalist fantasies and self-fashioning. Yet there is a darker side to the satire, foreshadowing the legacies of guilt that underpin the likewise largely offstage representations of foreign spaces in realist domestic narratives throughout the 1850s. It is these legacies of guilt that become channeled into elaborate plots of detection in the sensational stock-market novels of the 1860s.

These plot developments are more than simply indicators of interstices between popular subgenres as they crystallize themselves in the quickly fermenting mass print culture of the century's second half. Instead, they drive paradigm shifts. Once Brown stands exposed as an impostor, and hence as not foreign at all, it is immediately argued that he cannot be guilty of the robbery of which he has been suspected. At the same time, fun is poked at the women of Cranford for their orientalist infatuation with the presumably "exotic" gentleman and their naïve xenophobia as they equate foreignness and the criminal. The revelation of Brown's camouflage urges an exposure of just such mistrust. The admittedly brief narrative of provincial orientalism prefigures the wrongful incarceration, on suspicion only, of the three Indians who turn up in front of an English country house in *The Moonstone*, published fifteen years later. In what is without doubt the recently most discussed aspect of Collins's novel, three unnamed, for the most part portentously silent, Brahmins are sent from India to search for a looted diamond. Their appearance at the great house necessarily generates some commotion, but it has nothing to do with the theft that takes place in the young lady's bedroom that night. The connection between an Indian diamond and Indians in an English town simply offers an all-too-inviting clue. The local police consequently "contrive, by committing them as rogues and vagabonds, to keep them at our disposal, under lock and key, for a week. They had ignorantly done something (I forget what) in the town, which barely brought them within the operation of the law. Every human institution (Justice included) will stretch a little, if you only pull it the right way. The worthy magistrate was an old friend of my lady's—and the Indians were 'committed' for a week, as soon as the court opened that morning."[7] What remains an indulgently depicted foible in Gaskell's mock-pastoral becomes an important false lead, "a clue [soon] broken in our hands" (94), in Collins's novel. Whereas the referencing of diverse financial ventures in the quaint society of Cranford chiefly serves to create a fine gradation of character, sensational detective novels extensively draw on familiar narrative structures in order to explode such established dichotomies within prevailing conceptualizations altogether. Admittedly, a straightforward rearrangement (including simple inversion) is at times more likely to reinforce cultural or racial typecasting than to expose it as a misconception. In such cases, seeming subversion may figure as nothing but an aberration posed against a "normalcy" it helps to uphold. Nevertheless, critiques of international commerce increasingly help to renegotiate the relationship between the colonial and the domestic. Transposition does more than expose the real villains as part of the eminently respectable middle classes. It puts them side by side, indeed identifies them, with alternative suspects whose foreignness is shown to mark them out as an obvious threat (the South Sea pirates in *Hard Cash*), even to render them vulnerable (the arrested Indians in *The Moonstone*). By doing away with expected structures, such sensational accounts often deliberately redeploy the paradigms of earlier novels that, like *Cranford*, feature colonial commerce to probe an undeniable interdependence within the indeterminacies of finance capitalism. The haunting presence of financial collapses linked to foreign spaces in *The Newcomes* and *Little Dorrit*, I wish to suggest, offers a particularly informative contrast to the reversal of moral accounting in *Hard Cash* and *The Moonstone* a decade later.

Circumlocuting Legacies of Guilt I
"Our Poor Old Friend the Cocoa-Nut Tree"

Foreign spaces occupy an essentially dual function in Victorian domestic fiction in that they form a place for financial ventures as well as a retreat for failed speculators. The circulating "silver cocoa-nut tree" in Thackeray's *The Newcomes* becomes an emblem of this twofold appropriation. It comically renders manifest an excessive production of the artificially exotic as an object of consumption and thus appropriately comes to symbolize a failed venture built on fictitious credit. At the center of a spectacle of consumption, it is moved along by satirized "campaigns" at home. Once the BBC, the Bundelcund Banking Company, has collapsed, and Colonel Thomas Newcome is declared bankrupt, his son is advised to take his family abroad. In a rush to carry off some of the plunder made in what has turned out to be a large-scale swindle, Clive Newcome's virulent mother-in-law, "the Campaigner," nearly foils all of the Colonel's endeavors to prove that "he has been egregiously duped."[8] Her attempt to concert a preemptive robbery of their former possessions is the only really piratical venture in the novel. The loot consists of the relicts of their short-lived revelry in highlife: "all the silver forks, spoons, and ladles, and our poor old friend the cocoa-nut tree, which these female robbers would have carried out of the premises. Mr Clive Newcome burst out into fierce laughter when he saw the cocoa-nut tree" (741). Representing commodified orientalism, this "superb silver cocoa-nut tree" (666) is a horribly sturdy and substantial specter of seeming solidity, a centerpiece overshadowing as well as ominously supervising company dinners as the sign of an avid consumption of exotic products that is all that is seen of foreign speculations at home.

India and Anglo-Indians have a central presence in Thackeray's fiction.[9] Their representation ranges from the account of Anglo-Indian society earlier in the century in *The Tremendous Adventures of Major Goliah Gahagan* (1838) and the chiefly comical description of Jos Sedley, the Collector of Boggley Wollah, "an honourable and lucrative post, as everybody knows," in *Vanity Fair* (1847), to almost morosely loyal, bumbling Captain Dobbin in the same novel.[10] Jos exemplifies the typical, satirized nabob. He stokes the fire in the middle of June, loves his pillau and curry, and appears first in "the morning costume of a dandy or blood of those days" (24), with almost his entire face concealed in multiple neckcloths—an all too obvious target for impecunious young ladies like Becky Sharp. *The Newcomes* dismantles this stereotype. Although prey to just such fortune-hunting women (Clive's late mother included), Colonel Thomas Newcome is perhaps the most good natured as well as genuinely innocuous colonial financier of Victorian fiction. He is an old-fashioned, almost preternaturally ingenuous character, "a gentleman who was quite a greenhorn" (8). That he is simultaneously "a most gallant and distinguished officer in the Bengal establishment of the Honourable East India Company" (35) and an "East Indian warrior" (36) may be somewhat at odds with his innocuousness, yet this also serves to underscore the emergence of a new form of (white-collar) crime that at the same time assists in a prizing apart of economic and military forms of imperialism. "The nabob of books and tradition," in any case, "is a personage no longer to be found among us. He is neither as wealthy nor as wicked as the jaundiced monster of romances and comedies, who purchases the estates of broken-down English gentlemen with rupees tortured out of bleeding rajahs, who smokes a hookah in public, and in private carries about a guilty conscience, diamonds of untold value, and a diseased liver; who has a vulgar wife, with a retinue of black servants whom she maltreats, and a gentle son and daughter with good impulses and an imperfect education, desirous to amend their own and their parents' lives" (84). The hookah is instead retained by "the celebrated Indian merchant" Rummon Loll, the nabob's double, and even he only smokes it "after dinner when the ladies were gone" (77). A "greenhorn" in more ways than one in the City of London, Tom Newcome could not be any more different from the nabobs of literary tradition. The colonial company is his "child" in a particular transposition, his speculation only a realization of his wish to make a fortune in order to bequeath it to his son: "Now this Bundelcund Banking Company, in the Colonel's eyes, was in reality his son Clive. But for Clive there might have been a hundred banking companies established, yielding a hundred per cent. in as many districts of India, and [he] would never have thought of speculation" (543). Given that the Colonel's touching innocence, in financial as well as in other matters, is well established early on in the narrative, the rumors circulating about "his reputation as a keen man of business, who had made his own fortune by operations equally prudent and spirited" (666), could hardly be any more ironic. It is chiefly to accentuate this irony that the novel fulfills the main paradigms of the comforting narrative of risk's expulsion through projection. The self-proclaimed Indian merchant prince embodies the financial threat as a typecast impostor from abroad to facilitate the carefully considered rewriting of the stage nabob. In other words, he helps to exorcise the guilt if not the guilty conscience.

This seemingly straightforward realization of geographical risk management, however, becomes disposed by the Colonel's ambiguous positioning. Throughout the novel, his own moral worth is continually highlighted, which further brings out the opaqueness of the business ventures he becomes embroiled in. Barbara Weiss lists this "most unworldly innocent of all" among the typical vulnerable individuals of 1850s financial fiction.[11] His incapability is of course part of his worthiness: "This worthy old Colonel, who fancied himself to be so clever a man of business, chose to conduct it in utter ignorance and defiance of law" (715–16). The bursting of the bubble comes as no surprise. As the first-person narrator, the eponymous hero of Thackeray's autobiographical novel *Pendennis* (1850), stresses, he has never intended this to be otherwise:

> Knowing, from the very beginning of our story, what was the issue of this Bundelcund Banking concern, I have scarce had patience to keep my counsel about it; and whenever I have had occasion to mention the Company, have scarcely been able to refrain from breaking out into fierce diatribes against that complicated, enormous, outrageous swindle. It was one of many similar cheats which have been successfully practised upon the simple folks, civilian and military, who toil and struggle—who fight with sun and enemy—who pass years of long exile and gallant endurance in the service of our empire in India. [...] The failure of the Bundelcund Bank which we now have to record was one only of many similar schemes ending in ruin. (729)

This diatribe not only pinpoints Thackeray's deeply ambiguous attitude to "the Orient" and, with an embarrassing invocation of imperialist jingoism, "our empire in India," but it encapsulates his reaction to a bank failure that had cost him dearly as well. Born in Calcutta, the son of a Collector in the East Indian Company's service, Thackeray lost his fortune in a major financial crisis. In 1830 the collapse of Palmer and Co undermined confidence in Calcutta agency-houses; by 1834 the majority of established houses had failed.[12] Financial crashes recur in Thackeray's fiction, and they tellingly almost always indicate something foul and not infrequently implicate someone or something foreign. With its almost exclusive Regency setting, *Vanity Fair* references the fictitious "great Calcutta house of Fogle, Fake, and Cracksman," which "failed for a million, and plunged half the Indian public into misery and ruin" (761–62). The West Diddlesex Assurance Company of *The Great Hoggarty Diamond* similarly satirizes the failure of the Independent West Middlesex in the 1840s. Boasting Brough is "a great man on 'Change," a religious hypocrite, a predictable upstart who courts genteel society and charges two of his four horses on his fraudulent company, while his victims, including the preternaturally innocuous narrator, really are deceived innocents.[13] The Diddlesex reappears again briefly—shorthand for financial crashes—in *The Newcomes*, where an investment in "West Diddlesex bonds" is equated with "luckless speculations" (91) in anticipation of the BBC's collapse.

In the 1840s, London agency-houses were once again reviving India's economic landscape, although confidence rose only to plunge the more drastically in the commercial crises of 1847–48. It is in the course of such a temporary revival that the Bundelcund Banking Company finds fecund grounds in *The Newcomes*. It is clearly meant to create a sense of foreboding when Colonel Newcome becomes *indebted* to Rummun Loll, even if at first for his advice alone (428). Credibility is the speculator's chief capital. Such indebtedness links the foreign swindler to the ruthless, similarly orientalized moneylenders who populate the financial district at the heart of the Empire. Now, the first time the "celebrated Indian merchant, otherwise his Excellency Rummun Loll, otherwise his Highness Rummun Loll, the chief proprietor of the diamond mines in Golconda," is introduced, Colonel Newcome symptomatically refuses to join the public encomium on "the black Prince" (77–78). Cultural fictions of the ancient diamond mines of Golconda as an El Dorado had become dated at least by the 1840s and were frequently used as a metaphor for enormous fortunes to be made by speculation. As Daniel Thorner has pointed out, since the most extensive movement of British capital to India took place in the course of colonial railway speculation, Golconda effectively became displaced by new ventures in international commerce.[14] Hence it is made abundantly clear from the outset that the fluctuations of trust in Indian agency-houses are to cause the Colonel's ruin. A "lucky escape out of one house in India" (422) really only means that the Colonel can all the more easily be tricked into a more risky venture, one that is explicitly erected "by association" (321): an offstage fantasy construction. Playing on the Colonel's gratitude and guilt, the self-inflated "prince" creates the Bundelcund Bank out of the very memory of the agency-houses' failure:

> Founded, as the prospectus announced, at a time when all private credit was shaken by the failure of the great Agency-houses, of which the downfall had carried dismay and ruin throughout the presidency, the B.B. had been established on the *only* sound principle of commercial prosperity—that of association. (521)

Just as this advertisement of a speculation that grows out of a notorious failure foreshadows its own crash, its foundation on association is ominous. That the company branches out by taking in (in more senses than one) officers, residents, and their connections makes it all the easier for

Barnes Newcome, the Colonel's nephew, to malign them all as "blundering, muddle-headed managers, black and white," who "owe no little to the assistance which they have had from our house" (665), the family business of Hobson Brothers and Newcome. When they refuse thirty thousand pounds' worth of bills issued by the BBC, selling out becomes "quite epidemic" (677). A bank failure, it is made clear, cannot be explained by economic causes alone. On the contrary, public confidence makes or breaks it. In a literalization of metaphors of disease (speculation fever, mania, and epidemics), Rummon Loll's death of cholera brings about the final crisis. "The Orient" as the origin or site of these financial "diseases" can therein be seen to infiltrate the metropolis through amorphously foreign speculators. Nevertheless, despite considerable typecasting, the novel's investment in "the Orient" and those associated with it is considerably multifaceted. Indeterminacy may be the stigma attached to any foreign money matters, yet the functions of India in *The Newcomes* are characterized by a far more intricate ambiguity that prompts us to reconsider their complexities.

The intrinsically fake, orientalist taste that smothers Colonel Newcome's bohemian dinners is emblematic of moral decline. In the face of the company's remoteness and hence comparative inaccessibility (and intangibility), the cocoa-nut tree as symbolic centerpiece is offensively solid. It is also overpoweringly ornate; embarrassing in its orientalist iconography. Its leaves "dexterously arranged for holding candles and pickles," lending their shade to "an Indian prince on a camel giving his hand to a cavalry officer on horseback," it boasts "a Brahmin, Britannia, and Commerce with a cornucopia" (666). Its theme is the spectacle of India's commodification. In this, it contrasts with more personal associations with India as a home, not a place of speculation. The business events arranged around this piece certainly are a pathetic burlesque of the impromptu dinners at which the Colonel, displaying quite a different kind of interest in consumable exotica, is "great at making hash mutton, hot-pot, curry, and pillau" (168). It is vital for an understanding of the multiple function of India in the novel that the two-way export of colonial products (including banknotes) is much more than simply an empire founded on different debts, financial or otherwise. The initial reception of the mock-prince foreshadows the Colonel's own wretched attempts to keep up appearances, with the Bundlecund Bank's impending crash hanging over them. At the company's heyday, a plethora of orientalia spins around the mockingly solid silver centerpiece in a dizzying excess. As Pendennis indicates in a telling invocation of the confusion pertaining to what is, after all, from the beginning portrayed as a scam, "[t]hese subjects are mysterious, terrifying, unknown to me. I cannot pretend to describe them" (666). Conversation about them is not only "about millions," but about a strikingly indiscriminate list of products and places: "cotton, wool, copper, opium, indigo, Singapore, Manila, China, Calcutta, Australia" (666); "Sydney, Singapore, Canton, and, of course, London. With China they did an immense opium trade, of which the profits were so great" (521).

This repeated climax in consumption is at once comical and ill omened. Opium trade was to lead to two wars in the course of the nineteenth century. The first Opium War (1839–42) would have been contemporaneous with, or taken place shortly after, the BBC's enterprises, while the second (1856–60) was impending when Thackeray was writing *The Newcomes*. In the novel, the moral critique is both implicit and vague. Its referencing of such trade routes implies that the BBC is primarily involved in somewhat shady business. Conversely, taking entire "possession of the native markets" in India means that Indian idols are produced in Birmingham, and while this may "make the Low Church party in England cry out," debate on the subject eventually helps "to send up the shares of the Bundelcund Banking Company very considerably upon the London Exchange" (522). The satire is directed foremost at hypocrisy in England, a hypocrisy combined with ignorance of the "exotic" markets conquered by the company. This comes out most forcefully when an election speech is given on behalf of the Colonel (in pursuit of a place in Parliament, which he wins only to resign as the bubble bursts). In the speech, his military successes in India become subsumed by Indian cuisine:

> Whereas for years and years past, when he was away in India, heroically fighting the battles of his country, when he was distinguishing himself at Assaye, and—and—Mulligatawny and Seringapatam, in the hottest of the fight and the fiercest of the danger, in the most terrible moment of the conflict and the crowing glory of the victory, the good, the brave, the kind old Colonel. (722)

This truly is a choice piece of satirized orientalism. Mulligatawny is a spicy East Indian soup, made with rice and boiled meat or chicken. It comes from Tamil "pepper soup," and hence its invocation as one of the Colonel's hottest fights is particularly ironic. According to the *OED*, from the early nineteenth century onwards, Mulligatawny had come to be used as a now obsolete colloquial term in Indian English to describe a "European official serving in the former Madras Presidency in southern India."[15] So while this approach appears to parody the rhetorical hot air of election speeches generally, the novel's referencing of commercial imperialism is not always that lighthearted. The cocoa-nut tree as plate, an epitome of commoditized exoticism, does more than simply witness misguided speeches on the consumption of India. The extended orientalist typecasting of "the East" implies that it is peculiarly apt that this "poor old silver cocoa-nut tree" is handled by "[s]warms of Hebrew gentlemen with their hats on" (731) after the company has gone bust. When Clive Newcome's mother-in-law attempts to retain this offensive icon, the identification of piracy and an attempt to carry off portable property to prevent its confiscation by creditors points forward to yet another exposure of an even more self-interested hoarding of spoils. After the bankruptcy, she pushes home Tom Newcome's responsibility for her losses and his consequent dependence on her money in order to cash in on his sense of guilt.

The assumption of fiscal responsibility that ultimately kills the Colonel is an outmoded ideal that is narratively, not financially, rewarded in the novel. He might have been "egregiously duped" (732), but his indistinct desire to make amends is evidence as much of the futility of such nebulous ideas as of his moral probity. He shares such impractical self-reproach with Arthur Clennam in *Little Dorrit*, but the latter's case, we shall see, is even more ironic in that it replicates and partly grows out of Clennam's original desire to provide restitution for what he suspects to be his family's guilt, an inherited responsibility that has nothing directly to do with his own losses at the stock market. What is more, while Colonel Newcome has made and lost his money in India, an amount of fiscal and emotional recompense is doled out to his son after all. There even is a connection to India, or rather, to its rendering as a paper fiction that asserts it as a narrative space of youthful fantasy that can be nostalgically reclaimed from the plots of economic imperialism. As a boy, the Colonel "had a great fancy for India; and 'Orme's History,' containing the exploits of Clive and Lawrence, was his favourite book of all in his father's library" (22). It is in this colonial history, the last book the Colonel's long resentful stepmother is reading at the time of her death, that a paper is found that expresses her wish to bequeath a certain sum to his son Clive. Still, this fortuitous inheritance clearly struggles to operate as a believable counterpoise in a society determined by complex financial speculation. Barnes, for one, refuses to acknowledge any demands on his family's finances made by this paper. It is his sister Ethel's feelings of personal moral obligation, fueled by her fondness for the Colonel and her love for Clive, that induces her to honor what she at least sees as her grandmother's last will.

So if this financial legacy can be authenticated only because financial generosity is driven by emotional rather than legal obligation, the inheritance that is really celebrated in the novel is Colonel Newcome's incorruptible ingenuousness: "He [Clive] has inherited that loving heart from his father, [. . .] and he is paying over the whole property to his son [the Colonel's grandson]" (814). It is a legacy of incorruptibility that can be passed on after all, without deductions of any kind, from loving father to son and presumably extended to Ethel (as a reward for her personal fiscal responsibility) when she marries Clive after his first wife's convenient death. As a triumph of fiscal, as of other forms of, innocuousness, it is preternaturally—one might well say incongruously—untouched by associations with imperialism, either military or pecuniary. It stands completely outside the otherwise all-encompassing presence of a speculative economy. In absorbing at least financial inheritance in two ways, speculation does not simply cause the loss of (inherited) money in the novel. It constitutes the origin of the company that so disconcertingly stands in for Clive in the Colonel's distorted system of moral accounting. Premised on what is depicted as a preposterous attempt to accumulate enough cash for a worthy legacy by deploying risky ventures as a strategy to save money, this system is essentially a perversion of his fiscal innocence. Yet Tom Newcome exhibits such naïveté that he needs to be seen as exempt from the speculative drive that determines all sectors of society, from mercenary marriages to conjectures on the future value of a rising artist's work that "wouldn't be a bad speculation for our friend Sherrick" (459). This good-natured but nonetheless stereotyped money-lending wine merchant additionally complicates the novel's representation of "the Orient" and its manifestation in "Hebrew gentlemen" (731) as well as fake Indian princes. The novel, in fact, employs such typecast figures both as doubles to bring out alignments between paralleled forms of financial transactions and as foils to the victimized nabob. At the same time, they embody the signs of the times.[16] Sherrick symptomatically sees everything as a speculation, and if his comments are comical, they are also ominous: "It's all a speculation. I've speculated in about pretty much everything that's going: in theatres, in joint-stock jobs, in building ground, in bills, in gas and insurance companies, and in [his future son-in-law's] chapel" (263). Although the rewarded characters are set outside such exchanges in a secure bubble of old-fashioned ideals, this proliferation of interlinked speculation is where the future lies, a future that renders the novel poignantly nostalgic.

Circumlocuting Legacies of Guilt II: "Anxious for the Family Credit"

The bequest that can be validated only by a personal exchange that replaces impersonal, international commerce at the end of *The Newcomes* reinstates a redefined inheritance plot by asserting the value of inherent qualities as the real legacy. Dickens's *Little Dorrit* proposes a similar form of recompense in which one paper, a long secreted codicil, can successfully make up for the damage done by a proliferation of largely fraudulent or meaningless papers. It is only the will's destruction that can allow the obsession with "family credit," which dominates so much in the novel, to make way for this resolution. This is much more than escape into a questionable domestic refuge from the business world. Couched in unmistakably financial terms of exchange, the revaluation of commercialized transactions between people is premised on a debt that becomes equated with an emotional deficit. It successfully disrupts any easy identification between fiscal and emotional contracts. Instead of creating a bigger shortage still, this renegotiation of multiple legacies of debt taps into a hitherto unrealized surplus. When Arthur Clennam and Amy Dorrit are finally credited with a love that grows where there is the greatest such deficit, this collapse of fiscal metaphors brilliantly brings to a conclusion the novel's exploration of moral accounting. Their give-and-take of emotions is well balanced and firmly based on the generosity of mutual self-abnegation. Circulating papers, meanwhile, operate as so many false clues, and yet this confluence of misdirected paper business brings together the novel's main plotlines. It unearths the long established linkage between the Dorrits' and the Clennams' fortunes. A suppression of inherited guilt may cause houses to crash (literally and metaphorically), but it also makes possible the final transformative exchange of debt and credit between two individuals who have almost been crushed by the system:

> "From the unhappy suppression of my youngest days, through the rigid and unloving home that followed them, through my departure, my long exile, my return, my mother's welcome, my intercourse with her since, down to the afternoon of this day with poor Flora," said Arthur Clennam, "what have I found!" His door was softly opened, and these spoken words startled him, and came as if they were an answer: "Little Dorrit." (165)

Such personal recompense ultimately achieves closure. *Little Dorrit* ends with the burning of an official document that lifts a mystery by disclosing the long suspected connection between the two families. But its contents remain concealed from the self-elected amateur detective. Instead, Arthur Clennam's preoccupation with past wrongs becomes channeled into one of the most notorious and often cited stock-market plots of Victorian literature. It could almost be said that his venture into speculation realizes his feelings of guilt—that it finally yields good reasons for his vague suspicions. Loosely associated with the family business, they are first projected onto China's commercial enclaves, where the Clennams' trade is concentrated. Their inheritance of guilt, however, is brought out by speculations at the heart of the Empire. By the end of the novel, the exposure of Merdle's speculative enterprises has brought Arthur to the debtors' prison that used to be Little Dorrit's home. Her destruction of a piece of paper that states a possible financial restitution completes the rejection of inheritance as an easy solution or even a prominent plotline.

An unexpected legacy may early in the novel restore the Dorrits' fortune, spectacularly lifting the "Father of the Marshalsea," the longstanding resident and self-proclaimed patron of the debtors' prison, into high society. Its somewhat precipitate realization of course already disqualifies the traditional inheritance plot as the means to effect closure. Instead, it becomes subsumed by the encompassing interest in "[t]he magic name of Merdle" (564)—and the stock-market plot it calls up—and both are converted into sources of guilt. Symptomatically, the Merdle enterprises' "magic" as the epitome of a speculative economy is over and over again associated with gold, coins, and various papers. As we have come to expect from financial swindlers whose name "is the name of the age" (484), "nobody knew with the least precision what Mr Merdle's business was, except that it was to coin money" (394). Yet despite the fact that Merdle is described as "a Midas without the ears, who turned all he touched to gold" (246), and hence becomes "the golden wonder" (570) in the popular imagination, he is really made of paper: "Mr Merdle's right hand was filled with the evening paper, and the evening paper was full of Mr Merdle," deriving its substance from such "fattening food" (558). The prevailing obsession with paper and paperwork (and its circumlocution) is therefore very appropriately exorcised by a verbally expressed "charm" that demands the burning of paper. This also brings any anticipations of the inheritance plot's possible reemergence to an end. As the closure of a narrative of detection, it surely comes as an anticlimax. But it also effects another conversion of gold, of an inscription on an old-fashioned gold watch, into a fragile paper that needs to be destroyed. *Little Dorrit*, I wish to argue, achieves a cleaving out of an emotional exchange from institutionalized circumlocution through a short-circuited detective plot that combines inheritance and speculation plots ultimately to dismiss both. The Clennam mystery and the Dorrit legacy form two connected strands that converge, appropriately in the debtors' prison, as it witnesses the burning of a potentially valuable paper in a differently valued exchange.

What renders the insistent pressure of foreign spaces so important in the novel's structure is that the aborted detective plot is lodged in the interstices of an intricate web of financial transactions in the Empire's center as well as abroad. On his return from China, having been absent from England for twenty years, Arthur wishes to believe that the hated family business involves some wrong for which he might make restitution. This is at least in part to overcome his sense of being such "a waif and stray everywhere," having been raised under the shadow of a religion of "gloomy sacrifice of tastes and sympathies [and then] offered up as a part of a bargain for the security of [his family's] possessions" (20–21) abroad. If this system has deprived him of "Will, purpose, hope," his complaint especially of having "no will" (20) adds to the novel's puns on various forms of papers, anticipating the codicil's retrieval and purging destruction. In the same vein, an inherited timepiece acts as a memorandum of the past that marks out guilty legacies. Arthur's only clue is the inscription on a gold watch: "Do Not Forget." It is evidence of his father's "secret remembrance which caused him trouble of mind—remorse" (48). For Mrs. Clennam, this inscription acts as a reminder as well, but one that attests to her regimen of self-punishment, exemplified by her uneaten oysters, which she is said to register as an act "to her credit, no doubt, in her Eternal Day-Book" (52). Much has been made of this virtual ledger, a religious bookkeeping that confines Mrs. Clennam to her wheelchair and her room, just as the Circumlocution Office's system of equivocation paralyzes the country. It is a doubly crippling system of "reparation" that does nobody any good.[17] As George Holoch has already suggested, if we can safely assume that it is "a commonplace of Dickens criticism that 'the informing symbol' of *Little Dorrit* is the prison," Mrs. Clennam is "the first fully developed figure" to express it, just as Arthur's unhappy childhood under her regimented supervision has produced his indefinable sense of guilt.[18]

This inherited system of moral accounting significantly motivates Arthur in his spurious detective work. It is a poignantly disheartening parody of the narratives of detection that begin to restructure Victorian popular fiction at the mid-century, producing professional detective figures that number Dickens's own Mr. Bucket in *Bleak House* (1853) among them. Uncertain about possible guilty links to China, Arthur begins to look for additional clues. In his mother's household, he encounters a seamstress, discovers that her father is imprisoned for debt, and suspects the business. In other words, he deduces a connection based on the familiar moral accounting of guilt and restitution, debt and recompense. "In grasping at money and in driving hard bargains," Arthur is convinced, "some one may have been grievously deceived, injured, ruined" (49). The Dorrits, as a proudly shabby-genteel prison family, seem as good a bet as any. This may all suggest an overeager jumping to the wrong conclusions, yet it is already premised on the transference of his first suspicions. This multiple projection structures the novel's transposition both of typified foreign spaces and of newly popular detective plots.

There is more than a hint at dubious business in "the East," so that even if Arthur's first deductions turn out to have been a red herring, China remains central on a number of interconnected metaphorical levels. It is the nodal point of interlinked metaphors of foreign "infections." Since Arthur comes "from the East, and as the East is the country of the plague" (15), we first find him quarantined in Marseilles. This incarceration externalizes not merely his feelings of being trapped, but the sense of psychological imprisonment that pervades the literally crumbling house of Clennam and Co. By extension, as if it were radiating out from the childhood home, it encompasses a typical London Sunday ruled by the same sabbatical stringency that determines Mrs. Clennam's household. In a chapter titled, with barbed irony, "Home," the returnee encounters a post-apocalyptic cityscape that appears to be plague-ridden. Disease is suspected to come from "the East," from China or Egypt (through which Arthur has traveled) to be contained in Marseilles, but it seems to have already decimated London's population:

> It was a Sunday evening in London, gloomy, close and stale. Maddening church bells of all degrees of dissonance, sharp and flat, cracked and clear, fast and slow, made the brick-and-mortar echoes hideous. Melancholy streets in a penitential garb of soot, steeped the souls of the people who were condemned to look at them out of windows, in dire despondency. In every thoroughfare, up almost every alley, and down almost every turning, some doleful bell was throbbing, jerking, tolling, as if the Plague were in the city and the deadcarts were going round. Everything was bolted and barred that could by possibility furnish relief to an overworked people. No pictures, no unfamiliar animals, no rare plants or flowers, no natural or artificial wonders of the ancient world—all taboo with that enlightened strictness, that the ugly South Sea gods in the British Museum might have supposed themselves at home again. (28)

In *Dickens and Empire,* Grace Moore has suggested that it is particularly ironic that Arthur is quarantined because he comes from "the East," yet his first vision of home is "a Britain far more blighted than the China he has left behind [. . .], bearing more than a passing resemblance to the Blakean city of the damned."[19] It recalls London's cholera victims of 1854 and, in its exposure of a general abjuration of responsibility, suggests a spilling over of the devastation of battlefields abroad.[20] In the evocation of foreign gods and taboos, moreover, the returnee's alienation foreshadows the idolization of magic Merdle and the spread of speculative fever as an exotic disease.[21] "The Progress of an Epidemic" (ch. 13) returns to the images of a plague sweeping through London: a "moral infection," "a disease [that] will spread with the malignity and rapidity of the Plague" (571). When Arthur withdraws from the family business, it is ironically to advocate just such "investments" in the domestic economy instead of ventures abroad, but his resignation at the same time bespeaks, as Jeremy Tambling has put it, "a colonial guilt that cannot be articulated" so that "colonial activity itself may be a useful means whereby guilt at home may be displaced."[22] This displacement works both ways, as Arthur's horribly perverted homecoming indicates. It is an inversion of narratives of return as a reward, a denial of any acquisition of embowered estates at home after commerce or conquest abroad.

In a reading of "silences" in the wake of Edward Said's influential discussion of Austen's 1814 *Mansfield Park*—a novel in which China remains a paper fiction of exotic travel that is consumed by the heroine as part of her Romantic education in contradistinction to the financial viability of West Indian plantations—recent reassessments have focused on China's marginalization after its initial referencing in Dickens's novel.[23] It is an elision that points at once at the mystification of speculation (and overseas trade more generally) and at an ambiguous interest in "the Orient." That business in China has been "progressively on the decline" and "the track [the Dorrits] have kept is not the track of the time" (46) could thus be read as a reference to the opium trade as a convincing source of Arthur's sense of guilt.[24] Although the novel is set thirty years earlier, in the mid-1820s, it has also been suggested that the careful charting of the timeline could fruitfully be seen to break down in the face of topical interest in China in the mid-fifties.[25] Serialized from 1855 to 1857 and hence largely during the second Opium War (1856–60), the novel references commercial settlements in China to draw attention to the obscurity of speculators all over the globe. Still, as Wenying Xu has pointed out, since it was not until 1833 that the East India Company's monopoly over the China trade was dissolved, the Clennams' choice of business would have been severely limited.[26] What is more, regardless of the fact whether they were, or were not, involved in the opium trade themselves, the Clennams would have been well aware of its effects on China.

China remains a mysterious, offstage space that is doubled within a network of interconnected port cities around the world. These trade hubs feed on and into an emphatically commercial cosmopolitanism. Marseilles, where the novel opens, is described as a point of convergence for traders from various parts of the globe, including China: "Hindoos, Russians, Chinese, Spaniards, Portuguese, Englishmen, Frenchmen, Genoese, Neapolitans, Venetians, Greeks, Turks, descendants from all the builders of Babel, come to trade at Marseilles" (1). The Dorrits' later stay in Venice similarly underscores connections between past and present commercial empires. Just as Marseilles establishes the dominant metaphors of imprisonment and disease, and China functions metonymically for the overall mystification that envelops society, it has been remarked that Venice offers "a kind of objective correlative for the parable of economic failure in England which the novel documents."[27] Within multiple projections of Arthur's alienation from the family and its business, London's post-apocalyptic cityscape is extended to financial centers around the world. Such a replication mimes the intensity of the self-styled "waif's" sense of directionless confusion, mirroring an additional projection through doubling. The place of quarantine in Marseilles is near a prison from which the foreign stock villain Rigaud alias Blandois emerges as a mockery of the commercial imperialist and the indeterminate cosmopolitan. Whereas Arthur considers himself "a waif and stray everywhere" (20), Rigaud proudly proclaims himself "a cosmopolitan gentleman" who "own[s] no particular country," "a citizen of the world" (9). In a stab at financial and political speculators, he boasts of having "lived by [his] wits—how do your lawyers live—your politicians—your intriguers—your men of the Exchange?" (10). It is therefore peculiarly apt that he produces important papers relating to the guilty legacy: Arthur's identity. The self-styled cosmopolitan acts as a catalyst for the short-circuited detective plot. This *doppelganger* embodies the indeterminacies of foreign trade in its extremes and appositely comes to grief in the literalized crash of the Clennams' business.

Conversely, the sheer mundanity of business abroad in the absence of any mystery is projected back on to commerce between people at home. A seemingly plague-ridden London is ominously linked to "the Orient" as the country of the plague, but at the same time, the exotic has seeped out of overseas trade. Arthur may be silent on China, because there simply is not all that much to say about his business there, except that it suggests itself prominently as a believable source of various forms of guilt. The expected account is replaced by the curiously jumbled Chinomanie streaming out of poor Flora Finching, Arthur's former sweetheart, whose overblown silliness is yet another blow to the disheartened returnee. Flora fears

> that you [Arthur] are married to some Chinese lady, being in China so long and being in business [. . .]. I only hope she's not a Pagodian dis-

senter. [...] [W]hat a country to live in for so long a time, and with so many lanterns and umbrellas too how very dark and wet the climate ought to be and no doubt actually is, and the sums of money that must be made by those two trades where everybody carries them and hangs them everywhere, the little shoes too and the feet screwed back in infancy is quite surprising, what a traveller you are! (152)

What the novel's China ultimately represents is the breakup of commercial empires and their orientalized attractions. Flora's flurry of words may well suggest that the Clennams' business is (or at least generally is assumed to be) engaged in both of those two profitable trades with China: tea and opium. The House's impending crash is a collapse that is brilliantly externalized at the end of the novel when the "house in the city [with] its heavy dullness" (339) literally tumbles down. Reinforcing the metaphorical connection to "the East," it is "haunted by the appealing face [Arthur] had himself seen fade away" (542–43), as his father lay dying in China. It is also in the face of this transposition of a haunting Far East that Flora's Chinomanie is just as misplaced as her parodied sentimental recollection of her youthful romance. Like Arthur's own love of the past, it has been laid by as a currency that cannot be exchanged. In the course of his "exile" in China, Arthur has stored up "all the locked-up wealth of his affection and imagination. That wealth had been, in his desert home, like Robinson Crusoe's money; exchangeable with no one" (150). On his return, he finds its exchange value void, until he can replace it in a final dismissal of precisely these fiscal metaphors. That it is Flora who is identified with an exoticized view of overseas trade additionally underscores the dismissal of commerce, abroad or at home, as anything magical or interesting to anyone not in a speculative fever, or like Flora, just as feverishly indulging in vague fancies of the exotic.

Far from eliding its significance, the novel's account of Arthur's experience not only accurately reflects commercial interest in China, the dullness of such work abroad, and the attendant rise of Chinomanie at home. Arthur, of course, has not been "a great traveller" at all. Before his father's death and his decision to abandon the business, it is unlikely that he could have ventured much out of European enclaves or seen more than offices with an uncanny likeness to those in the City back in the Empire's capital or in port cities elsewhere. Even after China was "opened" at the end of the first Opium War in 1842, it was chiefly seen as a powerful incentive to commercial exploration.[28] The usefulness of foreign spaces as a point of projection collapses into a stark denial of expected narratives of homecoming. It is a symptomatic narrative shift. The childhood home, the sweetheart of the past, and the stern mother are all still there and essentially unchanged. Even Flora's fault is not that she has changed physically, but that she has remained "diffuse and silly," and having "been spoiled and artless long ago, was determined to be spoiled and artless now" (143). Arthur's carefully stored up memories seem to have been void investments in the idea of home and homecoming that residence abroad generates.

This seeming dismissal of stored up nostalgia needs to undergo a conversion that operates through a process that does away with, even while it mimics, fiscal transactions. The father's gold watch is a bequest to his son and a remembrance of guilt that is more than once converted into something else. The inscription's meaning keeps shifting: for Clennam senior it spells out a fond as well as a guilty memory of the woman he once loved and who bore him his illegitimate son, Arthur; for Mrs. Clennam it is a reminder that she has been wronged, and that she believes she has made proper restitution by raising Arthur in ignorance of his birth, while she is aware of the existence of quite a different debt, the suppressed legacy bequeathed in the missing codicil; for Arthur, it ironically assumes the most amorphous signification of imperialist guilt; for Rigaud, by contrast, it simply reinforces the power of the papers in which he trades. The purloined document immediately becomes "a commodity to sell," a "precious commodity [with a] price" (745). As such, Rigaud calculates, it "might be worth, to [Mrs. Clennam], a sum of money" (770). While this paper discloses a peculiarly twisted version of an inheritance plot, it is both the object of a purely financial transaction to Rigaud and has to do with monetary debts linked to a suppressed wrong. Motivated by feelings of guilt, Mr. Clennam's uncle—who had arranged the mercenary marriage of Arthur's father and cut him off from Arthur's biological mother—bestowed a legacy on the younger daughter, or niece, of the former employer of Arthur's mother, a singing girl. This helpful employer improbably turns out to be Little Dorrit's uncle. Meant as a pecuniary reward for kindness bestowed on the wronged girl, the legacy becomes the object first of guilty suppression and then of yet another business exchange. Arthur has partly been right all along, although he has been chasing an assortment of red herrings, homemade and imported.

The disclosure of the suppressed legacy is also the other side of the coin of the spuriously invoked inheritance plot. Mr. Pancks trades on what he hears of the Dorrits. Like the stock-market villains of Braddon's later sensation novels, he speculates on the Stock Exchange (in what he insists are secure investments) and supplements this further by secretly operating as an amateur tracer of heirs-at-law. This inheritance plot, in other words, is itself already the outcome of detection as speculation. To establish Mr.

Dorrit's right to a fortune, Pancks takes risks, contracting debts in order to proceed with his "speculation as to what a surprising change would be made in the condition of a little seamstress, if she could be shown to have any interest in so large a property" (410). He is proud of having "[m]oled it out" (410), of risking "time and trouble [and] industry" (319). Pancks's inversion of risky speculation and safe investment is symptomatic. The tracing of inheritance is a speculation, whereas his "investment in one of Mr Merdle's certain enterprises" (571) is repeatedly termed "safe" and "certain" (582): "Yes. Investments is the word" (581). Even after Merdle's emblematic suicide, Pancks holds on to this spurious distinction: "for it was my misfortune to lead him [Arthur] into a ruinous investment. (Mr Pancks still clung to that word, and never said speculation.)" (765).

What is perhaps most disconcerting in this rejection of inheritance as compensation or resolution is Arthur's sense of relief when Pancks assures him that his discovery does not implicate anyone: "'How implicate, sir?' 'In any suppression or wrong dealing of any kind?' 'Not a bit of it'" (387). The failed business that has brought about Mr. Dorrit's ruin has nothing to do with either Merdle or the Clennams. This of course all the more emphatically proves the commonness of such failures. It is nonetheless disturbing that before this reassurance, Arthur has been thinking of the restoration of the Dorrit fortune with as much trepidation as with a longing to make restitution himself: "A frequently recurring doubt, whether Mr Pancks's desire to collect information relative to the Dorrit family could have any possible bearing on the misgivings he had imparted to his mother on his return from his long exile, caused Arthur Clennam much uneasiness at this period" (319). He is "doubtful," "uneasy," and "perplexed," as he dreads that Pancks's "moling" might unearth legacies of guilt before Arthur has been given the chance "to repair a wrong that had been done in his father's time, should a wrong come to light, and be reparable" (319). This surely is a somewhat odd qualification as he muses on his own wish to make recompense. Daniel Born has described this ambivalence as "the first fully developed case of liberal guilt in English literature."[29] Still, Arthur's fear of any untimely revelation and almost jealous guarding of the ability to make restoration are much more complex than a simple transposition of spiritual bookkeeping into an equally distorted "liberal" version would suggest. His emotional distress is as much the result of a general depression, in which disappointment in love and unhappy childhood memories merge, as of a concept of fiscal responsibility that is part and parcel of prevalent business ideals. In his desire to claim the "right" to repay a debt, whatever it is, Arthur exhibits a peculiarly patronizing stance towards East Londoners as well as towards commerce with "the East." The sense of guilt that accompanies the returned commercial imperialist helps to investigate social and personal accountability at home after all.

In this network of symbolic transpositions, China represents the returnee's alienation, underlining what Grace Moore has termed his role as an outsider who encounters in the prison-like city something that might have been the norm for Londoners, but which is at once "remarkable and deeply depressing" to Arthur.[30] Correspondingly, his vague wishes to interest himself in the Dorrits' fortunes stand in for imperialist anxieties about Britain's supposed "protection" of commercial hubs abroad. As opium appears as a glaring red herring, it is only one of the many objects of Arthur's speculations that come to nothing. Their vagueness hints at a diffusion of guilt and an all-pervasive circumlocution. The Clennams' business in China has nothing to do with the Dorrits, and likewise, there is no direct link between the Dorrits' imprisonment for debt and Mrs. Clennam's concealment of Arthur's identity. But if it is with an ironic twist that the collapse of the Merdle enterprises finally gives Arthur reason enough to feel guilty, the novel takes its multiplication of the word "speculation" further by posing both monetary and moral calculation against daydreaming as an ultimately more profitable, rewarded occupation: "For, it had been the uniform tendency of [Arthur's] life—so much was wanting in it to think about, so much that might have been better directed and happier to speculate upon—to make him a dreamer, after all" (40). Hence, just when he counts the costs of the "unhappy suppression" of his childhood, his guilt-ridden work in China, and his depression at his return, the solution is "Little Dorrit" (165).

This answer to his conflicting conjectures is repeated in the final exorcism of commercial exchange. What is burned when Little Dorrit puts the undisclosed codicil into the fire is the plotting of inheritance, speculation, and the regularly referenced "family credit" in which both are rooted. Although primarily connected to the Dorrits' spuriously sustained fictions of gentility and their desperate elision of the Marshalsea from their memories of the past—something Amy's nostalgia, which so aptly matches Arthur's own daydreaming, does not permit—"family credit" also means a heavy burden and a debt to the Clennams. It is in this interlinking of family, business, and different forms of credit that the Dorrits' elaborate pretenses emerge as a striking parallel to Mrs. Clennam's spiritual system of wrong and retribution. Being "anxious for the family credit" (485) may be a convenient excuse for Amy's siblings to police their gratitude. But as this play on "credit" to bespeak a suppressed awareness of a shameful or guilty legacy denotes it as a debt (its opposite), it collapses the all-pervasiveness of finance in the novel. This is why it is particularly appropriate that a "charm" countermands fiscal language. It is a re-mystification of the power of paper: "'Does the charm want any words to be said?' asked Arthur, as he held the paper over the flame. 'You can say (if you don't mind) "I love you!"' answered Little Dorrit. So he said it, and the paper burned away" (825). As the power of paper is destroyed, it is not just property (a portion of the estate) that is exorcised here, but fiscal exchange itself.[31]

This also brings to a pointed conclusion the elided mystique of Arthur's guilt-driven ventures into different parts of "the East" (China and the East End). The "charm"—the burning of the paper offering—is conjured up in the sordid surroundings of the debtors' prison. Throughout the novel, mystique or magic is associated repeatedly with the East, from Mrs. Clennam's sphinx-like air of secrecy (543), and Flora's bizarre queries about "Pagodian dissenters" (152), to the "unholy rites" performed by her late husband's aunt, his only legacy: bent "over a steaming vessel of tea, and looking through the steam, and breathing forth the steam, like a malignant Chinese enchantress" (534). Disenchantment is inevitable in mundane spaces, at home or abroad. After his suicide in a public bath, the magic Merdle finds his end in a grotesquely comical version of "a grave or sarcophagus" that strips any mystique from him: all that lies revealed is "the body of a heavily-made man, with an obtuse head, and coarse, mean, common features" (705). Yet the charm invoked by Little Dorrit reverses disenchantment's ascension, as it does so many rules of exchange or commerce in the novel. If it fails to break through the interlocked systems of circumlocution and speculation as the determining factors in the financial organization of society, it makes this personal exchange all the more precious. In the burning of the codicil as a paper offering, the novel compellingly imbues the destruction of official papers with a peculiar magicality of its own.

Hard Cash and Paper Diamonds

Consisting solely of paper notes, the eponymous Hard Cash Captain Dodd collects in Calcutta as his "hoard" or "treasure" (91–92) in Reade's novel is curiously tangible, even as the definition of its real value continues to fluctuate. What is the most startling, however, is the explicitness of its evoked spirituality, which becomes part of its sensationalization. Independent of monetary exchange rates, the Cash means very different things to different people at different times. It is not only more than just paper, but also more than a convertible currency. For Dodd, it embodies his love for his wife and children; for his daughter, hope of marriage in a conflux of narratives, of

"'Love' and 'Cash,' the converging branches of this story [flowing] together in one stream" (157); for the fraudulent banker, Hardie, a final temptation: "the fatal Cash" (191). It becomes the ultimate object of desire, an absolute value redefined. A consistently capitalized, anthropomorphized entity, the Hard Cash is not just powerful, magical, and the novel's main protagonist. Its elevation to a divine level is curiously devoid of irony. Its ultimate apotheosis disconcertingly illuminates its centrality and justifies its power:

> O immortal Cash! You, like your great inventor, have then a kind of spirit as well as a body; and on this, not on your grosser part, depends your personal identity. So long as that survives, your body may be recalled to its lawful owner from Heaven knows where. Mr Compton [legal advisor to the banker's son] rushed to Pembroke Street, and put this hard, hard Cash in David Dodd's hands once more. (467)

Crucially, it is this tangibility that makes the Hard Cash's role in the novel such an unusual recycling of the notorious fictionality of paper currencies on which financial speculation relies. That the stress is on the "hardness" of the anthropomorphized stack of banknotes despite its alternate floppiness and brittleness is in itself an ironic reversal of traditional narratives of old and new money and of gold's precedence over paper, what Brantlinger has described as "the fiction of gold or of absolute value."[32] Pointing out striking inconsistencies in the condemnation of "filthy lucre" and the ways in which it was worked out through conceptualizations of the taboo, Christopher Herbert refers to "the nineteenth-century divinisation of money."[33] As money is both "filthy" and magical, it negotiates concepts of the sacred and of the polluted within a "powerful force field of attractions and revulsions that surrounded the idea of money in the nineteenth century."[34] From Karl Marx's 1844 "The Power of Money in Bourgeois Society" to Max Weber in the early twentieth century, the fetishization of money as a "visible divinity" in nineteenth-century middle-class ideologies was regularly condemned.[35] That the Hard Cash's tangibility is continuously stressed in Reade's novel makes its ultimate apotheosis only the more perplexing.

The majority of nineteenth-century narratives that focus on the power of paper money certainly make the most of its fluctuating value. Gaskell's Miss Matty, we have seen, needs to learn that a note issued by a joint-stock bank is, after the bank's failure, nothing but worthless paper. This familiar plotline becomes embedded in Reade's novel as an almost cursory reminder of exploited trust at home. It does more than add to a panorama of fraudulent transactions in that it serves at once to characterize the villainous banker and to demonstrate the intrinsic instability of financial systems in general. Markley, a rural miser, wrongly believes his money to be safe once he has retrieved it from the doomed bank. The miser as a capitalist gone mad can only think of holding onto the tangible reality of paper. Its inherent worthlessness is completely obscured by his belief in a wrongly assumed universality of paper currencies: his "nice new crisp note [...] 'tain't money at all, but only a wench's curl paper," for "what vally be Hardies' notes when Hardie's be broke?" (197). This realization plunges him into violent insanity, foreshadowing the banker's own monomania at the end of the novel. Evidence of the Hard Cash's all-pervasiveness and power, in fact, Dodd and Hardie are both driven out of their senses by its loss. Hardie's son is wrongfully incarcerated in an asylum in its name. At the same time, the eponymous Cash is at once victim and villain, the object of a detective plot and the central subject of a social critique.

"You Have Read of Bubbles": Tracing Paper Treasure in Hard Cash

In its juxtaposition of pirates at sea and the modern banking business, *Hard Cash* uncovers the schemes of an established banker who speculates with his son's money and then capitalizes on the believability of the latter's presumed insanity only to fall himself victim to a monomania that turns the desperate speculator into an obsessive miser. It is a strikingly sensational plot that comprises an array of startling incidents. If it clearly makes the most of the melodramatic plot devices that foreign spaces can provide (pirates, shipwrecks, storms), however, it does so in order to project this climate of danger onto the seeming tranquility of provincial England. It engenders a decisive reversal that situates the novel's speculation plot at the interstices of variously reworked plots of detection, including their ongoing negotiation within domestic realism. Most strikingly, the power of money is additionally confirmed as it becomes completely justifiable to run mad at home once colonial spoils (the imported wads of cash made abroad) are subsumed by failing financial houses in England. Captain Dodd suffers from amnesia after Hardie appropriates his anthropomorphized Hard Cash. Luckier in his first rescue of the Cash in India, Dodd has already experienced a revulsion of his simple faith in commercial integrity that prefigures the subsequent inversion of this predictable plotline: "a blind terror took the place of blind trust in him" (91). As he retrieves his savings from "a great Calcutta house, which gave eight per cent for deposits," he does not so much finally heed "the common-sense cry, 'Good interest means bad security'" (91), as that he considers his fortuitous escape as a deliverance from a danger that is explicitly coded as foreign. His emotions nevertheless continue to sea-saw like stock-market graphs: as he "[finds] himself somehow safe in the street clutching the cash," he is propelled from a "natural chill" into "triumphant glow," topped by "a novel and strange feeling [. . .], a sense of personal danger [so that the] material treasure, the hard cash, which had lately set him in a glow, seemed now to load his chest and hang heavy round the neck of his heart" (91–92). Still, this dread of personal danger is preferable to blind reliance on banks, at home and abroad.

The all too workable projection of any indeterminate threat onto the foreign ominously foreshadows financial fraud at the Empire's center. As Daniel Thorner has discussed in *Investment in Empire: British Railway and Steam Shipping Enterprise in India, 1825–1849*, "[r]ailways for India were 'in the air' in the early 1840's," and the general repercussions of the railway mania caused crashes throughout the Empire.[36] *Hard Cash* may not go into much detail in discussing the situation of East India businesses at the time, but it is vital to its representation of foreign speculation that Dodd's savings are nearly swallowed up by bank failures in Calcutta. Ironically, because they occur in "the East," they fail to prevent Dodd from considering his neighbor's bank the ideal haven for his imported treasure. On the contrary, in distinguishing between bank failures in India and what he deems a safe investment in homely respectability, his one-sided vilification of foreign banks is built on a near fatal misconception:

> He and It landed on the quay. He made for home.
> On the way he passed Hardie's bank, a firm synonymous in his mind with the Bank of England.
> A thrill of joy went through him. Now it was safe. [. . .] He longed to see It safe out of his own hands and in good custody.
> He made for Hardie's door with a joyful rush, waved his cap over his head in triumph, and entered the bank with It.
> Ah! (156)

The threat posed by banks in India can be all too easily explained away by the fact that they are situated abroad. They are part of colonial, inherently indeterminate commerce. Although Dodd's logic is exposed as flawed, what Reade terms the novel's "nautical" scenes (ii) in the preface ironically pay into the same dichotomous structure. Valuable time is lost as the ship has to wait to get a "chop," permission to leave China (89). In a direct alignment with this official form of commercial piracy, the South China

Seas are reputed to be swarming with symptomatically indeterminate pirates whose origins remain indecipherable: "the crew was a mixed one" (92), "a wild crew of yellow Malays, black chinless Papuans, and bronzed Portuguese" (109)—Asians and Europeans united by the common goal of making profit in a parody of international commercial agreements. In a reinforcement of racial alignments with commercial rapacity, the Cash is moreover nearly stolen by a passenger's servant. A peculiarly obnoxious by-product of imperialism, a colonialist's wife arrives as part of Dodd's shipment, with "brat and poodle" as well as with a string of servants: "item her white maid, item her black nurse, item her little boy and male Oriental in charge thereof, the strangest compound of dignity and servility, and of black and white" (89). The latter's hybridity aligns him with the pirates' version of an international corporation, a result of commercial imperialism both.

The retelling of familiar narratives is explicitly addressed. The Hard Cash's journey is a colonial adventure tale Dodd plans to recount breathlessly in what he deems the safety of home. Its picaresque voyages are brought out by a staccato invocation reminiscent of chapter headings in travel narratives "How would he tell them Its adventures—Its dangers from pirates—Its loss at sea—Its recovery—Its wreck—Its coming ashore dry as a bone; and conclude by taking It out of his bosom and dropping It in his wife's lap with 'Cheer, boys, cheer!'" (154). But instead of thrusting the capitalized "It" into the safe lap of the embodied domestic bosom, he deposits the money in the local bank on the way home. Warning of the bank's impending crash comes too late, and Hardie stands exposed as a pirate: "I saw you put It into that safe: a liar is always a thief. You want to steal my children's money: I'll have your life first. My money! ye pirate!" (175). In his rage, Dodd suffers an apoplexy and is carried home not only unconscious, but amnesiac, until the fortuitous double restoration of his money and his sanity, his social and his personal identity, at the end of the novel. However unexpectedly the bank's failure may come to Dodd in his "nautical or childlike confidence" (91), it is firmly situated within the repercussions of stock-market speculations on national and international businesses. Recounting a history of bubbles, the novel at once evokes the expectedness of the ups and downs captured by stock-market graphs as well as novels and pinpoints an acceleration. It is a picking up of speed in the recurrence of crashes. Having successfully negotiated company scams in the 1820s, Hardie is both villain and victim in the railway mania of the 1840s. Yet the recycling of popular paper fictions in *Hard Cash* accomplishes a lot more than simply a referencing of lists of bubbles. A crash in the past has set up the banker in more senses than one. During the financial crises of the mid-twenties, Hardie saves the bank by reclaiming it from a multiplication of bubbles:

> You have read of bubbles: the Mississippi Bubble and the South Sea Bubble. Well, in the year 1825, it was not one bubble but a thousand; mines by the score, and in distant lands; companies by the hundred; loans to every nation or tribe; down to Guatemala, Patagonia, and Greece; two hundred new ships were laid on the stocks in one year, for your dear papa told me; in short, a fever of speculation [. . . .]. [Y]ou must try and realise that these bubbles, when they rise, are as alluring and reasonable as they are ridiculous and incredible when one looks back on them; even soap bubbles, you know, have rainbow hues till they burst: and, indeed, the blind avarice of men does but resemble the blind vanity of women: look at our grand-mothers' hoops, and our mothers' short waists and monstrous heads! (82–83)

The respectable banker has been made by his management of bubbles. Mrs. Dodd's retelling of the financial romances of the Regency period, however, operates on three interconnected levels. First, it establishes Hardie's traits, including his "'sound commercial principles'—that means, I believe, 'get other people's money, but do not risk your own'" (83). Simultaneously, it accounts for Hardie's past as a parvenu banker. Once an unsuccessful suitor for Mrs. Dodd's hand, he has his son confined in an insane asylum when the latter proposes to Mrs. Dodd's daughter. This has less to do with personal resentment (yet another red herring) than with the fact that he has embezzled his son's money. Still, it is an important undercurrent in the condemnation of the upstart banker that he thereby also cheats the children of a neighbor of aristocratic lineage. A quickly rehearsed silver-fork prehistory establishes this great house family as "the fruit of a misalliance" between "a young lady well born, high bred, and a denizen of the fashionable world" (1), and the captain of an East Indiaman, a gentle, simple, man whom "they call Gentleman Dodd" (93) at sea. But if Mrs. Dodd thinks that her saved "loose cash, to speak *a la* Hardie" (84) might make up for Hardie's perceived financial superiority, she has miscalculated. Any social or financial estimates have meanwhile burst as part of "a respectable bubble" (99).

This is the third, and most important, revision of financial plots in the novel. The bubbles of the 1840s cannot be contained as easily as those of the 1820s. The railway mania may have started as a common "speculative fever due to the whirligig of time" (100), but it has become unmanageable. Because he "itche[s] for a share of the booty" (101) in a clear reference to the South Sea pirates who are likewise after the Hard Cash, Hardie decides to profit from others' credulity. But with the coming of the railways, the recurrence of financial panics has gathered speed as well. The effect on the banker is a crash of his belief in the representational value of paper money. It is clearly dangerous "to be a convert, real or false, to Bubble" (101). The tracking of a progressing corruption is scattered throughout the narrative. First Hardie only starts, "like thousands before him, [...] fabricating and maturing a false balance-sheet" (103). Then he embezzles his children's trustee money. Subsequently, he resorts to bribery to silence a clerk who has acquired knowledge that gives him a dangerous hold over his employer. So far he has been calculating on cash flows; now he lusts for the sheer physicality of the cash deposit he refuses to return:

> He must have a look at It.
>   He stole back, opened the safe, and examined the notes and bills.
>   He fingered them.
>   They seemed to grow to his finger.
>   He lusted after them. (177)

This handling of money issues a conversion featured as a frightful physical transformation. Hardie's clerk, the ominously named Skinner, functions as a double to act out its literalization. A speculator and miser on a smaller scale, he keeps shiny sovereigns in a torn mattress, "rubb[ing] them with an old toothbrush and whiting every week" (439). At the end of the novel, Skinner is found dead, with the purloined "Receipt, the soul of the lost Cash" (455), still grasped in his fingers. These clutching claws are as shriveled and dry as the brittle piece of paper itself: "they peeped at the Receipt: they touched the weird figure. Its yellow skin sounded like a drum, and its joints creaked" (455). The money has absorbed Skinner's life. The Hard Cash's legal possessors are grouped "motionless round the body that held the Receipt, the soul of the lost Cash, and still, as in life, seemed loth [sic] to part with it" (455). This spectral invocation of the dead man's miserly hold over the Cash's "soul" as embodied in a particularly brittle, shriveled piece of paper underscores paper money's preternatural power. Hardie likewise lusts after paper before the last stages of his madness conjure up imaginary sovereigns. His obsessive belief in the transmittance of value breaks down the relationship between paper and what it represents: "He had converted the notes into gold direct, and the bills into gold through notes; this was like going into the river to hide his trail. Next process: he turned his gold into L. 500 notes" (188). The repeated conversion of the coveted object induces him to believe in the fictionality it incorporates to the extent that he ends up living in a nightmarish fiction. The son he has had institutionalized for erotic monomania and a "little delusion" (259) about his father's illegal hold over the Cash ironically escapes from the asylum to find the banker "a monomaniac" who "writhe[s] under imaginary poverty" and dies soon after, "his end being hastened by fear of poverty" (472–73).

The novel may have been originally conceived as an exposure of manipulative diagnoses of insanity, but speculation underpins the central madhouse narrative and links it to the nautical, suburban, and romance plots.[37] Both loss of money and a too obsessive retention of it (i.e., monomaniacal miserliness) can cause madness. Financial speculation leads as naturally to manias and bubbles as to fraud and embezzlement. Once Hardie has begun to fabricate a false balance sheet and to speculate with his children's money (inherited from his dead wife), he needs to rid himself of his son. As in numerous sensation novels—Collins's earlier *The Woman in White* famously among them—the insane asylum offers a convenient containment of undesirable relatives. The chief irony is of course that it is the speculating banker who turns out to be deranged. In addition, Reade's novel makes clear that madhouses themselves promise a profitable speculation. The madhouse in which the unsuspecting young man is locked up is the property of "a full-blown pawnbroker of Silverton town, whom the legislature, with that keen knowledge of human nature which marks the British senate, permitted, and still, permits, to speculate in Insanity, stipulating, however, that the upper servant of all in his asylum should be a doctor; but omitting to provide against the instant dismissal of the said doctor should he go and rob his employer of a lodger—by curing a patient" (273). Private asylums are included in large-scale building speculations, but beyond that, papers recording false statements have the power to entrap Hardie's son. Certificates of insanity are a paper fiction created at and for the maintenance of madhouses erected as a financial speculation. The Hard Cash alone drives no fewer than four men mad in its name: Dodd, Hardie, Skinner, and Markley. This manifold vilification of paper is effectively counterpoised when the spiritualized Cash literally finances the happy end of the romance plot. It operates within a proliferation of paper that accentuates its versatility, its malleable, multidirectional, essentially ungovernable power. A cryptic advertisement in the newspaper gives Dodd's daughter hope that her lover has not deserted her, at the same time "keep[ing] her in his power" (360); a note written in blood and pinned to her parasol reaches Mrs Dodd after her visit to the asylum; a published letter on "Private Madhouses" spells out the novel's exposure of more than just Hardie's scheme. As the only uncorrupted physician in the novel (a largely comical character) puts it, "Justice is the daughter of Publicity" (408). In other words, if paper can do a lot of damage, it can also set everything right again. Much more than a rehearsal of truisms about the mighty pen, this addresses a fascination with paper currencies and, by extension, with any circulating paper.

Hard Cash ultimately reinstates paper as a viable currency, as Hard Cash, and certifies the power of its receipt (an even thinner paper fiction) to call back "the magic sum": "Thus rose the Hard Cash a second time from the grave" (473). This is not to say that paper is no longer dangerous. It can be manipulated, but never safely managed. This ambiguity issues a crucial warning that additionally underlines its binding power. Even among close relatives, the following rule applies: "Catch me signing a paper without reading it" (243). An assumption of trust would mean playing into the hands of those who make a profit out of others' credulity. It is, in fact, not so much that the novel exposes piracy at home, but that it asserts the value of suspicion in a modern financial world anywhere. Dodd is right to retrieve his money from the collapsing East India houses, but he is wrong in thinking that an English bank would be any safer. Just as he fights for his spoils with South Sea pirates, he should not expect piratical bankers to be any less ruthless. After the restitution of the Cash, the insane banker is kept on a fictitious salary until his death of imaginary poverty. Those who survive have accepted the necessity for mutual distrust: to read carefully what they sign, to ask for receipts, and not to rely on the outwardly solid. The conversion of foreign currencies, or of colonial financial practices, into threats at home functions as a warning in a bubble economy that leaves no safe haven even in the immediate family.

Converting Guilty Legacies:
Colonial Property Lost at Home

In a diametrically opposed trajectory, the titular diamond of Wilkie Collins's *The Moonstone* is turned into paper. Its concealment in the Empire's financial center brings to light swindles at home in a twofold rewriting of traditional inheritance plots. In the often-cited words of the butler Betteredge, "here was our quiet English house suddenly invaded by a devilish Indian Diamond—bringing after it a conspiracy of living rogues, set loose on us by the vengeance of a dead man" (46). A contested diamond in precolonial times as well, the moonstone is carried off as part of an illegal looting after the battle of Seringapatam in 1799. Although this appropriation provides the impetus for a plot of guilty legacies, this is not the theft under investigation. The moonstone's elusive presence throughout most of the text determines an intricate interrogation of inheritance, colonial guilt, and personal debts that generates a self-reflexive adaptation of prevailing financial plots. Presented in the form of embedded family papers, the moonstone's previous history promises a revising of predictable cultural fictions through a reordering of such papers. Briefly, Colonel Herncastle has pilfered a sacred diamond from a Hindu temple. Given that he is aware that in its wake follows a "conspiracy" with the purpose to retrieve it, he makes it a very dubious birthday present when he bestows it posthumously, in token of his "free forgiveness" (53), on his estranged sister's daughter, Rachel Verinder. "Free forgiveness" is a tautology that bespeaks a conflation of various exchanges that need to be revisited in the new set of papers that make up the structure of *The Moonstone*.

Trading on the expected mystique of foreign spaces, the dangerous legacy denotes the Colonel as a peculiarly preposterous incarnation of the wicked fairy. It promises an intrinsically sensational narrative revolving on "[t]he wicked Colonel's will," "the wicked Colonel's executor," and "the wicked Colonel's Diamond" (42). As a replication that simultaneously operates, ironically, as an orientalist appropriation of the curse that comes with the plundered diamond, the Colonel's own rewriting of his past is matched by the novel's conversion of the moonstone's story into paper. Once it is stolen for the second time, and this time from within the great house, the three Indians who have been sent to retrieve it are put in custody without proof. This leaves the only person who endeavors to profit from the theft free to turn the diamond into paper: into a moneylender's receipt and cash. The real thief is Rachel's cousin, Godfrey Ablewhite. A respectable barrister of aristocratic lineage as well as a popular philanthropist, Ablewhite unites a good background with a new professionalism, just as he fuses interest in the law and institutionalized charity. His concealed character is brought to light by a temptation that is offered not so much by the mysterious diamond itself as by the monetary value it represents. Its conversion into paper, he wrongly believes, might be able to divorce it from its origins and thereby rid it of its original functions as a religious icon and a symbol of colonial guilt.

In this retracing of repeatedly converted papers, *The Moonstone* offers a multilayered rewriting of popular financial narratives. Their very familiarity promises an intricate detective plot premised on false leads. In a twofold projection, the Colonel's intrusion into sectarian conflict in India is matched by a long-standing family feud in England. The circulating paper fictions of the looted diamond link distant relatives together even as they bring out conflicts at home that center on inheritance. Franklin Blake's father, it is therefore important to note within the English prehistory of the narrative, has been drawn into the affair of the moonstone through an exchange of papers that relate to potential legacies. In a deliberate reversal of speculation plots that are contingent on remote possibilities of an inheritance. Blake senior has had "the misfortune to be next heir to a Dukedom, and not to be able to prove it" (28). Like the bulk of expected fortunes in the novel, it remains a "mis-fortune." What makes him responsible for the moonstone's "safe custody" (48) is Herncastle's "possession of certain papers which were likely to be of service to him [Blake] in his lawsuit" (47). The "exchange of friendly services" (48) Herncastle proposes to Blake is a fateful transaction that legitimizes the moonstone's importation into the great house. As Blake has agreed to manage Herncastle's affairs (which boil down to his obsession with the moonstone) after his death, the arrangement brings Blake junior to Lady Verinder's estate and then, guided by opium-enhanced feelings of responsibility, into Rachel's bedroom in an involuntary, because unconscious, attempt to take charge of her treasure. The unrealized lawsuit that induces Blake senior to trade his services thus plays a crucial role in setting the plot in motion. As a typical inheritance plot, it is left at the margins of the narrative through a symptomatic substitution. The disputed dukedom is displaced by plots involving traceable pawnbrokers' receipts and checks, contrasting histories of debt, and foreign incursions within the moral economies of the great house.

This parallelism may invite (and has amply invited) colonial discourse analysis, but at the same time, it also has an important impact on the novel's structure.[33] Within its dual plotting of incursions, the sexual connotations of Franklin Blake's entry into Rachel's bedroom are of course compelling as is the linkage between the looting of India and the symbolic violation of Rachel. It bespeaks an emasculation of "the Orient" that identifies women and the colonized "East," while projecting this violation onto a foreign penetration of domestic space. Franklin takes the diamond under the influence of opium (a colonial import) and thereby just as unwittingly renders it available to Ablewhite, who secretly observes the "thief." However, the narrative use of foreign contaminants does not stop there. In an additional spin on colonial invasion, or physical infection, a matter of opium is turned into a matter of fact after all: "The Colonel had been a notorious opium-eater for years past; and, if the only way of getting at the valuable papers he possessed was by accepting a matter of opium as a matter of fact, my [Franklin's] father was quite willing to take the ridiculous responsibility imposed on him" (48). The "ridiculous responsibility" turns out to be his son's only inheritance, while the lawsuit projected by Blake senior is replaced by the written enactment of a courtroom scene that structures *The Moonstone* itself. So far from being expunged, foreign elements extricate complicated interrelationships at home and abroad.

The real legacy is the diamond's conversion into paper, into the written accounts that make up the novel itself. It is a conversion that countermands its exchange for a receipt or banker's check. As Betteredge hopefully suggests, this bequest rewrites the diamond's history: "I picture to myself a member of the family reading these pages fifty years hence" (197). These new family papers have successfully written out the inherited extracts with which the novel opens. The tracing of the receipt has generated a mass of papers, ranging from the transcribed mutterings of a delirious doctor commenting on his "experiment" with opium on the hapless Blake to the commissioned accounts of a series of witnesses of the moonstone's history. For the novel's brilliantly parodied arch-hypocrite, the cash-poor, but "spiritually-wealthy" (201), Miss Clack, a worshipper of Ablewhite, the account is tellingly supplied only in exchange for a check. Matching her ethical bookkeeping, in which dry pamphlets need to be circulated to amass credit in the afterlife, her "wealthy relative's cheque [as] the incubus of [her] existence" (208) is accepted as an expression of "self-denial" (202).[39] Her free distribution of the pamphlets she deems of value is a mock-version of Herncastle's present of the moonstone as a sign of his "free forgiveness." As Ilana Blumberg has suggested, such unwanted gifts puncture the larger system of moral accounting, and in its referencing of colonial legacies of guilt, the novel "reminds us that the identity of a circulating object is hardly stable, that it takes its identity in exchange."[40] Not only might theft be turned into gift giving, which is again a placing of a debt that implicitly demands a return, but when the doubly stolen and bequeathed diamond eventually resurfaces in the forehead of a deity in India, its recirculation has clearly put it back where it came from.[41]

The repeated transposition of the foreign, however, is not so much about the return of the Indians or of the diamond than about the exposure of the seemingly respectable at home. In tune with the paradigms of the sensation novel's domestic Gothic, Franklin Blake's cosmopolitanism functions as another red herring. The result of his father's exasperation with England, English law, and English society—an exasperation that additionally links Blake senior to misanthropic Herncastle—Franklin has been (in Betteredge's words) "sorely transmogrified" (56) by "[t]hat foreign training of his—those French and German and Italian sides of him" (80). This is the result of having "lived here, there, and everywhere; his address (as he used to put it himself) being 'Post Office, Europe—to be left till called for'" (29). Contrary to appearances, the villain is not this debt-ridden cosmopolitan either, but big, rosy, respectable Able*white*. If his final exposure in the disguise as a black sailor reinstates the identification of colonial guilt as a threat to domesticity, it is done so with a marked irony. His identification is achieved through an unmasking that reveals seeming foreignness abused as a convenient camouflage: "He's washing off his complexion now!" (447). After his death, his shady past comes to light: he has sold out trustee money by forging a signature, and what chiefly accounts for his debts is his expensive mistress, who is at the heart of his double life: a "side kept hidden from the general notice" in "a villa in the suburbs which was not taken in his own name, and with a lady in the villa, who was not taken in his own name, either" (452). This abandonment of "[t]he Indian clue to the mystery" (94) for a dubious suburbia simultaneously identifies different alterities.

Reade's novel uses piracy as a metaphor to criticize financial speculators at home, in a suburb by the sea. In Collins's novel, the exposure of the villain's double life in Victorian suburbia aligns it with various alterities. As these two novels rewrite the threat that foreign trade may pose at home, they both suggest a startling connection between suburbia and "exotic" territories. The connection between the indeterminacy of dubious financial transactions and foreign spaces clearly provides one of the most often used structures in Victorian speculation plots. Its redeployment within the metaphorical projections onto domestic spaces at once parallels and reinforces an ongoing rewriting of popular plotlines based on these shifting alignments. The pairing of two realist domestic novels of the 1850s and two sensation novels of the 1860s pinpoints the significance of these shifts. *The Newcomes* and *Little Dorrit* question the most common stereotypes connected with mysterious forms of speculation, at home and abroad; the latter by eschewing a plot of detection that prefigures sensational narratives of speculation to instate instead a personal emotional economy of free exchange at home. *Hard Cash* pivots on the inversion of untrustworthy commerce abroad, taking further the rewriting of the stage nabob that is already present in Thackeray's novel. *The Moonstone* locates the villain within the great house to show that the foreign element's infiltration can act as an expulsion of intrinsic corruption. It becomes a purging process, wherein the metaphorical alignment between colonies and marginal geographies at home indicates a further complication that plays with the villain's camouflage. But what is more, like Ablewhite's fatal disguise as a black sailor, his secret second home in the suburbs suggests a doubly dubious association with spaces that are foreign to domestic moral economies.

Four

Speculators at Home

The most pertinent narrative function of Victorian stock-market villains remains grounded in the mysteries attached to their dubious financial transactions. Cunning speculators who place bets on their victims' greed or gullibility have consequently received more attention than less glamorous, more exculpable moral vacillators. Unlike such helpless would-be entrepreneurs, scheming swindlers are the makers of fiction themselves, of fictitious commodities and identities. While they might end up embroiled in their own plots or lose control over conflicting narratives, there is something almost admirable, or awe-inspiring, in their large-scale scams that appeals to the imagination. However, when the paradigms of clichéd stock-market villainy become transposed, inverted, and exploited as cultural fictions within increasingly self-reflexive stock-market novels, they produce some of the most intricate plotlines. What I wish to explore in detail in this chapter is that it is primarily through metaphorical alignments that the speculator's at times vaguely denoted foreignness engenders and then queries the indeterminacies most commonly associated with this figure.[1] Financial transactions conducted abroad imbue even homebred stock-market villains with the requisite mystique as they cash in on the tantalizingly risky allure of foreign markets while remaining—securely, they believe—at home. But when these villains' reliance on exotic spaces is exposed as a false sense of security, the ejected components fold back upon them, disallowing such an easy divorce of business from the confines of the home.

This "domestication" of speculation plots—a relocation that at once situates financial crises in domestic space and renders them mundane and often dull—hinges on the rupture of the established literary functions with which specific spaces have become associated. While colonies, including former colonies such as parts of the Americas, serve as a major import and export center of swindlers and fraudsters, the Continent traditionally functions as a refuge for absconding bankrupts and nobility in straitened circumstances to form a set of clichés that likewise invites their reordering. Altogether, the mock–Grand Tour in search of retrenchment becomes inextricably linked to unpaid debts, so much so, in fact, that Dickens's Little Dorrit considers English society in continental Europe "a superior sort of Marshalsea" (511). After the crash in the wake of the 1873 World Exhibition in Vienna, central and eastern Europe began to displace the United States as an offstage financial Gothic: a "Wild East."[2] An anonymous article on "Romance in Business," published in *Blackwood's Magazine* in 1882, symptomatically denounced "those *bourses* of Eastern Europe which are the creations of yesterday" with a sense of resignation when faced with an apparently unstoppable development.[3] Welding together steamers to America as a place of opportunity for "the biggest capitalists, and the boldest ventures" on the one hand and "[t]he imposing architectural proportions of the new Bourses of Berlin and Vienna [as] the outward and visible signs of a financial revolution that has subverted social relations and levelled the old landmarks" on the other, the article spelled out a prevalent connection.[4] British novelists were not slow to capitalize on the ambiguous international reputation of any rival empire or commercial hub. Trollope's Melmotte has connections to suspicious ventures across the globe. He has passed through a series of migrations to and from New York, Paris, and Vienna, as well as Ireland, and his businesses see him involved with China, the Americas, and continental Europe.[5]

On an additional, metaphorically more intricate level, foreign locations are not merely combined with such an amorphous cosmopolitanism. Rather, they encompass fears and allures of indeterminacy that go far beyond a rehearsal of familiar types. Ellen Wood's cursory novella of a suicidal speculator, *Adam Grainger* (1876), lists transactions in both the Austrian-Hungarian Empire and the United States and contains one of the perhaps most outlandish speculations in Victorian popular culture. The "vast scheme of all" literally reaches for the moon: the "'Grand Atmospheric Moon and Middlesex Line,' with a branch (projected) to the tail of the new comet—which, you may all remember, appeared that year."[6] The railway to the moon had of course already featured as an epitome of overly ambitious speculative ventures in fiction ever since the railway manias of the forties. Robert Bell's *The Ladder of Gold* (1850) refers to a new gullibility nourished by railway speculation's reliance on scientific progress as a tactic of persuasion: "The people had believed in the South Sea, in the Mississippi, in the Unknown Tongues. Why should they not believe in the conquest of time and space by practical science?"[7] Just as "the skies were to be scaled [and] hissing locomotives were to rush over the tops of houses," it is in the same vein that it "was not quite decided whether an attempt would not be made to run a railway to the moon" (1:274). It is an expression of sheer hubris, as vast speculations are fed by a blind belief in progress. In the final decades of the century, such stellar enterprises became a reference to the exotic, indeterminate spaces in which fraudulent transactions could conveniently be placed. What makes Melmotte's major bubble project last so long in Trollope's satirical stock-market novel of 1875 is predictably its location at a great distance, in the hitherto unreachable regions that his fictitious railways are meant to open up. The South Central Pacific and Mexican Railway line is hardly less alluringly exotic and inscrutably remote than the juxtaposition of Middlesex and the Moon in Wood's novella a year later. Both narratives involve connections between exoticism as an additional attraction of the speculations in question and a twofold localization of the attendant indeterminacy in continental Europe and America.

It consequently comes as no surprise when Mrs. Cheveley in Oscar Wilde's 1895 play *An Ideal Husband* arrives from Vienna to import knowledge of foreign speculations to create havoc in London high society. In a reworking of the Victorian stock-market novel's paradigms that persuasively attests to its cultural impact as a recognizable subset of popular fiction, English aristocrats have to come to terms with the pressing need to adjust moral economies in domestic politics. By the end of the century, financial fiction's main clichés clearly could be conjured up with remarkable ease. Frequently, they served merely as shorthand for a cluster of associations. Precisely through such typecasting, however, their familiarity itself had paved the way for more experimental redeployments of the most common cases of gender, class, and ethnic stereotyping in ever more self-reflexive treatments of established topoi. In Wilde's play, it becomes almost comically symptomatic that the businesswoman from abroad is a would-be speculator of English origins. In this, she replicates, and yet also parodies, the genre's most favored resolution when she returns to the Continent. This is why Wilde's parodic restaging of financial plots provides such a good comparison to their reworking in the fiction of the time. As an insightful take on the much-used juggling with stereotypes and their inversions, it offers an ideal point of entry into a discussion of variously "domesticated" speculations.

While ultimately reasserting moral economies, *An Ideal Husband* plays with overtly realized typecasting. It does so by turning common alignments inside out. Mrs. Cheveley is a heavily exoticized woman with a dubious past connected to seductive financial affairs. Wilde's explicit stage directions suggest that she "looks rather like an orchid, and makes great demands on one's curiosity."[8] And yet she is really an English émigré, remembered as a thieving schoolgirl. Behind the veneer of carefully cultivated exoticism, she has simply moved into a large-scale realization of petty theft. What takes her back to England is a mixture of white-collar crimes that stretch from shady stock-market speculation to extortion. In order to appreciate fully the play's multiple reversals of established plotlines and clichés, it is necessary briefly to rehearse the offstage speculation plot of the past. In Vienna, Baron Arnheim has induced Mrs. Cheveley to "invest" (as she insists on putting it) in a canal scheme, a "brilliant, daring speculation" that, to "call things by their proper names," really is only "a commonplace Stock Exchange swindle" (30–31). The dichotomy of investment and speculation boils down to a swindle that is to be cemented by blackmail and deliberate misrepresentation. An incriminating letter reveals that Sir Robert Chiltern, under-secretary for foreign affairs, has made his fortune by selling a Cabinet secret to the foreign baron. Joseph Bristow has suggested that this makes Chiltern a feminized figure in that he "has prostituted himself, if not sexually, then to the God of Mammon" under the influence of a foreign aristocrat.[9] Underscoring this linkage of promiscuity and foreign speculation, Mrs. Cheveley refers to the current swindle as the deceased baron's "last romance" (32)

This echoes a favored resolution of earlier stock-market narratives, but in Wilde's play, it backfires with tragicomical effect. Chiltern's initial outrage at the proposition made by Mrs. Cheveley is vitiated with irony: "You have lived so long abroad, Mrs Cheveley, that you seem to be unable to realise that you are talking to an English gentleman." (34). Like so many typecast stock-market villains of mid-century fiction, she wishes to realize, to cash in on, the power of the paper she holds. Despite the juggling with moral economies, however, she is triumphantly outmaneuvered; the swindle publicly denounced; any streamlined ideals, including the "ideal husband" of the title, put up for revision. The play, in short, dramatizes the cultural impact of the Victorian stock-market novel even as it sets out to parody the values that are most commonly seen to underpin it. While capitalizing on the comically typecast seductiveness of foreign affairs, it eventually validates a moral realignment of economic and domestic matters within Chiltern's reassessed marriage. If the concomitant domestication of finance repeats an expected structure after all, it does so in a deliberately overdrawn fashion that sums up defining elements in the fictionalization of foreign financial transactions and their impact on the Victorian home.

This concluding chapter, in fact, analyzes the diverse attempts at "domesticating" stock-market narratives. Foreign speculation encapsulates the fear and the fascination with which various forms of indeterminacy are invested. Its attendant projections, however, are further complicated when they become addressed as a theme themselves. The businesswoman from abroad presents an inviting opportunity to showcase the resultant complexities, as Wilde's play clearly shows. Victorian domestic fiction by women writers, by contrast, deliberately sets out to retrieve just such typecast figures. The recuperation of women in business, of the suitable professional stockbroker, as well as of the innocuous would-be speculator, is one of the most direct approaches. But domestic fiction can also be seen to build on the admixture of threat and hope implied by a growing acknowledgment that the effects of business simply cannot be kept separate from the home. In order to highlight the zones of intersection across what may seem diametrically opposite ways of thematizing speculation's impact on private life, I therefore seek to track markedly divergent engagements with this domestication. As in previous chapters, this discussion is divided into two sections that provide complementary explorations of a specific structure or topos. The first part, "Building Speculation at Home," explores the figures and tropes of mobility that were being formed in the course of the century's second half, including the haunted commuter and collapsing building speculation. Their analysis simultaneously interrogates the use of "colonization" to describe what was happening in the suburbanization of Victorian Britain. From the building boom of the 1850s onwards, the representation of expanding suburbia continuously remade ideals of the domestic as defined against business transactions that ironically erected the suburban home on more than one level. If mid-century fiction such as Trollope's *The Three Clerks* (1857) already staged an ambiguous critique of such expansion, in the wake of the sensation craze fictional suburbia became literally haunted by spectralized speculators. Victorian suburban Gothic, Charlotte Riddell's *The Uninhabited House* (1875) will illustrate, literalizes this incursion of the otherworldly into the home.

"Romancing the Stock Market," the chapter's second section, then proceeds to revaluate the thematic as well as structural significance of financial speculation in late-Victorian domestic fiction. Oliphant's *Hester* (1883) and Ouida's *The Massarenes* (1897) both show foreign-born young women handle domestic and business matters capably as they redeem their father's legacies of failed speculation. They offer a solution to the recurring question of how to integrate domestic moral economies into the business world. In breaking through the divides of domestic/foreign, romance/business, and investment/speculation, commercial and love interests converge, allowing redemption for financial recklessness while business is shown to continue as before. Domestic fiction by women writers increasingly demonstrates that the promise of the sensational in speculation plots needs to be all the more securely contained since business itself cannot be expelled from the confines of the home. Oliphant's "The Stockbroker at Dinglewood" (1868) already dramatizes the incursion of predominantly sensational paradigms into domestic realism. An additional twist propels Oliphant's perhaps most ambiguous version of the sensational stock-market novel. *At His Gates* (1872) thematizes the problems of artistic production in a speculative economy by channeling business's manifold impact on literature and art into a self-reflexive consideration of competing narrative modes. Situated within a plethora of diversified stock-market fiction, the texts chosen for a more detailed analysis—*The Three Clerks, The Uninhabited House, At His Gates, Hester,* and *The Massarenes*—are not only representative of specific phases in the ongoing representation of the effects of speculation on Victorian domesticity. They contribute to an emergent literary tradition with an amount of self-reflexivity that issues a significant revaluation of the functions of finance in fiction.

Building Speculation at Home

In Trollope's *The Three Clerks*, the coming of commuter railways generates a peculiarly modern image of suburbanized, starfish-like London: "London will soon assume the shape of a great starfish. [. . .] The old town, extending from Poplar to Hammersmith, will be the nucleus, and the various railway lines will be the projecting rays."[10] As the novel traces the starfish's sprawling members along suburban railway tracks, it invites a careful reconsideration of suburbia's dual indebtedness to financial speculation: to building projects and to the growth of the stockbroking belt that rendered commuting necessary for a growing number of the City's workforce. In Trollope's mid-century novel, both ventures are shown to collapse traditional structures at home and at work: "It is very difficult nowadays to say where the suburbs of London come to an end, and where the country begins. The railways, instead of enabling Londoners to live in the country, have turned the country into a city" (21). The starfish reaches out;

the last rural refuges are no longer impervious to the effects of expanding urbanization or to the fluctuations of "ticklish stock, sir—uncommon ticklish" (433). An exotic animal rises up to finger the English countryside. Although evoked lightheartedly, it is a monstrous outgrowth, to be understood only as an otherworldly creature. Suburban developments in the Victorian imagination, I wish to suggest, emerge as an expanding field for fictional explorations in which the association between urbanization and ventures into foreign spaces powerfully draws into debate the promotion of "suburbanism" as the ultimate manifestation of the divorce of home and workplace. The construction of suburban fiction consequently takes place within a negotiation of domesticity that brings home the problems associated with different, yet interlinked, forms of expansion and mobility. In cutting across subgenres, it brings forth conspicuous clichés of "the suburban," but in an ambiguous process of redefinition that prompts us to reconsider still-current cultural myths of Victorian suburbia and its multifarious role in the representation of financial speculation.

After a brief sketch of suburbia's cultural as well as architectural construction as a speculative venture in the second half of the nineteenth century, I seek to trace metaphors of imperialist expansion in the literary and journalistic investigation of the countryside's "colonization" in fiction by popular writers as different as George Sala, Charles Lever, and Wilkie Collins. Crucial to middle-class self-definition, the creation of Victorian suburbia worked through the expulsion and containment of elements with which an upwardly mobile middle class was becoming uncomfortable. As Elizabeth Wilson points out in *The Sphinx in the City*, nineteenth-century planning reports, journalism, and government papers initiated a "campaign to exclude women and children, along with other disruptive elements," from inner-city spaces, a campaign that created suburbia as "this familiar, oppressive ideal of Victorian family life."[11] Coined in Mary Ward's 1888 *Robert Elsmere*, "suburbanism" as a colonization of cityscapes and minds came to be at the center, as it were, of this marginalization.[12] When T. W. H. Crosland published *The Suburbans* in 1905, he only consolidated an understanding of degeneration that was to prove notably persistent: "man was born a little lower than the angels and has been descending into suburbanism ever since."[13]

The suburban imaginaries of mid-century fiction, however, constituted a contested space that reflected an explosion of building speculations. This imaginative representation of suburban space has been elided, often shamefacedly, much as orientalist imaginaries had been before Edward Said resituated canonical nineteenth-century novels among imperialist discourses. Whimsical as such a linkage between suburbia and the colonies might seem, it symptomatically originated in nineteenth-century popular culture. Wilkie Collins's first sensation novel, *Basil* (1852), introduced this newly sensationalized space in all its "newness and desolation of appearance" as a "colony of half-finished streets, and half-inhabited houses."[14] A timely criticism, it appropriated the rampant building projects of the midcentury as a promising locus of sensational narratives. Although suburban areas had long been part of London's social and fictional cityscape, as a conceptualized space, "suburbia" was created by the construction boom of the 1850s.[15] It was a concerted effort to offer escape from overcrowded city spaces. The irony was that the rush in building rapidly devalued land. Overspeculating condemned oversized villas to almost instantaneous conversion into subdivided tenements. Slums formed in their wake, following and unleashing railway lines, making future developments "leap-frog" them, as H. J. Dyos and D. A. Reeder have put it in their seminal "Slums and Suburbs."[16] Suburbanism as a cultural concept might have been discussed only in the last third of the century, but journalists and novelists in the early 1850s were particularly outspoken about the effects of overspeculation.

Anecdotal accounts in the periodical press of the time regularly issued warnings against the purchase of developments in the suburbs. Printed in *Household Words* in 1852, George Sala's "Dumbledowndeary" satirizes the impact of the building boom in a fictional Kentish town. The Dumbledowndeareans are shown to speculate so ardently on the prospective financial outcome of its suburbanization that it "may be called without much exaggeration a Town to Let."[17] They throw "themselves upon bricks [and] extensive operations and speculations in bricks" in an apogee of capitalist expansionism, conjuring up "one grim brick mausoleum of dead capital."[18] In practical terms, this meant either demolition or conversion into lodgings. This did not prevent ruthless speculators from advertising devalued areas as new, quiet, even rural. In "A Suburban Connemara" (1851), likewise published in *Household Words*, T. M. Thomas took up this vexing issue: a clerk searches for a suburban home by drawing a semi-circle on a map to indicate the desired distance from his office. Yet when he views developments in the area, there are only slum-like tenements. What is remarkable is that the article refrains from criticizing the living conditions themselves. Instead, it exclusively aims to expose a shocking fraud. The speculators simply have not managed the property in an appropriate way to be able to offer it to the middle classes. The solution is to turn the boggy land to some use by building working-class tenements.[19]

Newly erected slums that anticipated "leap-frogging" bourgeois suburbia were soon peppered all over London's outer-city belt. The self-consciousness bred by a continuous progression from downgraded suburbs only further drove the colonization of surrounding villages. If this identification of sensationalized suburbia and the colonies quickly became hackneyed, it was precisely because it formed a convenient connection that worked for divergent ideologies. By 1884 an unsigned article on "Suburbanity" in *The Spectator* could glibly refer to the "numberless middle-class colonies which encircle London."[20] It is an intensely claustrophobic image, reminiscent of Trollope's starfish. Such images were eclipsed by the grasping tentacles in H. G. Wells's *The War of the Worlds* (1898): the Martians' targeting of London's suburbs provides a metaphorical vehicle for this emerging space's disturbingly "other" cartography.[21] By the 1890s, this had become almost a standard imagery (and standard complaint) with reference to urban sprawl. In Arthur Conan Doyle's *The Sign of Four* (1890), Sherlock Holmes traces a legacy of colonial riches (and colonial guilt) through "the howling desert of South London" to a "forbidding neighbourhood" reached along "the monster tentacles which the giant city was throwing out into the country."[22] Although the suburban homes of Conan Doyle's domestic narratives can seem an antithesis to the mysterious London of his detective stories,[23] Holmes's suburbia is not only an extension of "dark London," but a marginal space in which crime can be concealed even better. In *Beyond the City: An Idyll of a Suburb* (1893), Conan Doyle describes the city's "long brick feeler [thrown] here and there, curving, extending and coalescing, until at last the little cottages had been gripped round by these red tentacles."[24] They invite comparison with the sprawling traces of blood left behind by the Martians' ships in Wells's novel.

In a twofold bind of colonial metaphors, the majority of journalistic and literary representations generally envisioned suburbs as a diseased growth. There was considerable irony in this since organizations like "The Home Colonisation Society" or "The English Land Colonisation Society" had been set up to promote healthy housing especially for lower-middle-class suburbanites.[25] Victorian fiction proved almost unanimously critical. In *The Nether World* (1889), George Gissing targets just such ostensible remedies for overcrowding in inner-city spaces as "a wholesome demolition" that robs slum dwellers even of the comfort of the familiar since these "model-lodgings" appear constructed on the principle of comfortlessness: "The economy prevailing in to-day's architecture takes good care that no depressing circumstance shall be absent from the dwellings in which the poor find shelter."[26] This dual critique of aesthetic and social disruption had significantly been prefigured by delineations of railway constructions from the mid-century onwards. Dickens's *Dombey and Son* (1848) perhaps most memorably presents the coming of suburban railways as "a great earthquake" that leaves in its wake "carcases of ragged tenements, and fragments of unfinished walls."²⁷ But throughout nineteenth-century fiction, from Sanditon's artificial enlargement in Austen's uncompleted narrative to the explosion of suburban constructions in the mid-nineteenth century, the critique of building speculation's colonization of the countryside continuously reengages with the putative civilizing mission of such projects. There is considerable ambiguity in often spurious attempts to disentangle the effects of building speculations (and the notorious "coming of the railways") from the dynamics of speculation itself. "A Tale of the Railway Mania," A. MacFarlane's *Railway Scrip; Or, The Evils of Speculation* (1856), for example, concedes that railways may "exert a beneficial influence over the trade and commercial interests," but speculating on them sets loose "a demon spirit [. . .] to delude and infatuate mankind—to call up the very lowest and worst feelings of the human heart."²⁸ Conversely, Charles Lever's *Davenport Dunn* (1857–59) connects stock-market swindles to the confiscation of land in Ireland by the means of a railway line that is supposed to "civilize" remote areas that are considered a hazardous speculation due to their resistance to such civilizing:

> The panic created at the first moment by a law that seemed little short of confiscation, the large amount of landed property thus suddenly thrown into the market, the prejudice against Irish investment so strongly entertained by the moneyed classes in England, all tended vastly to depreciate the value of those estates which came first for sale; and many were sold at prices scarcely exceeding four or five years of their rental. An accidental disturbance in the neighbourhood, some petty outrage in the locality, was enough to depreciate the value; and purchasers actually fancied themselves engaged in speculations so hazardous that nothing short of the most tempting advantages would requite them for their risk.²⁹

Lever's contribution to stock-market fiction may follow its paradigms with a notable predictability, yet as it trades on a widespread preoccupation with internal colonization through the coming of the railways, it also dramatizes the Irish Question within this new medium of financial fiction. The controversial Irish Encumbered Estates Bill of 1849 permits the novel's titular speculator to buy up Irish estates embarrassed by debts.³⁰ Ireland is mapped out as "the bush," a "wild and untravelled country" to which even fraudulently supported ventures may constructively introduce progress (2:158). There certainly is nostalgia for "this Ireland of long ago [of which] there will soon be no vestige" (2:158), although the reference to such vestiges builds on the pervasive terminologies of evolutionary discourse—

rendered notorious by Robert Chambers's *Vestiges of the Natural History of Creation* (1844)—to suggest an inevitable step. Nevertheless, a warning is premised on metaphors of imperialist expansion: "It will be interesting, doubtless, to see the last receding steps of a departing race. [. . .] I am not, however, one of those who think that to promote the advancement of this country you must treat the Irishman as the Yankee does the Red Indian" (2:165). Building speculation as a form of internal colonization is associated with the worst atrocities of colonialism.

Colonial metaphors and their literalization, in short, critique speculative ventures and vice versa. Throughout the century's second half, popular writing in the periodical press and in novel form as well as in advice manuals, studies of urban planning, and the first sociological reports thus amply attested not only to the pressing urgency, but also the narrative potential, of urban expansion. What Dickens had already memorably indicted as "Telescopic Philanthropy" in *Bleak House* became exposed as an extended analogy in General Booth's influential *In Darkest London and the Way Out* (1890). In one of the most elaborate uses of imperialist rhetoric to explore slums at home, Booth mimicked Henry Stanley's *Through the Dark Continent* (1879), an immensely popular account of "'Darkest Africa' and his journeyings across the heart of the Lost Continent," to expose neglect of the urban poor in the wake of commercial speculations abroad and at home.[31] Stanley's descriptions may offer "a terrible picture, and one that has engraved itself deep on the heart of civilisation," but there is a "darkest England" as well as a "darkest Africa" that demands as much attention: "May we not find a parallel at our own doors, and discover within a stone's throw of our cathedrals and palaces similar horrors to those which Stanley has found existing in the great Equatorial forest?"[32]

While this suggests a counterpoise to the adoption of the tentacles of urban sprawl in social satire, detective fiction, and early science fiction, there is an additional irony in what becomes a curiously twofold (and inadvertently contradictory) deployment of colonial metaphors. Booth suggests the exportation of slum dwellers to colonies abroad as a solution to the problem of overcrowding, exemplifying an ambiguity that permeates such parallels throughout Victorian writing. Since "City Colonies" at home are to prepare future colonists for exportation, the analogy becomes reversed. An accompanying graphic features a map of England that breaks it up into these "City Colonies" leading to the outer "Farm Colonies" in the countryside, from which the colonists are then dispatched. After using colonization as a metaphor to condemn neglect at home, Booth thus advocates emigration, promoting the construction of what he terms "Over-Seas Colonies" as "pieces of Britain distributed about the world, enabling the Britisher to have access to the richest parts of the earth."[33] Reactions at the time deplored both the solution and the analogy of imperialist exploration underpinning it. In *General Booth's Book Refuted* (1890), for example, H. M. Hyndman regretted this connection to "the last infamous journey of the canting and murdering filibuster Stanley through 'Darkest Africa,'" suggesting that this alone would already give rise to prejudice, before proceeding to criticize the idea of the overseas colony itself.[34]

Beyond this pervasive linkage of exploration and the "dark Continent," the creation of the suburban home as the space of the exile's and the commuter's desire, the bungalow as the product of a two-way exportation of suburban and colonial consumerism,[35] and the simultaneity of building speculations and colonial expansion, including the emergence of colonial suburbs,[36] clearly pervaded the conception of Victorian suburbia. In more than one way, slippered City men at home encompassed the armchair imperialist within. Probably the best-known satire of Victorian suburbia, George and Weedon Grossmith's 1892 *The Diary of a Nobody* lays bare the commuting clerk's bourgeois utopia as a space of "miserable mediocrity" suitable for self-satisfied members of the lower middle classes.[37] Pooter proudly declares: "After my work in the City, I like to be at home. What's the good of a home, if you are never in it? 'Home, Sweet Home,' that's my motto. I am always in of an evening" (27). Pooter's railway suburb as domestic retreat marks out the endpoint of suburban building speculation as a cultural and social as well as financial construct. The commuter embodies the ultimate realization of the dichotomous split of home and business on which Victorian ideologies of domesticity are premised. The ways in which this figure can be pictured as riding through distinct subgenres help disclose overlaps created by the emplotment of speculative ventures at home. Trollope's first stock-market novel, *The Three Clerks*, engages with the everyday negotiation of suburban commuting in an ambiguously defensive fashion that expresses the complexities of shifting attitudes towards the suburban ideal. Suburban Gothic such as Riddell's can then be seen to make the most of what had by mid-century already become a rapidly evolving space characterized by immense fluidity. The figure of the commuter opens up new narrative structures by converting pressing anxieties into some of the most startling developments in Victorian fiction.

The Commuter's Refuge: Speculators on the Move

Numerous Victorians undoubtedly longed to be able to say with Wemmick in Dickens's *Great Expectations*, "the office is one thing, and private life is another. When I go into the office, I leave the Castle behind me, and when

I come into the Castle, I leave the office behind me."[38] This split certainly denotes the suburban clerk, with his miniature drawbridge, his livestock, kept securely within the Castle's boundaries, and his likewise well-guarded cucumber-frame, as an "emblem for the conflict of public and private life," as Alexander Welsh has memorably phrased it.[39] But it is one of the main ironies of Wemmick's Castle—and exactly these ironies are vital in Dickens's account of such self-enclosure—that this "little wooden cottage" is located among a "collection of back lanes, ditches, and little gardens [that] present the aspect of a rather dull retirement" (193). In the course of the nineteenth century, a lengthy commute became more and more common as homes within walking distance increasingly meant living in the slums. As John Tosh has shown in his study of "a man's place" in Victorian England, in representations of homecoming, imperialist traveler and commuter became (con)fused. The "penchant for the exile's sensibility was reflected in the homecoming rituals of middle-class homes: the waiting wife and daughters on the threshold, the proffered slippers, the armchair ready at the fireside."[40] In the figure of the commuter, a new fascination with the City met an opportunity for spatial exploration that presented suburbia as an evolving place that colonized the countryside.

As the commuter shuttled between city and suburb, between social spaces, along the lines of random junctures, or interchanges, he (seldom she) mapped out an emerging conceptual and literary landscape. Novelists took up such movements to find in them an apt representation of instability and uncertainty. In one of the most powerful descriptions of nineteenth-century commuting, Riddell's *The Race for Wealth* (1866) describes suburbanites being washed up in the City "on the tops of omnibuses, or hurrying from the various railway termini" in the commuter's new race.[41] The pressing crowds, the stress on speed, railway tracks restructuring urban space, all flow into a list of suburbs spewing out commuting employees:

> Work!—every man's mind is full of it. See you, as you walk along the streets in the early morning, men hurrying city-ward, men going forth to their labours. The pavements are crowded; the omnibuses are laden; [....] [from] all outlying towns and villages they come to work; they are to be met with in the back streets as in the main thoroughfares; they are to be found taking short cuts on foot,—beheld in the regular roads seated on the tops of omnibuses, or hurrying from the various railway termini. (193–94)

There is excitement as well as a resonating evocation of mindless pressure in Riddell's depiction of modern life in "city and suburb," as one of her novels is entitled. Suburban Gothic as it emerges in the mid-nineteenth century claims commuting as part of a new urban horror, a shifting space for supernatural encounters that feature as a projection of the commuter's experience. In J. Sheridan LeFanu's "Green Tea" in *In a Glass Darkly* (1872), for example, a mysterious demon appears when an omnibus passes a deserted mansion on a late-night ride from the city center to the suburbs.[42] Overall, suburban living is rarely presented in a favorable light in Victorian fiction. Trollope's *The Three Clerks* forms a notable exception and is clearly conceived as such. If the contested concept of the suburban home as domestic refuge is not entirely sustainable even as the narrative goes to great lengths to assert its moral economies, this only the more glaringly illuminates the ambivalence with which the growth of the stockbroking belt around London had come to be regarded.

In imagining one of the few positively presented suburban homes in Victorian fiction in *The Three Clerks*, Trollope carefully measures out its ideal distance from the city center, satirizing attendant class alignments. Located in Hampton, maintained by the widowed Mrs. Woodward and her three daughters, Surbiton Cottage at first only offers a feminized weekend shelter for the three eponymous clerks. It may exert a "salutary effect" (21) on Charley Tudor, the youngest and at first most irresponsible, but it does so in comparison with the cheaper suburb that would await him should he not extricate himself from an entanglement with a barmaid: "what would be the joy of returning to a small house in some dingy suburb and finding her to receive him?" (373). Since suburbs constructed for the working and lower-middle classes function as a foil to bourgeois ideals, the novel utilizes a recurring argument in public discussions of urban sprawl at the time.[43] But if Charley escapes the undesirable connection to the working-class suburb, his cousin, Alaric Tudor, moves too close to the city center after marrying Gertrude, the eldest Woodward daughter. There is no more refuge from the business world, and Alaric soon succumbs to the temptations of finance capitalism, including both stock-market speculation and embezzlement. They do not so much function as a corruptive influence as that they bring out an underlying competitiveness that needs to be expelled from a domestic ideal removed from the city's vicinity without merging into expanding slum areas.

The pressing social and aesthetic issues pertaining to devalued locations become an ominous joke in Trollope's novel. When would-be fashionable Mrs. Val advises Gertrude to "come down somewhat nearer to the world; indeed you must" (418), the relish Gertrude takes in shocking this snob is invested with a sense of doom: "'We are thinking of moving; but then we are talking of going to St. John's Wood, or Islington,' said Gertrude, wickedly. 'Islington!' said the Honourable Mrs Val, nearly fainting" (418–19). This proposed move foreshadows their plunge in social status and subsequent exile at the antipodes. Alaric's involvement in fraudulent transactions is a moral degradation that mirrors as well as propels their downward movement. He slips down the "[e]asy, very easy, [. . .] slope of hell" (352). He becomes a "rogue; despite his high office, his grand ideas, his exalted ambition; despite his talent, zeal, and well-directed official labours," and thus worse than Bill Sikes, the notorious brutal robber and murderer of *Oliver Twist*: "a robber, doubly disgraced by being a robber with an education, a Bill Sykes [sic] without any of those excuses a philanthropist cannot but make for the wretches brought up in infamy" (345–46). After Alaric has served his prison sentence for having embezzled trustee money he needs for his speculations, they emigrate to Australia.[44] They forfeit any return to Surbiton Cottage, the reward of the reformed clerk, Alaric's cousin Charley.

Trollope's idealization of suburbia has important limits. Surbiton Cottage can qualify as an acceptable prize only after it has been duly upgraded, re-formed as well. The novel's opening introduces it as "a desirable residence for a moderate family with a limited income [with] no pretension to the grandeur of a country-house" (21–22). But "sundry changes" render it almost unrecognizable so "that were it not for the old name's sake, we should now find ourselves bound to call the place Surbiton Villa, or Surbiton Hall, or Surbiton House" (541). It becomes a place of work through the very erasure of the divorce of the domestic from the workplace that has prompted the construction of bourgeois suburbia in the first place. After marrying the youngest Woodward daughter, Charley commutes during a five-day workweek, but during his leisure time he dedicates himself to his writing (his real vocation) at home while still enjoying a secure civil service income. In other words, suburbia can be reclaimed through the elision of its class, work, and gender specific conceptualizations. The plodding clerk becomes a successful writer and paterfamilias, and the suburban home is somewhat incongruously returned to the countryside.

This retrieval of the great house may embrace even commuting as part of the Victorian ideal of the home as a refuge from the dirt, noise, and stress of the city—elements that suburban spread of course brought along with it. Still, what Charley eventually attains is premised on a dual escape from "some dingy suburb": he is saved from an insalubrious working-class home; Surbiton Cottage from the "thronged multitude of men, women, and children" who bear down onto the country at weekends and increasingly in search of tenements to spoil bourgeois suburbia with "dirty bits of greasy paper which were left about on all sides" (47). It is an erasure of the ideal villa's working-class *doppelganger*, underscored by the parallel removal of Alaric and likewise of his fellow clerk Harry Norman, who marries the second Woodward daughter after Alaric has outdone him in their competition for the first. In contrast to the upstart Tudors, Norman is solid, patently honest, bears his genteel poverty with fortitude, and remains out of place in the City.[45] A small property, substantial enough to allow him to retire from the civil service, turns "Harry [into] Mr Norman of Normansgrove' (493) and thereby removes him from the novel's center. Whereas Harry is returned to the landed gentry as a world apart from urban modernity, and Alaric's emigration identifies financial business with a criminal history, the suburban home can be retrieved only through its transformation into a hall or house.

Such nostalgia for the elusive great house becomes more and more difficult to sustain. *The Three Clerks* indeed simultaneously prefigures the speculator's preoccupied spirit in suburban Gothic, if in a tongue-in-cheek fashion: "If any spirit ever walks it must be that of the stock-jobber, for how can such a one rest in its grave without knowing what shares are doing?" (458–59). The most memorable Victorian ghost, we have seen, is shackled by chains made of "cash-boxes, keys, padlocks, ledgers, deeds, and heavy purses wrought in steel" (17), as Gothic paraphernalia are updated to suit Scrooge's late business partner in Dickens's *A Christmas Carol*. A new urban and suburban Gothic elaborates on concerns introduced in mid-century stock-market narratives. Suburbia as a sensational space, in fact, evolves so rapidly into an established topos that Braddon's 1864 self-reflexive defense of sensation fiction, *The Doctor's Wife*, describes a "neglected suburban garden upon the 21st of July 1852" (31) as an instantaneously recognizable reference to the speculative building boom of the 1850s. The suburban household is complete with a cursorily sensationalized forger of checks. It is similarly on a suburban road that the eponymous Woman in White appears for the first time in Collins's influential sensation novel of 1860, and in St. Johns Wood that she is secretly divested of her identity. Anticipating the fully fledged realization of colonial metaphors in *The Moonstone*, Collins's *Armadale* (1866) describes suburbs in different stages of completion in the year 1851 and poses them against colonial settings. Their most extensive delineation is of a degenerating space in which evolution has been aborted: "Builders hereabouts appeared to have universally abandoned their work in the first stage of its creation."[46] Near this "atrophy of skeleton cottages," only "waste paper float[s] congenially to this neglected spot [. . .]. No growth flourished in these desert regions but the arid growth of rubbish" (453–54). Building speculation creates wastelands that harbor wasted heroes, bring forth a new species of villain, and set loose ghosts of a demolished past as the victims of building booms.[47] In Riddell's *The Uninhabited House,* the abandoned great house is literally haunted. Her increasingly sensationalized fictionalization of Victorian London and its expansion maps out most strikingly the significance of this emergent form of Gothic for narratives of financial speculation.

"Out for Compound Interest": Haunted Commuters

Although Charlotte Riddell is now chiefly remembered for her ghost stories, contemporary praise was foremost for her realist chronicling of City life.[48] Invitations to the reader to embark on virtual "city-tours" permeate her novels to such an extent that the opening of *George Geith of Fen Court* (1864) already refers to them as a commonplace: "I should like to take my readers thither. We have paced the City pavements together before now, and I am glad to be threading the familiar streets and alleys in good company again."[49] But while her fiction is structured by minute accounts of often dubious business, ranging from food adulteration in *The Race for Wealth* (1866) to color patents in *Mortomley's Estate* (1874), based on the Riddells' own experience of patent offices and subsequent bankruptcy, the City is embraced for its rich history as well as its present vibrancy. The hero of *The Race for Wealth* "loved London—loved it as those only who have grown thoroughly sick and weary of the country ever can come to love the mighty city" (77). In *Mitre Court: A Tale of the Great City* (1885), the City is a sublime space that promises various sensations: "O City! once interesting beyond all power of speech."[50] Such eulogies, however, at the same time indict urban planning as the destruction of the City's heritage to make way for a "mere aggregation of offices and warehouses" (68).[51]

Suburbanization especially constitutes a sore spot. However exhilarated Riddell's novels may be about the city center, they remain ambiguous about suburbia. Its promising title notwithstanding, *City and Suburb* (1861) only has a sickly woman escape "the bustle and the turmoil of London" to "the comparative quiet of Marsh Hall [. . .] [q]uite in the country."[52] *The Race for Wealth* traces Stepney's gradual absorption by London as a narrative of decline: "Of great antiquity and of great importance," it is "sinking in the social scale, sinking slowly and surely" (47). A nostalgically described "grand old mansion [. . .] is now a common lodging-house, and up the staircases and along the passages tramp John, Tom, and Harry—free of the premises at so much a night" (49).[53] In the same vein, Riddell's heroes and heroines frequently boast of (lost) legacies of landed wealth. Wellborn gentlemen enter the financial heart of London to prove themselves, as if in a foreign country. This certainly imbues the mundane business of the clerk, the engineer, or the speculative merchant with a narrative interest that goes beyond, even as it circles around, their attempts "to gain a prize in the business lottery" (68), as it is put in *The Race for Wealth*. In the same novel, nevertheless, Mr. Barbour, the hero's father, is said to have "shed natural tears at the idea of one of his sons demeaning himself by entering trade" (14). The chosen trade is sugar manufacture and food adulteration, controversial issues at the time. Young Barbour consequently sinks, like suburbanized Stepney, slowly, but surely, and his story is soon overtaken by that of Percy Forbes, a young gentleman who has a substantial inheritance to invest in more respectable business. The titular hero of *Mortomley's Estate* is likewise neither an upstart nor a born businessman, "at best as wretched a financier as he was an admirable inventor," and sports a pedigree: "Pedigree is one of those intangible and incontrovertible commodities which never commands a premium in the busy, bustling, practical city of London. [. . .] And yet the fact remained that the Mortomleys had once been country squires of some reputation."[54] What saves their business is symptomatically its relocation to the periphery. About to be liquidated at the novel's opening, the eponymous "estate" is a factory, posed among "a new class of building [that] has, mushroom like, sprung up in the Metropolis" (29). If it thrives in its suburban location, it is because this is the right place for factories, securely removed from country and city.[55] As the mirror image of these City novels, Riddell's ghost stories fully realize the sensational potential of speculation in still largely uncharted suburban spaces.

The eponymous property of *The Uninhabited House* is not simply a haunted house, but a house that haunts. In a departure from her realist fiction, the revaluation of inheritance plots makes way for a spectralization of property investments that turn on speculations so dubious and risky that they involve the supernatural. This play with the speculative opens up an additional dimension of the urban ghost story. As Julian Wolfreys has argued, the Gothic becomes "truly haunting" once it is divorced from traditional structures: the specter of modernity manifests itself in the various apparitions of "an uncontrollable spectral economy."[56] In Victorian urban narratives, Sharon Marcus has similarly suggested, spectral eruptions accompany domestic disruption as they "broadcast the urban deformation of the domestic ideal."[57] Ghosts become a commercial liability, as haunted houses understandably fail to retain anyone willing to rent them at their market value. It is with a tongue-in-cheek recognition of this fall in value that futile advertisements are said to "haunt" the lawyer's office at the novella's opening: "If ever a residence, 'suitable in every respect for a family of position,' haunted a lawyer's offices, the 'Uninhabited House,' about which I have a story to tell, haunted those of Messrs. Craven and Son."[58] When Harry Patterson, one of Craven's clerks, investigates its mysteries, he becomes obsessed with the house, its story, and the woman who owns it. The place itself forms the haunting specter: "The place haunts me. Believe me, I suffer less from its influence, seated in this room, than when I am in the office or walking across the Strand" (148). The resulting narrative of detection issues a startling revaluation of speculation and inheritance plots.

Inheritance itself is the curse. The eponymous troublesome legacy is the property of eccentric Miss Blake's niece, Helena Elmsdale, the offspring of a misalliance between a Cockney moneylender and a penurious Irishwoman. A double narrative of financial misspeculation structures this prehistory. The "Demoiselles Blake" inherit money, come to England to marry dukes and lords, but are said to have "missed their market" (92). Instead, they are cheated by their trustee to be rescued by Elmsdale, in Miss Blake's words, "a dirty money-lender" (94), who marries her sister. Shortly after his wife's death, Elmsdale, it is believed, shoots himself because of reputed gambling debts. All that is left of this quickly summarized courtship-*cum*-inheritance plot is a ghost-ridden property in a "lonely suburban road" (127). In a multiplication of speculators, the specter that haunts it needs to be evicted. The son of a country gentleman who has lost his fortune in a "dabbling in shares, and [its] natural consequence—ruin, utter ruin—" (66), and likewise died of it, Harry Patterson is doubled by the moneylender's murderer as well as by the spectralized speculator (former clerks both). The man who, it transpires, has shot Helena Elmsdale's father is a building speculator by the name of Harringford. The spectral resonance of elusive aitches links both Harry and Harringford to Elmsdale (or Helmsdale, as the Cockney himself pronounces it). The only debtors ever to escape the moneylender are "a Mr Harrison and a Mr Harringford—'Arrison and 'Arringford, as Mr Elmsdale called them when he did not refer to them as the two Haitches" (95). The urban uncanny is realized through such spectral doubling.

A building speculator and moneylender himself, Elmsdale embodies yet another level of spectralization. The son of a builder, he has "wash[ed] his hands of bricks and mortar," having seen "that people who advanced money to builders made a very nice little income out of the capital so employed" (94). Instead, he possesses buildings virtually: "whole streets were mortgaged to him; terraces, nominally the property of some well-to-do builder, were virtually his, since he only waited for the well-to-do builder's inevitable bankruptcy to enter into possession" (95). He capitalizes on the virtuality of the buildings' projected exchange value. Formerly one of his desperate debtors, who has (following his example) attempted "to start as builder and speculator on [his] own account" (160), Harringford shoots Elmsdale and makes it look like suicide as the failed speculator's prerogative or inevitable end. But in an intriguing literalization of the very spectralization of financial discourse on which the story is premised, his victim's ghost is back for compound interest: "He [Elmsdale] thought a great deal of money, and he has come back for it. He can't rest, and he won't let me rest till I have paid him principal and interest—compound interest" (161). The specter appears hunched over papers, counting banknotes; his spectral existence notwithstanding "wett[ing] his fingers in order to separate them" (107). As Harringford is fittingly struck down "in the midst of his buying, and bargaining, and boasting" (158), his almost instantaneously fatal encounter with his ghostly creditor compels him to bequeath his money to Elmsdale's daughter. In ways equally mysterious, a construction plan is passed on from the afterlife to Harry Patterson. A spooky inheritance, it aptly epitomizes the intangibility—the spectrality—of speculation. It is therefore particularly appropriate that at the end only utter demolishment can complete the building speculator's exorcism.

In what seems at first sight a sudden swerve back into an inheritance plot that turns the detective story into a courtship plot, the clerk into an heir, and a social critique into a preternatural resolution driven by poetic justice, Harry inherits money from an uncle, marries the murdered man's daughter, and gets rid of the uninhabitable house she brings into the marriage. The suburban villa, however, fails to be redeemed. Demolished, it is reduced to an unmentionable ghost story: "Helena and I have always been town-dwellers. Though the Uninhabited House is never mentioned by either of us, she knows I have still a shuddering horror of lonely places" (171). In a recent article, Lara Whelan argues that such exorcism is about normalizing domestic space in a reassertion of middle-class values through a fantasy of putting the haunted house in order.[59] But when the ancestral ghost is driven out, the end of a petit-bourgeois fantasy of the home-as-castle is converted into a property investment. Like so many other buildings erected by overspeculation, the devalued stand-alone house makes way for "desirable tenements" in a "fine terrace" (171). Ironically, although the ghost as the most objectionable item is the real cause of a court case for willful misrepresentation in its advertisements, there is more than a hint that the description may have been generally misleading. The eminently suitable residence is, in fact, located in "a most unhealthy part" (153). It is an insalubrious suburban location in a "neighbourhood [that] has gone down" (112), and when Harry volunteers to stay in it to find a clue to the mystery, he catches a feverish cold that renders him more amenable to the expected ghostly experience. This is a common ambivalence in nineteenth-century ghost stories. Nevertheless, when the ghost of a murdered building speculator haunts a suburban villa, walking the corridors clutching bundles of banknotes and construction plans, then surely Victorian fiction's investment in suburban speculation has found its most startling form. Increasingly, the reworking of financial plots becomes concerned precisely with the solidity of the domestic as a desired counterpoise that suggests that the management of speculation's attraction needs to be domesticated within reset structures.

Romancing the Stock Market

"[T]hat little speech about the jam and the strawberries brought her to herself. She felt herself to come back with a sudden harsh jarring and stumbling to solid ground. 'The strawberries!' she said."[60] A chance reference to strawberries and the making of strawberry jam startles the titular heroine of Oliphant's *Hester* (1883) out of "a wild sensation of freedom [...], an intoxication of feeling," as she considers "final and sudden flight" with a reckless speculator. In a deliberately overdrawn, reiterated identification of financial and sexual risk taking, the seductions of the stock market are part of a planned elopement. This projected narrative is unwittingly balked by the mother's "talk of all the little household things as she took her tea; of how the strawberries would soon be cheap enough for jam" (394–95). The ripening of seasonal fruit and the fluctuations in the market prices this entails are a reminder of domestic duties. But if this seems all too easily to pit the confines of domesticity against the City's dangerous allures, Hester Vernon is prompted to refrain from eloping by a larger sense of responsibility that revolves around the family business. Vernon's bank offers desirable employment for the most responsible members of the family (notably the women), while the business becomes domesticated, aligned with the demands of strawberry jam. The bank comes to personify domestic solidity. In an additional twist, it is the young woman from abroad who reasserts moral economies, whereby she unknowingly makes up for her father's defalcation in the past. Standing expected plot developments on their heads, this retelling of a clear-cut stock-market narrative fascinatingly plays with its juxtaposed romancing and domestication.

As late-Victorian novels engaged critically with a conscious revisiting of familiar financial plots, the indeterminate foreigner and the successful businesswoman presented two sides of the same coin in a questioning of the problematic cultural enterprise of risk management at home. In contrast to self-indulgently reckless amateur speculators (including untrained women and foreign-trained outsiders), the specialized stockbroker became depicted as a personification of order, of professionalism, of risk under control. Such a promotion of the professional additionally marginalized the role of women in large-scale economic activities. Ellen Wood's *In the Dead of Night* (1874) defends a young gentleman for choosing stockbroking as his profession, whereas speculating women remain bored titled ladies notorious for their risk taking. It is strongly suggested that it simply serves them right that the professional considers them "like any other pawn that may be on [his] chess-board."[61] Despite growing interest in working women filling various occupations, in the majority of late-Victorian financial novels, female clerks are de-sexed and speculating upper-class women irresponsible amateurs *par excellence*.[62] The "Bucket-Shop Portraits" of C. J. Scotter's 1890 *Lost in a Bucket-Shop: A Story of Stock Exchange Speculation* provide an illustrative example. Women in business fall into two categories: high-class amateur speculators (notably foreign) and female employees who are both dull and "unfeminine." The punning reference to having a lady's company in the office is a sarcastic stab at the absence of anything ladylike in the company's women: "I must not omit to mention that the company included a lady. She was old, wrinkled, quaintly dressed, and, when I first entered the room, was reading with close attention the 'Money Article' of a daily paper."[63] The satirical array of City types reflects not only public perceptions, but also the ossification of literary representations of women in business.

    Domestic fiction by women writers describes a distinctly different trajectory. In Craik's *Olive*, we have seen, the effects a failed speculation has at home remain confined to a disturbing disruption. It is quickly ejected from the narrative structure. Since this pattern becomes more pronounced once domestic fiction explicitly reacts against sensationalism, this is where the overlaps between subgenres as narrated sites of conflict engender a particularly intriguing restructuring. Oliphant and Ouida are by no means alone in their rewriting of familiar financial plots, yet their "domestication" of financial plots significantly targets specific preconceptions and their perpetuation in fiction.[64] When an absconded speculator's foreign-born daughter steps in at a crucial moment in *Hester*, her rescue of the family business issues a return of what could be seen as the loose ends of common stock-market narratives. From "The Stockbroker at Dinglewood" in the sixties onwards, Oliphant's adaptation of speculation plots works through an assessment of opposing narrative modes that pivots on their reworking.

Chapter Four

Domesticating Financial Scandal in "Dinglewood"

Literary sensationalism functions as a metonymy of commercialized art in Oliphant's most complex narratives of speculative enterprises. If she notoriously tapped into the sensation genre's marketability in her novels of the "sensational sixties," her renewed recourse to its formulae in subsequent decades became part of an intricate working out of competing demands at the book market.[65] The consequent welding together of divergent narrative structures, therefore, is not a lopsided bifurcation generated by an attempt to boost sales figures, but an interrogation of the production and reception of popular culture. Oliphant's ongoing adaptation of financial speculation plots therefore also demonstrates how the convergence of literary, aesthetic, and economic values becomes differently thematized. Her first fully fledged foray into stock-market fiction, "The Stockbroker at Dinglewood," appeared in the *Cornhill Magazine* in September 1868. As it details a stock-market swindle from the point of view of suburban, middle-aged Mrs. Mulgrave, this first-person narrative retells a typified tale of a financial scandal by evoking it with a mixture of nostalgia and self-irony. Filtered through this specific lens, financial fraud as a plot device becomes domesticated: it is absorbed by a narrative that focuses on domestic concerns, attitudes, and approaches to economic crises. Even as the exposure of a stock-market swindle unfolds according to predictable developments that feature sudden scandal, bankruptcy, and the villain's attempt to abscond, its sensationalism is safely contained within the confines of domestic realism. This containment is structurally expressed through a framing that introduces additional layers of irony, prefiguring the self-reflexivity that characterizes Oliphant's later fiction.[66]

The satirical conscription of sensational financial plotlines in "Dinglewood" hinges both on the outcome's predictability and on the irony that underpins the framing. The parallelism of the stockbroker's introduction and expulsion marks this out most clearly. The story opens up with a nostalgic reference to the times before the Greshams' arrival in a genteel suburban neighborhood called the Green. Harry Gresham is a businessman in the city, the son of a stockbroker who has made a fortune in speculation—"and, they say, not even the best kind of that."[67] When the Greshams move into Dinglewood, a once old-fashioned yet "popular house in a quiet way" (312), they introduce questionable improvements "just like those nouveaux riches" (316) would. Thus, "these millionaires" change "Poor Lady Sarah's drawing-room, which was good enough for her" (313), into a billiard room, for example. Unsurprisingly, Dinglewood's previous owners, Mr. Coventry and Lady Sarah, are recalled with a nostalgia that radiates through memories of a time when "the sunshine lay warm and still round them, and the leaves rustled softly" (312). "[A]ll this has nothing in the world to do with my story," the narrator adds, pinpointing the main function of the evoked memories: "But it was a pretty sight in its way. [...] I like to think of them even now" (312). In contrast, the concluding sentence sums up the Greshams as a symptom of an unstable, changeable society: "But the Greshams and their story, and all the brief splendours of Dinglewood are almost forgotten by this time" (343). As the likes of the Greshams come and go, their tale's timeliness undercuts nostalgia for their loss.

Such a neat parallelism becomes fissured when it emerges that Mr. Coventry introduced "new money" in his own time as well: he "was an old Indian and a salamander, and could bear any amount of sunshine" (312). This ruptures more than the nostalgic sunshine imagery. As his identification as a nabob suggests an ongoing absorption of class climbers, it additionally exposes the neighborhood's (and, by extension, traditional society's) bias. Much of the satire, in fact, is at the expense of the shabby-genteel suburbanites. The narrator dwells on "social differences" (314), describing "us" standing "thunderstruck" at nouveau riche "improvements" as "a great piece of presumption" (313). In addition, the social circles introduced by the newly rich become an "important quarry" (317) for marital speculation. For "poor Lottie," an aging young lady, the Greshams raise "a terrible chance before her [...], a chance, for her family and for herself" (317). It is "anything but an amusing sight" (317). The resulting ironic double lens becomes accentuated when the newcomers host writers and artists because "having no real rank, they appreciated a little distinction, howsoever it came; whereas the second cousin of any poor lord or good old decayed family was more to the most of us than Shakspeare [sic] himself or Raphael" (315). Nevertheless, while this introduction stirs up the neighborhood—"[waking] us all up" (315)—this also makes Harry Gresham's business enterprises disconcertingly offstage. While his wife organizes society events in the suburbs, nothing is seen or heard of the husband's business.

Closely following the paradigms of sensational financial fiction, the crash happens suddenly. Unexpected by the main protagonists and largely unspecified, it is followed by the exposure of fraudulent speculations. The news breaks in at a ball that marks the Greshams' social acceptance in an undisguised sensational scene. After receiving a telegram, Gresham exhibits such pallor that the sight of him comes upon the narrator "like a touch of horror" (325). His wife gives "a loud sudden shriek" before "turn[ing] her despairing eyes on me [Mrs. Mulgrave]" (330). It is a cry "so piercing and sudden that it rang through the house and startled every one" (330). The languages of sensational terror and satirical detachment are oddly mixed as Mrs. Mulgrave deliberately understates her involvement. Assisting in Gresham's escape from London detectives, she acts within a typified sensational narrative, feeling "grieved and disgusted and sick at heart, remembering all the wicked stories people tell of mercantile dishonesty, of false bankruptcies, and downright robberies, and the culprits who escape and live in wealth and comfort abroad. This was how it was to be in the case of Harry Gresham. [. . .] When one reads such stories in the papers, one says, 'Wretches!' and thinks no more of it. But these two were not wretches, and I was fond of them, and it made me sick at heart" (336). This retelling of a common tale pinpoints three interconnected concerns with established plotlines. First, the retrospectively framed account shuttles between a satire of the genre and a redeployment of sensational elements. Second, this ambiguity is central to a containment—and consequent domestication—of sensationalism. In a twist of a recurring cliché, "[t]he happy house [that] had toppled down like a house of cards" (333) refers to Dinglewood, a suburban household hosting a successful ball, and not a business. What is more, the fraudulent activities that lead to this collapse are reported from a domestic, feminine vantage point. In his wife's simple words, Gresham "has taken some money that was not his, and lost it; but he meant to pay it back again" (337). For sympathizing female neighbors, allegations of illegality look like persecution: "The men say there was no excuse for him, and I can see that there is no excuse; but he never meant it, poor Harry!" (341). The son of a disreputable stockbroker who loses money irresponsibly and then absconds to America, "poor Harry" certainly is a typical stock-market villain, yet he is pitiful rather than malicious or designing. Despite Mrs. Mulgrave's acknowledgment that she can "see that there is no excuse" (341), her personal account is more likely to provide the full story than the presumably more impartial delineation in the newspapers. This rejection of their typecasting sensationalization brings us to the third central aspect of the story's redeployment of sensational financial plots: the simplifying "stories in the papers" of typified "wretches" are posed against complexities that cause the narrator's heartsickness because she knows "these two were not wretches" (336).

The distorted newspaper stories also remind us that the sensation novel was from the beginning associated with the most sensationalizing tendencies in the popular press. In his 1863 critique in the *Quarterly Review,* Henry Mansel tellingly termed this rising subgenre "the criminal variety of the Newspaper Novel."[68] When "Dinglewood" frames financial crises within a domestic narrative, it does not merely domesticate sensational paradigms. In showing what happens behind the scenes of the simplified tales supplied by the newspapers, it revises a narrative that has otherwise "melted away like a tale that is told" (340). This anticipates the self-reflexivity with which *At His Gates* literally brings back the presumably guilty and self-destructive speculator when all sensational reporting has been "done with, and put aside like a tale that is told."[69] The consequent move from the domestic to the sensational and then ultimately back to a domestic containment is additionally complicated by the fact that this irresponsible speculator is an artist who successfully absorbs sensationalism in his startling comeback.

"Very Saleable Articles, Indeed": Sensationalized Commerce as Art

When Oliphant draws on financial speculation as a metaphor for the artist's vulnerability in a commercialized society in *At His Gates*, she uses the figure of a painter to reflect her own artistic dilemma. Briefly, Robert Drummond is a mediocre portrait painter whose plodding work has disappointed his more ambitious wife, Helen. Partly because of her disappointment, he takes up the offer of her cousin, Mr. Burton, to become involved in a joint-stock bank despite the fact that he knows "as much about business as Mr Burton's umbrella" (1:99). Burton, by contrast, is an eminently respectable businessman who "won't run any sentimental risks" (1:104). One "can't afford" them in business: "Money is money, and has to be dealt with on business principles. God bless me! If I were to reflect about the people whose lives, &c., I could never do anything" (1:104). True to his business principles, he is a typecast stock-market villain and a hypocrite who never engages in any illegal activities. Instead, he and his manager, Mr. Golden, prudently withdraw from the bank's board just before its collapse. It subsequently transpires that they have known all along that it is a failing affair. Yet the press condemns Drummond alone, driving him to a suicide attempt. His seeming self-destruction further feeds into the publicized sensational tales Testifying to the novel's essentially ambiguous redeployment of popular paradigms, he returns years later with a startling success: a painting inspired by his despair.

At His Gates thereby repackages the conventions of sensational financial fiction to suggest new ways of working out sensationalism's attractions in order to produce something better than "very saleable articles" (1:2). Critics at the time significantly remarked on the success of the novel's depiction of villainous speculators. The *Athenaeum* particularly praised the creation of the typical characters of "joint-stock rascality" as "pictured to the life."[70] Yet the expected cycle of temptation, sudden success, and cataclysmic crisis is over before the end of the first volume. A proliferation of clues ensures that the culprits' identity is certainly no secret to the reader. In addition, frequent references to familiar plot developments firmly establish the novel as a rewriting of, rather than an addition to, sensational financial fiction. Even at the height of their brief business success, Robert Drummond's daughter Norah questions the intentions of Burton and Golden by considering what their motivations would be in a novel: "Do you think they are papa's friends? I suppose there are no villains nowadays, like what there are in books [where] there is always somebody clever enough to find out the villains" (1:123). Norah is promptly scolded for having "read too many novels" (1:123). Her mother's caution reflects the characterization of the hypocrite Burton: "In the world people are often selfish, and think of their own advantage first; but they don't try to ruin others out of pure malice, as they do in stories" (1:123). Such comments invite a rethinking of the structures of popular fiction more generally, and the remainder of the novel significantly features and discusses reworked elements of courtship and sensational detective plots.

This two-pronged deployment of popular paradigms is premised on an intriguing ambiguity that may seem merely paradoxical at first sight. Some of the most typecast formulae function as effective sensational devices despite the self-reflexivity of their critique. Norah Drummond, for example, is repeatedly right whenever she suggests developments she herself would employ as plotlines if she "were writing a novel" (2:164). Her mother's rejection of typical joint-stock rascality, moreover, is exploded by her subsequent condemnation of Golden as "her enemy, the wicked man *par excellence*, the incarnation of wrong and cruelty" (2:270). His very "face is like a curse" (2:274). The appearance of sensational language helps to highlight that the novel operates on two intersecting levels. In the same vein, both Drummond's suicide attempt and his farewell letters retain their startling effect even as their appropriation by the popular press is at once condemned and pastiched. After the bank's collapse, Drummond leaves cryptic notes and then walks to the river without really knowing why. On the way he encounters Burton "fresh and clean and nicely dressed" with a "certain golden atmosphere surround[ing] the man of wealth" (1:163). Their confrontation short-circuits the detective plot by giving away the mystery, and yet it nonetheless creates a sensational effect:

> "Shall you lose much?" said Drummond dreamily, and he turned round without meaning anything and looked in his companion's face. His action was simply fantastical, one of those motiveless movements which the sick

soul so often makes; but it was quite unexpected by the other, who fell a step back, and grew red all over, and faltered in his reply. (1:165)

The poignant delineation of the suicide's emotional experience can compete with Wilkie Collins's finest explorations of such despair,[71] yet it becomes rewritten within the novel's satirical exposure of sensational newspaper reports. Drummond's supposed suicide makes "a great sensation" (2:127): "A watery grave may not be pleasant for the occupant of it, but it is a very fine thing for the press. The number of times it appeared in the public prints at this period defies reckoning" (2:123–24). The pastiche of the newspaper reports is filled with references to fictionalization and especially to the distorting factors of sensationalization. The story of "Robert's guilt" is a "fable" and "the most horrible farce, a farce which was a tragedy" (1:289). The result of a "lively commercial imagination" (2:127), it works all too well as "an exciting story" that is "dramatically complete" (1:209). It is writ large in more ways than one, "printed in large type" (1:210), "announced in big capitals on the placards of all the newspapers" (2:123), in "great placards up with headings in immense capitals, '*Great Bankruptcy in the City.—Suicide of a Bank Director*'" (1:209). Nor is sensationalization restricted to the daily papers. The "history [of] 'the wretched man'" similarly "furnishe[s] a text for a sermon to the *Daily Semaphore*" (1:265). Such moralizing is as distorting and as damaging as the most morbid dwelling on watery graves.

Clearly, there is more than one way to feast on such a death. In an additional irony, the painter's posthumous notoriety includes a special exhibition of his work. Not even covering expenses, it is a failure that chiefly testifies to the public's proverbial fickleness. After the media have cashed in on a widespread scandal, its sensational attraction has simply been exploited in all its possible variations: "The public did show its enthusiasm—for two days. [. . .] [A]nd Drummond's story came to an end, and was heard of no more" (2:135). This fickleness is further paired with the restrictions exerted by special-interest groups. Just like artistic circles get up a special exhibition to boost the art scene, specific denominational magazines make the most of events of widespread interest. Nor is such an impulse necessarily generated by sensationalism. Drummond's friend Stephen Haldane, a partly paralyzed former minister, abuses his position as editor of an evangelical magazine to write back to the daily papers in order to vindicate his friend. Mirroring the novel's revision of expected narratives, this attempt brings out the difficulties involved in catering for different market forces. Haldane's participation in the paper war over the speculator's missing body exposes his longstanding endeavor to find an outlet for his literary talents within a narrowly confined medium. He nearly loses his position over having turned a publication not meant as "a mere literary journal" into a "vehicle of private feeling" (1:295). Forced to issue a formal apology, he concedes to the pressures of his readership.

Oliphant emphasizes the artist's dilemma through a series of genre moves that transcends such constraints by evoking typical plotlines self-reflexively. After the formulaic financial plot has seemingly run its course, a decisive shift is signaled by Helen Drummond's figurative escape into traditional courtship novels from the circulating library. It is couched within a commonplace defense of novel reading: "The reader, perhaps, is doing the same thing at this moment, and yet, most likely, he will condemn, or even despise, poor Helen" (2:137). Underscoring the need for a "world of fiction," Oliphant further deplores that "so little provision is made" so that "the love-story keeps uppermost in spite of all," although in facilitating escapism "perhaps the love-story is the safest" (2:138). This discussion concludes with a reference to Norah's impending entrance into society, and the following chapter opens with "A Girl's first ball!" (2:140). With this, the novel seems to have left sensational finance behind to enter exclusively into the conventions of the courtship plot. This shift is externalized by a geographical move from London (and the vicinity of the City) into provincial England. Burton's suppressed sense of guilt has induced him to invite both the Haldanes and Drummond's wife and daughter to live rent-free at the gatehouse on his estate. Interconnected courtship plots that appear to be taken from the novels Helen borrows from the library center on Norah Drummond and Burton's children, Ned and Clara. They also involve young Rivers, the son of the aristocratic figurehead whose name has falsely lent credibility to the failed joint-stock bank. It is therefore very apt that Golden's incursion into this plotline constitutes a turning point in the novel's overall structure. His narrative function is both to bring news of the collapse of Burton's enterprises—news delivered, as in a number of Victorian financial narratives, including "Dinglewood," at a triumphant ball—and to elope with Burton's daughter Clara. While this may be read as an instance of poetic justice, it also marks the return of the novel's main driving force: the sensational financial plot has only been suspended.

The courtship plots ruptured by this return are so pointedly straightforward as to engender some of the novel's most self-reflexive passages. The young aristocrat, Rivers, appears "with the air of a hero of romance; bearded, with very fine dark eyes and hair that curled high like a crest upon his head" (2:152–53). Compositionally, he is reduced to a type, "look[ing] as if he had just walked out of a novel with every sign of his character legibly set forth" (2:153). His replacement by Ned Burton likewise follows expected paradigms in their competition for Norah's hand. Struggling against "being subjugated like a young woman in a book by this 'novel-hero [Rivers],'" Norah has already identified the emergence of this suitable *contre-hero* (Ned) as "an understood rule" of fiction (3:46-47). Its predictability undercuts any narrative tension derived from the courtship plots. Although Norah ultimately accepts Ned, neither a social snub by Rivers's mother nor her rejection of Ned's first proposal elicits the same amount of emotion that financial crises occasion: "Would he [Ned] go away, and never be heard of more? Would it—and the very thought of this thrilled through Norah's veins, and chilled her heart—would it do him harm? Would he die?" (2:218). Norah is to be disappointed. Humdrum, yet consistently loyal, Ned shows no despair. Financial scandal, not love, is a cause for suicide. Conventional courtship plots have been upstaged by sensational finance.

What remains the most important, however, is that the novel retains a sensational appeal throughout. Although the financial plot appears to be merely a preliminary for a more traditional narrative structure, references to the unsolved case of Drummond's guilt and disappearance continue to reverberate throughout the text. The echo of the novel's title in Haldane's wary acceptance of Burton's offer to live in the gatehouse is ominous: "I wonder if he is comfortable when he reflects who are living at his gates?" (2:57). This very wariness revives Helen's suppressed memory of a clue embedded in her husband's suicide note. That "Burton and Golden have done it all" is added in "a postscript which nobody read or paid any attention to" at first (1:190). The impact of this postscript is symptomatically smothered by the proliferating reports in the newspapers. But as a nearly forgotten warning, it becomes an important clue: it "seemed to haunt" Helen (2:85). Just when the novel shifts from financial to courtship plots, Haldane's suspicion triggers a flash of memory that foreshadows the reactivation of the sensational:

> It seemed to kindle a smouldering fire in her, of the nature of which she was not quite aware. "Burton and Golden" suddenly flashed across her thoughts again. Where was it she had seen the names linked together? What did it mean? and what did Stephen [Haldane] mean? She felt as if she had almost found out something, which quickened her pulse and made her heart beat—almost. But the last point of enlightenment was yet to come. (2:57-58)

The final resolution is held in abeyance. While this suspense generates narrative tension, the detective plot is nonetheless never fully realized.

Chapter Four

Instead, Burton's sudden bankruptcy reintroduces the novel's original investment in financial plots, but with an additional emphasis on their rewriting. Repeating Mrs. Mulgrave's involvement in the Greshams' escape in "Dinglewood," Helen shelters the absconding Burton, outmaneuvering the detective force. Yet Helen also takes advantage of the situation by demanding a literal rewriting of the past: a signed statement declaring her husband's innocence (3:147). She simultaneously dismantles "those fables about feminine weakness" (3:147) that arise from the introduction of economic crises into domestic settings. They are red herrings in a rewriting of sensational financial fiction that makes simple domestication from a sympathizing, neighborly vantage point (such as Mrs. Mulgrave's in the earlier story) problematic: "He [Burton] had forgotten everything but those fables about feminine weakness which are current among such men, and had half laughed in his sleeve half an hour before at her readiness to help and serve him" (3:147). Ultimately, Helen forfeits her revenge only because her reunion with her husband means that the "tale of seven long years" (3:89) has now truly come to a close. And yet, his return is the novel's most sensational plot twist.

The return of characters believed dead most clearly abides by popular sensational paradigms. The fact that Drummond's body cannot be found after he has presumably drowned himself already promises a reengagement with his unknown fate.[72] Nevertheless, it is not only that his innocence proves the standard plotlines of the newspapers and of typical "newspaper novels" wrong. This plot twist turns on the intertextual reworking of the literary trope of the portrait: Drummond's return is prefigured by the exhibition of his recently finished painting. This adds to the interconnected levels in which pictorial representation structures the novel. Their thematic, symbolic, and structural function can be seen to hold otherwise disparate elements together, creating a sustained interrogation of market forces and its effects. Paintings and their reception thereby help to articulate the novel's main concern with competing popular trends. Mirroring the shuttling in Oliphant's own work between domestic realism and the more commercially successful sensational writing, Robert Drummond achieves fame when both his life and his art move from the domestic into the sensational. He is driven to despair by the combined pressures of commerce, but this despair is then translated into the production of a startlingly intense piece that thematizes a return from the dead. The novel's critique of sensation becomes complicated by the narrative praise that is bestowed upon Drummond's art. His new work functions as the final clue to his disappearance. In disclosing the cost of such an intense—sensational—work for the artist, the novel again questions the preference for such art. Its interrogation of sensationalism is therefore twofold in that it addresses the competition of narrative modes at the level of its own structure and the commodification of sensational events in both art and writing.

Drummond's most successful painting expresses a despair that reveals the true story behind the circulating "fables" of his guilt. At the same time, it prefigures the artist's metaphorical return from the dead, a return that is also the painting's theme. This expression of a truth or "reality" beyond mimetic realism is anticipated by an early invocation of the potentially supernatural power of paintings. From the beginning, this sensational motif is intricately entwined with financial plots. When considering Burton's offer, the Drummonds "defy all omens," including the wind wailing "like a spirit in pain" and Drummond's unfinished portrait crashing onto the floor: "*Absit omen!* It is my own portrait" (1:51). This jocular reference to a possible omen comes back to haunt his wife when the picture is damaged in another fall at the moment of Drummond's suicide attempt (1:185). That his return is partly facilitated, partly prefigured, by his new work years later circles back to a complex metonymic connection between the portrait and the artist it depicts. At the end of the novel, a painting appears at an exhibition that is "exactly his style, his best style" (3:73). It is at once the apotheosis of all his work and a literalization of the foreshadowed identification, or substitution, of painter and work.

This sensational success is a portrayal of Dives, the rich man suffering in hell after spurning the beggar Lazarus (Luke 16:19–31). Its theme underlines the novel's moral critique of commercial greed, while linking the perhaps most easily sensationalized plot device—the return from the dead—to biblical references as if to remind us that this trope is by no means confined to current sensational writing. On the level of plot development, meanwhile, Helen's recognition of the painting from sketches made just before Drummond's disappearance directly leads to their reunion. In an inversion of the cliché of the absconding speculator, Drummond has been working as a portrait painter in America ever since he was fished out of the river by a steamboat. He makes a comeback once he has produced his best work. Not only is this work a success with both the critics and the public; it also represents the realization of Drummond's full potential. His mediocre art is for once elevated beyond what his critics have dubbed—echoing the predominant reception of Oliphant's own work—"very saleable articles, indeed" (1:2).[73] This contrast structures the novel's thematization of the artist's struggle with commercial pressures. The plodding portrait painter of the novel's opening refuses to go in "for anything sensational" (1:48). Instead, he produces saleable works that are criticized for having "no energy of emotion, no originality of genius about them" (1:2). Whenever he makes "a spasmodic effort to break through his mediocrity," moreover, Drummond is "warned [. . .] against the sensational" by critics said to be "very well pleased on the whole with his mediocrity" (1:9). Such dubious praise encapsulates the paradoxical demands of popular culture. Although the exhibition organized in his memory is a notable failure, posthumous accounts by critics ironically appreciate his focus on the domestic and the quiet more than during his lifetime, suggesting that his works shine in "harmony of conception, true sense of beauty, and tender appreciation of English sentiment and atmosphere" (2:125). Yet this does more than exemplify the critics' essentially confusing directions. In stressing domestic realism's moral, if perhaps not aesthetic, preeminence, such an endorsement of harmony, tenderness, and English sentiment prefigures the final move back to such domestic qualities after Drummond's return and sensational success.

The biggest irony, however, is that a financial and consequent emotional breakdown has been transformed into art. Intense suffering has induced Drummond to take "to his work in a way which made it a very different thing from the paint which is done for bread and butter" (3:234). Thus, he rises "above that pleasant, charming level of beautiful mediocrity" (3:274), but at what price? For once, it is stressed, he has "painted, not in common pigments, but in colours mixed with tears and life-blood" (3:274). "[S]uch a cost" is considered too high, and after their happy reunion the Drummonds are content "to descend to the gentler, lower work—the work by which men earn their daily bread" (3:274). The portrait painter never creates another masterpiece. With this, the sensational is once again safely locked away in an embrace of "the dear common life—the quiet, blessed routine of every day—that ordinary existence" (3:275). This final twist encapsulates the ultimate containment of sensationalism within a self-affirming domestic realism. In a critical assessment of the aesthetic, moral, and commercial requirements for a successful work of art or literature, Oliphant addresses the novel genre's status by dramatizing a popular painter's dilemma. If the artist manages to combine all required elements, it is only through symbolic death and rebirth, and even then, the effect is expressed—or contained—in one single piece. Literary sensationalism functions as a metonymic representation of a commercialized culture that can thus be repackaged. Such a morally and aesthetically perfected sensational success exemplifies Oliphant's ideal, yet it remains elusive. The consequent swerve back to an endorsed domesticity is accomplished in a tone of contentment more than of resignation. This additionally underlines Oliphant's critical judgment of the domestic as aesthetically and morally superior to sensationalism, although domestic fiction may well profit from a reworking of the sensational.

The Bank's Heiress:
Inheriting a Genius for Business

When Oliphant returns to the domestication of financial speculation in *Hester* (1883), she departs from this idea of containment or projection by newly engaging with the possibility of managing financial speculation. She does so by pairing sets of doubles that embody various levels of negotiating the conflicting demands of business and domesticity. The running of the family bank is redirected after a household detail (the making of strawberry jam) explodes risks associated with escape abroad. Household economies provide the solid grounding that pushes aside instability's attractions. While tentatively invested in the proto-feminist issue of women in the banking business, the novel firmly foregrounds this domestication as an essential part of the heroine's successful integration of business and the domestic while dealing with risk in both areas. In reworking popular plotlines of stock-market fiction, it interweaves three distinctive developments, or strands First, the family history of bank failures is relegated into the past, quickly rehearsed as a predictable speculation plot to resurface again in an intriguing doubling. Second, the already modified figure of the responsible, professional stockbroker as the opposite of the recklessly speculating amateur becomes subsumed by a triangulation of speculators. Doubling as Hester's would-be suitors, three young men become involved in speculation to different degrees that reflect a spectrum of attitudes to risk. Third, through such doubling, the narrative's circular structure reasserts domesticity's preeminence through a female takeover of the family bank when Hester becomes its heiress.

The triangulation of doubles is realized with a self-reflexivity that foregrounds the porosity of the paper fictions that become confronted with the strawberries' comparative solidity (even as jam). The temptingly risky speculation plot in which Hester has projected herself at this point stands exposed as simply an inappropriate fiction. Edward Vernon has proposed an elopement that is to coincide with his attempt to abscond after his secret speculations have jeopardized the bank. In a drafted response, Hester has just captured this dual temptation, yet in her sudden realization of the narrative structure she finds herself in, the eventually unsent note becomes reduced to a meaningless paper. The strawberries' incursion into her indulged fiction of risk taking renders her letters "obsolete, and out of date, as if her grandmother had written them. [...] [T]hey were as fictitious as if they had been taken out of a novel" (396). It is not her narrative, as Edward's reuse of yet another paper fiction easily proves. After Hester's refusal, he recycles the marriage license he has prepared by engaging in a completely chancy runaway match with another woman. It is the climax and, at the same time, a parody of risk taking, achieved in a determination "to make the adventure complete, to cut every tie and tear every remnant of the past to pieces" (417). They go abroad, leaving the bank to "[t]he usual panic" (446), which precipitates a financial crisis that replicates the run on the bank with which the novel opens.

This financial prehistory sets the scene for a reversing of familiar plotlines in order to issue a new engagement with women's roles in the business. The questioning of prevailing preconceptions is achieved through a juggling with clichés borrowed from popular fiction, including such outmoded forms as the silver-fork novel. The paradigms of Victorian stock-market fiction are evoked for their established associations with sensationalism and filtered through a likewise partly parodic rehearsal of older narratives of high risks in highlife. Beyond mere pastiche or parody, they become reworked as part of a literary tradition of women's writing. At the same time, the predictability of the typified speculation plot plays with concepts of economic cycles that need to be taken into account at home. The narrative is, then, an interrogation of popular plotlines, leading to a synthesis of changing paradigms that redefines the boundaries of domestic fiction. The speculation plot of the past is a symptomatically cursory summary of typical, primarily sensational stock-market fiction: Hester's father speculates with the bank's money and absconds to continental Europe. Catherine Vernon, his cousin, proves to be the true "heir of her great-grandfather's genius for business" (22) when she offers her fortune to save the bank. A generation later, this displacement is repeated when Edward, the young male relative Catherine has singled out as her potential heir, risks the family fortune on the Stock Exchange, leaving John's daughter Hester, returned to England after her father's death, to support Catherine and the business. If this retelling of past events suggests the cyclic nature not merely of financial crises, but of a hereditary propensity towards irresponsible risk taking within the family, there is an important shift that becomes quintessential to the representation of women in business. Hester achieves a better balance between the demands of domesticity, romance, and business than her predecessor. For her the bank is more than an alternative to a family, which remains its main function for Catherine: "What flagging and loneliness might have been hers—what weariness and longing had ended at that time. Since then how much she had found to do! [...]

She was an old maid, to be sure, but an old maid who never was alone" (24). For Hester, the integration of romance and business needs to be premised on a different domestication of the family bank. It can no longer be simply a substitution for marriage. Nor should it become tantamount to a romancing of risk taking.

Within this revaluation of women's business in different economic activities, a projection onto generations of women poses Hester not only against Catherine, but against her own mother and against the woman Edward Vernon ultimately marries: Emma Ashton, the flirtatious sister of a professional stockbroker. This intricately patterned pairing forges additional links between past and present crashes. Catherine's management of the first crisis throws the naïve irresponsibility displayed by Hester's mother into sharp relief. This fashionable lady of Regency highlife can hardly be expected to know anything of business: "it was the fashion of the time to be unpractical just as it is the fashion of our time that women should understand business and be ready for any emergency" (10). In spotted muslin and sandals, a "fine lady, sitting in her short sleeves on the edge of the volcano, and knowing nothing about it" (10), she embodies an outmoded feminine ideal reminiscent of silver-fork fiction. She retains the family pearls and even her settlement because she really does not understand that it should all have gone to the creditors. In contrast, it is repeatedly reiterated that Catherine has "a head for business" (20, 297). With her "masculine mind" (329), she may admittedly come close to being branded as a de-sexed businesswoman, yet she also suggests a new female heroism that is emulated by her successor as part of her inheritance. It is a hereditary business sense that has become confined to the female line. Hester is of "the old stock, with a head for business" (29). She longs for a "chance" like Catherine's:

> Hester felt that she, too, could have done this. Her breast swelled, her breath came short with an impulse of impatience and longing to have such an opportunity, to show the mettle that was in her [...], to have that golden opportunity—the occasion to do a heroic deed, to save some one, to venture your own life, to escape the bonds of every day, and once have a chance of showing what was in you! This was not the "chance" which Emma Ashton desired, but it appealed to every sentiment in Hester. (300)

The juxtaposition of this "golden opportunity" and a "chance" in the marriage market probes business's various roles at home. Roland Ashton, the professional stockbroker, reintroduces speculative business into the quiet country society in which Vernon's bank has once again become an icon of stability after Catherine's takeover. In contrast to the fascination he exerts on the bored country bankers, Edward Vernon and his plodding cousin Harry, Roland himself cautions against romanticizing his occupation: "A man may lose his head in love or in war, or in adventure, or in pleasure, but he must not lose it on the Stock Exchange" (309). Edward flies to his papers "as another man might have flown to brandy or laudanum" (131). Correspondingly, when such risk taking as profit making guides marital schemes, the result is Emma's "chance." It is, she insists, "like helping young men on in business" (230). Catherine may be before her time and remain in many ways a singularity, investing moreover her hopes in a surrogate son (Edward) who betrays her trust. But Emma adapts the new demand for women's understanding of business to the marriage market. It is therefore comically appropriate that it is after forfeiting her gamble on the Vernons' social circle that she chances upon absconding Edward, who promptly recycles the specially procured marriage license meant for Hester to propose to Emma instead. It is an excess of identified financial and sexual risk taking that eschews any romanticizing.

Within the narrative arc described by this circling back to the original crash, Hester the domestic businesswoman in the making becomes the focus of two sets of triangulated doubles. In an intriguing cutting across conventional gender paradigms—worked out through this overstated identification of the stock and the marriage market—Edward as well as Emma serves as Hester's double. Points of intersection between narrative modes become externalized by overlapping sets of doubles. One comprises Catherine Vernon and Mrs. John Vernon (Hester's mother) and Emma Ashton and Hester herself as their younger versions. In its intersection with the second set, there are not only the three young men involved in the banking business (Edward, Harry, and Roland), but also Hester's father. He is a contrast to Catherine and Hester as well as Edward's counterpart. His daughter may have inherited the Vernons' genius for business, yet she simultaneously carries her father's legacy of an attraction to risk taking. In exorcising her fascination with risks, her unsent letters spell out her flirtation with the stock market. Indeed, Hester enjoys long conversations with various young men about the mysteries of the Stock Exchange, so much so that Roland begins to think that "even stockbroking will do as a vehicle for flirtation" (312). Ironically, at this point, she is interested more in tracing Edward's alluring instability than in Roland's professional approach. The eventual double expulsion of Edward and Emma and what they stand for not only establishes Hester in the family bank, but her promising future includes a choice of partners (Roland and Harry). Their "chance" with

Hester is fascinatingly left unsolved at the end of the novel. The courtship plot is pushed aside by the preeminence of financial fiction: "And as for Hester, all that can be said for her is that there are two men whom she may choose between, and marry either if she please [...]. What can a young woman desire more than to have such a possibility of choice?" (456). Born abroad, the absconder's daughter becomes rooted in a domestic space which is determined by the economies of seasonal fruit, and yet which is also identified with the family bank. The popular narrative of exciting risk taking has been contained: professional stockbroking as well as banking managed as part of household economies.

Capital Women:
Whatever Happened to Mrs. Melmotte?

Replicating the main plotlines of Trollope's *The Way We Live Now,* Ouida's *The Massarenes* similarly seeks to achieve a new integration of business and romance that simultaneously rewrites gender and ethnic alignments. Since this study opens up with Trollope's notoriously indeterminate speculator, it is fitting that it should close by situating the significance of his self-destruction within the wealth of financial narratives that cut across, while they help newly to forge, the divergent subgenres of nineteenth-century literature. One of the most memorable Victorian financial novels, *The Way We Live Now* itself already condenses a range of related images, fictional types, and structures. It encapsulates a central satirical thrust of stock-market narratives by registering an all too eager embrace of the symptomatically unclassified new businessman. But if foreign shares in British business are shown to be ruling Victorian homes, what role do women, and especially foreign women, play? As a pointed conclusion, this final section compares Mrs. Massarene's detailed unhappiness in Ouida's novel with Madame Melmotte's marginal and, given her comfortable size, bizarrely shadowy presence in Trollope's. Like her husband, Madame Melmotte is indeterminately foreign, yet unlike this sought-after speculator, she is an object of pity, a pawn in a speculative society at large. Reading these two novels side by side helps to reveal what had clearly become easily recognizable stereotypes and plotlines of Victorian financial fiction. Before looking more closely at the multiple rewriting that underpins the curious bathos of Mrs. Massarene's death in Ouida's novel, I shall therefore first briefly discuss Trollope's treatment of speculators' emblematic suicide in his novels of the 1870s. Their end reflects central shifts in the Victorian stock-market novel's most lasting images. Trollope redeploys these clichés to boost a satire that encompasses all levels of society and all levels of involvement in financial speculation.

Melmotte crystallizes speculative interest among the leading members of "the way we live now." Far from importing this modernity, he arises from the fermenting grievances and desires of an impecunious, greedy, speculative aristocracy: a specter realizing a wish fulfillment that turns into a nightmare of their worst fears about new money and new businessmen out of control. While his vulgarity's solid prominence performs this spectralization as comical, its reception casts a different light on the attraction of indeterminacy. In a society living on credit, solidity is no longer reassuring, as the deceptively visible building that houses the Anglo-Bengalee Disinterested Loan and Life Assurance Company, with its "massive blocks of marble in the chimney-pieces, and the gorgeous parapet on the top of the house" and its name "painted on the very coal-scuttles" (430), is in *Martin Chuzzlewit*, for example. Instead, elusiveness is welcomed. It is a quality that makes the indeterminate a promisingly unobtrusive tool. Melmotte famously grows more in demand on shares in a railway that does not exist, and the majority of shareholders could not care less. On the contrary, in their (geographically limited) imagination, its fictitious location in the Americas denotes it as securely offstage. Melmotte's career satirizes their fantasies of easy risk management.

Trollope's mapping out of the attendant speculations' very real, solid effects on England's countryside (through Melmotte's incursion into aristocratic estates) is of course much more complicated, purposely to satirize this willful misreading of the foreign speculator's promise. Ferdinand Lopez, the commodity trader of *The Prime Minister* (1876), is similarly an outgrowth of a dangerous exoticism ingrained in the guano, coffee, and bios in which he speculates, but which he is careful to possess only on paper. He is a more cursorily evoked, but curiously also more vulnerable, altogether less glamorous figure and hence a revealing point of comparison. Exhibiting a linkage of the luxurious and the excremental, his elusive commodities also constitute a fictional construct, much like the rumors circulating about Lopez's falsely flaunted value, or in a by then already clichéd conflation, personal values. As it is put in a chapter ominously titled "He Wants to Get Rich Too Quick," "the deceit had come from the fact that his manners gave no indication of his character."[74] Lopez is moreover marked by his "foreign" physiognomy (indeterminate like Melmotte's). He fails to fool his father-in-law, who has "amassed a large fortune, mainly from his profession, but partly also by the *careful* [italics added] use of his own small patrimony and by his wife's money" (1:21–22). Hence this upstart feels entitled to dismiss Lopez's speculations as "a sort of gambling" and to be wary of entrusting either his money or his daughter "to a friendless Portuguese,—a probable Jew,—about whom nobody knew anything" (1:29, 31). As in Melmotte's case, anti-Semitic stereotyping converges with social indeterminacy, although Melmotte ultimately stands exposed as most likely the son of an Irish forger. Embodying the bubble economy's self-destructiveness, Melmotte and Lopez both exorcise its worst effects by committing suicide. It is largely thanks to their memorable exploits that both foreignness and suicide have become established as the Victorian stock-market villain's defining characteristics.[75]

The association of their cosmopolitanism with anti-Semitic stereotyping may be disconcertingly conspicuous, although critics have recently focused more on the ambiguity with which it is treated in Victorian literature and especially by Trollope.[76] This of course does not mean that it could not all too easily be shorthand for any seeming infiltration. In *Guilty Gold: A Romance of Financial Fraud and City Crime* (1896) by Headon Hill (Francis Edward Grainger), a moneylender-*cum*-stockbroker "of Hebraic extraction" tellingly sports a self-proclaimed cosmopolitan identity: "Gus Eppstein, who used the more alluring name of 'Sydney Engledue' in his dealings with the public, kept a 'bucket shop' in Moorgate Street, whence he flooded the country with circulars setting forth the advantage of employing him as a stockbroker."[77] Trollope's indeterminately foreign speculators (Lopez and Melmotte prominently among them) reflect and further consolidate such typecasting, obscuring the full significance of a much more encompassing satire that is directed at a speculative society at large. The stock-market villain as the careful businessman's double is a recurring figure from early-nineteenth-century writing onwards. As we have seen, containment through ejection is a favorite cliché in sensation fiction, and its reworking perhaps not surprisingly focuses on the more problematic figure of the inside trader. Trollope's own *Can You Forgive Her?* capitalizes on this cliché. When he returns to this plotting of the (seemingly) "other" speculator as a contaminant a decade later, it is in a satirical spin on society's expectations and desires. All that is foreign about Lopez is his name and, of course, his speculations. Melmotte invites a tracing of global networks that situate the British Empire within a multiplicity of financial exploitations that cannot be delimited through transposition or projection.

Linked to China and Mexico, traced from New York to Continental Europe, Melmotte all too glaringly embodies the threats most commonly associated with foreign commerce. He is rumored to have provisioned "the Southern army" during the American Civil War, supplied the Austrian-Hungarian Empire with arms to put down Italy's fight for independence, and at one time bought up all the iron in England in a larger critique of new imports. Elected representative of the English merchant classes to host the Chinese emperor, he rapidly progresses from being regarded as so indiscriminately foreign that he might well be Chinese himself to hosting a foreign dignitary as the representative of the British commercial Empire. His suitability is doubly ironic: "Some men said that Melmotte was not a citizen of London, others that he was not a merchant, others again that he was not an Englishman. But no man could deny that he was both able and willing to spend the necessary money" (270). In a similar vein, Hamilton K. Fisker, Melmotte's indisputably American counterpart, is even pronounced to be "a 'Heathen Chinee' such as he had read of in poetry" by an indiscriminately speculating lord who does "not understand much about the races of mankind" (78). In that Fisker functions as Melmotte's double, they both become connected to American exports to such an extent that Melmotte has been seen as an embodiment of what Trollope considered "the American business ethic."[78] However, what remains the most symptomatic about this ironically very apt embodiment of a commercially oriented Empire is his incommensurability. Melmotte's varied career on both sides of the Atlantic, with stopovers in Paris and Vienna, has consequently puzzled critics as much as the clueless aristocrats in the novel itself. At one end of the spectrum, he has been described as "an Austrian Jewish financier" and hence a definitely foreign character; at the other end, it has been suggested that Melmotte "was almost certainly modelled after Albert Grant," one of the fraudulent company promoters who became "notorious villains of the Victorian era."[79]

The disclosure that Melmotte might "only" have been Irish or American-Irish certainly comes as an anticlimax. After his exposure and suicide, "[t]he general opinion seemed to be that his father had been a noted coiner in New York—an Irishman of the name of Melmody—and, in one memoir, the probability of the descent was argued from Melmotte's skill in forgery" (747). His daughter ends up "not even knowing what was her father's true name, as in the various biographies of the great man which were, as a matter of course, published within a fortnight of his death, various accounts were given as to his birth, parentage, and early history" (747). His only legacy consists of the contradictory narratives of his indeterminacy and its identification with a new, global business sense. Marie Melmotte turns out to be an "excellent [. . .] woman of business [. . .] her father's own daughter" (746–47). A "very enterprising young lady," she has "been able at an early age [. . .] to throw off from her altogether those scruples of honesty, those bugbears of the world, which are apt to prevent great enterprises" (227–28). She impresses even the effete baronet whom she empowers to elope with her (only he oversleeps), surprises her father in refusing to sign over money kept under her name, and matches Fisker's "thorough contempt for scruples" (703), a way of doing business associated with the encroaching New World: "how excellent a woman of business she had become, and how capable she was of making the fullest use of Mr Fisker's services" (746). Miss Melmotte eventually returns to America, importing money made out of European scams. The speculator's daughter thus embodies the worst outgrowth of his cosmopolitan identity as well as of his exploitation of various commercial practices.

But if Melmotte is determined by a heavily stereotyped indeterminacy, and his daughter conforms to the stereotypes of the unfeminine American heiress,[80] Madame Melmotte remains a dubious nonentity. As a result, her significance in the novel has been largely overlooked. Yet in showcasing the hypocrisy of a speculative society through her prominent, and yet precarious, positioning within it, Trollope accords considerable sympathy to her, without scaling down her vulgarity, silliness, or general inability to fit in. In contradistinction to Miss Melmotte, the financier's wife remains a mere pawn, not only in her husband's financial gambles, but also in London society. Just as cash-poor landowners vie over seats on Melmotte's boards, their wives have to put up with Madame. In the chapter "Madame Melmotte's Ball," introductions to the aristocracy are accomplished in a "very business-like manner," and "Madame Melmotte, who had been on her legs till she was ready to sink, waddled behind, but was not allowed to take any part in the affair" (39). When hosting the Chinese emperor, she is likewise visibly marginalized:

> Madame Melmotte during the evening stood at the top of her own stairs [...], longing only for the comfort of her bedroom. She, I think, had but small sympathy with her husband in all his work, and but little understanding of the position in which she had been placed. Money she liked, and comfort, and perhaps diamonds and fine dresses, but she can hardly have taken pleasure in duchesses or have enjoyed the company of the Emperor From the beginning of the Melmotte era it had been an understood thing that no one spoke to Madame Melmotte. (472)

It is in this incongruous position of the seemingly courted outsider that Ouida's *The Massarenes* redeploys the speculator's indeterminate wife as a typecast figure. Madame Melmotte is a blank space in the social events she hosts; Mrs. Massarenes serves as a hilariously unwitting mouthpiece of criticism. She pinpoints the superficiality of English highlife, "not intending any sarcasm," as it is put more than once.[81] Thus, she reassures five-year-old Jack (Lord Kersterholme) that he need not worry about being clever: "'My lord don't want to be clever; he'll be duke,' said Mrs Massarene, intending no sarcasm" (29). Jack and his sister Boo have good reasons to think the wealthy American woman they encounter at a dubious Continental resort must either be "a cook or a nurse" as they survey her "with puzzled compassion" (13), while willingly accepting her presents: "Shrewd little beggars, getting' things out of the fat old woman" (157), as their parents, Cocky and Mouse (Lord and Lady Kenilworth), consider it. Since the Kenilworths' "financial embarrassments were chronic" (47), they consider the Massarenes a panacea offered for their convenience. They count on Massarene's spending power as an expected deliverance from their impecunious state by purchasing the family estate. In being served up landed wealth, Massarene succeeds all too fast in what Melmotte strives for. In both novels, however, it is clearly established from the beginning that calculative aristocrats are by no means simply the victims of a changing economic and social structure.

The resemblance of circumstances of the Melmottes and the Massarenes is indeed compelling. Like the Melmottes, the Massarenes penetrate high society after their return from America via the Continent. They likewise turn out to be originally from Ireland, but unlike in Trollope's novel, this is revealed almost perfunctorily, as neither a mystery nor an anticlimax. What is more, Melmotte may be "purse-proud and a bully," yet there is "a wonderful look of power about his mouth and chin" strong enough "to redeem his face from vulgarity" (31); Massarene simply resembles a "grazier or cheesemonger" (32). While "shirt-sleeves and butcher-boots, with a brace of revolvers in his belt" can render him "a formidable and manly figure," dressed-up in a gentleman's clothes, "he looked clumsy and absurd, and he knew it" (32). Still, despite the absurdity, his hybridity is endorsed by the "freemasonry of business" in the City in a balancing out of simplifying stereotypes: "He united the American rapidity, daring, and instinct in business with the Englishman's coldness, reserve, and prudence. The union was irresistible" (342). Having started his career in the American West by keeping a pork shop, Old Billy joins the list of threatening returnees in Victorian fiction as "William Massarene, late of Kerosene City, North Dakota, U.S.A., miner, miller, meat salesman, cattle exporter, railway contractor, owner of gambling saloons, and opium dens for the heathen Chinee, and one of the richest and hardest-headed men in either hemisphere" (17). This renaming parodies the returnee's traditional camouflage as well as an assimilation that becomes an infiltration. This is indeed his main goal: "buyin' the old uns out" and marrying his daughter "to a lord duke" (39–40). Appropriately, he is eventually supplanted in his fashionable townhouse by "an Australian wool-stapler [. . .], a big burly heavy man, who owned many millions of sheep on many thousands of pastures, and had as much taste as one of his woolly wethers" (573–74). Returnees come to gobble up the imperial capital.

This reassessment of the legacies of commercial imperialism's expansion and infiltration at home plays a central role in the novel, partly rehearsing alignments it wishes to disentangle. As in so many earlier financial novels, an embarrassment of riches, even when not illegally obtained, can be a guilty burden, a "loathsome inheritance" (390). In contrast to Trollope's Miss Melmotte, who has at an early stage in her life divested herself of any scruples, to Miss Massarene, the exposure of the making of "[m]ost self-made men [. . .] by questionable means" (433) comes as a sensational shock: "like electric light shed on a dark place where murdered bodies lie" (428). This is despite the fact that, unlike the majority of stock-market villains, Massarene has consistently stayed within the law. This distinction marks out an important shift for financial speculation's use to indicate gradations of character. Such legalized success not only arraigns the financial system that supports such transactions, but singles out Massarene's clever calculations as "all the worse because of that cold-blooded caution which had kept him carefully justified legally in all which he did" (423). Although he never resorts even to white-collar crime, he has exchanged his sausage shop for an office that "seemed like a very charnel-house" (396). It is the apposite location of his violent death. The breaking in of a pistol-wielding, one-armed ex-miner, a rival returnee from the Wild West, certainly is a far cry from Melmotte's convenient and, it has been argued, ennobling suicide.[82] Conversely, the exportation of Madame and Miss Melmotte is reworked as Mrs. Massarene's sad, yet tranquil, death. It is a resigned giving in that is a form of suicide.

Much of the novel's poignancy rests in Mrs. Massarene's social isolation. She is the successful speculator's marginalized wife of Trollope's satire transposed into a domestic novel that reworks numerous clichés of high-risk speculation in highlife. An easily typecast figure becomes invested with unexpected emotional poignancy. Her lack of polish does not detract from the sympathetic evocation of her misery: "What was the use of having an income second only to Vanderbilt's and Pullman's? There are things which cannot be purchased. Manner is chief amongst them. Margaret Massarene was very lonely indeed" (6). "[S]ad and silent" (8) in society, she finds that "her natural sincerity, simplicity, and good nature were all homely instincts, no more wanted in her new life than a pail of fresh milk was wanted at one of the grand dinners" (106). She is frequently in tears and heard to heave "a heart-broken sigh" (25). Her absence from her husband's last will is meant and fully understood as his final "injustice and insult" (387). Since it is indicated that this "great wrong" could only be of a pecuniary kind, Mrs. Massarene's transfiguration is tragic-comical: "The fat, homely, vulgar woman was transfigured by the noble endurance of a great wrong" (386). Having "no powers of assimilation" (388), she dies a misunderstood foreigner, her death rendering the marriage of the successfully assimilated daughter, Kathleen (anglicized into Katherine), to Mouse's brother, Ronnie Hurstmanceaux, more acceptable.

The duly conscripted daughter's marriage is somewhat incongruously conjured up as an apt counterpoise to the "irresistible" union of the worst of cool English calculations and American enterprising powers in the person of the infiltrating returnee, her father (342). Whereas Mouse thoroughly deserves her mistreatment at Massarene's hands, so that he serves as a desirable visitation upon a speculative aristocracy, the elision of Katherine's foreignness partly obscures the novel's most complex realignment of the stock-market novel's conventional structures. A less intriguing substitute for her inadvertently criticizing mother, she becomes a more articulate outsider who can arraign imperialist policies, so that when Hurstmanceaux first encounters her, her comments on India make him believe that she "must surely be a Russian" (146). Allegations of vulgarity—and it remains a cardinal sin in the novel—are leveled at the English abroad: "How vulgar, how fussy, how common the conquerors look beside the conquered!" (142). Importantly, Katherine needs to renounce "that barbed legacy of the dead" (403), her "blood-stained and accursed" (428) fortune, which she does by devoting it to charities in the United States as well as in England and Ireland. The money is allowed to flow back, undercutting the financing of estates at home through speculations abroad at least for the novel's most laudable characters. Standing outside modern financial flows is their reward in a narratively satisfactory assertion of poetic justice.

This union of the anglicized daughter and one of the last honorable aristocrats, in short, constitutes an ideal, albeit elusive, alternative to the infiltration of a "modern and American civilisation" (38). Contrary to the standardized development arising from this pairing, however, the latter does not simply rupture an outmoded way of life by externalizing the worst of an intrinsic move towards a modernity characterized by financial transactions' predominance in social intercourse. As Talia Schaffer has recently argued, in depicting a society ruled by commodity fetishism, Ouida reintroduces elements of silver-fork fiction—elements of a decidedly outmoded narrative structure. This is more than a recycling of a "style derived primarily from Catherine Gore" with its favorite focus on aristocratic fracas as Ouida attacks "a world whose debased standards had made a better kind of womanhood impossible."[83] Silver-fork clichés are adapted to interrogate the insistent pressures of modernity in all spheres of life. In an excess of references to "the modern," Massarene is described as "an essentially modern product of modern energies" (201). But precisely this identification with modernity links him to Mouse, indicating that it is by no means an importation alone. A "modern woman of the world," she is "a terribly expensive animal" (225), and whenever her daughter Boo is at her most mercenary, she is described as "the true child of modernity" (33), exhibiting "the fine instincts proper to one who will have her womanhood in the twentieth century" (9). Hurstmanceaux, by contrast, stands outside time. He is "not a man of his time; he was impetuous in action, warm in feeling, sensitive in honor; he had nothing of the cynical morality, the apathetic indifference, the cool opportunism of modern men of his age" (118). Ironically, the ultimately successful absorption of the speculator's offspring realizes one of the returnee's main calculations on his incursion into highlife: to marry his daughter to a "lord-duke." The endorsed cross-class marriage may twist the standardized endings of, by then, classic stock-market novels (Trollope's prominently among them), but it significantly does so through an ambiguously nostalgic recall of narrative modes.

If *The Way We Live Now* satirizes the willingness of aristocrats to follow where the indeterminate speculator leads them, the remake of its main plotlines in *The Massarenes* reactivates marital and inheritance plots, co-opted by the central representation of financial crashes and their interrelationship with paralleled emotional and moral collapses as they are. Trollope's novel indeed already anticipates the most prominent inversions of the seemingly foreign businessman. Still, Melmotte's suicide is as emblematic as Merdle's in Dickens's mid-century novel, and when his daughter pursues the failed financier's other form of expulsion (exile to America), she successfully carries off money made out of England's speculative upper classes even after their speculations on the promising foreign enterprises have signally plunged. What makes the novel so compelling is, after all, the extension of the satire to various, significantly interconnected spheres of life along the exposed networks of financial speculation. Ouida's version ultimately offers a more nostalgic reconstitution after all. This closure may be narratively satisfactory as Mrs. Massarene's slow death imbues the killing off of the foreign element with a new kind of pathos that locates culpability more specifically within a speculative society at large, yet the elision of Katherine's foreignness rights the reinstated silver-fork world perhaps too effortlessly. Precisely this reintroduction of the narratives of highlife, combined with the romance plot's desirable closure, however, engenders a reworking of financial fiction and its association with particular narrative modes. It is through such a remolding of specific structures into new forms that the interstices between subgenres—highlighted and partly created by financial speculation plots—become the most accentuated.

Conclusion

The proliferation and attendant stratification of emergent subgenres in the nineteenth century map out the fascination with which financial speculation was being depicted and taken up as a source of narratives at the time, illustrating the formative influence of financial plots in the development of the novel during the genre's most defining period. While revaluating fiscal relationships in Victorian Britain, I have therefore also sought to highlight flows of influence and interchanges in literary formations. Nineteenth-century fiction certainly gained from the climate of anxiety about financial liabilities and instabilities, while at its best, it refused simply to rehearse moral or economic discourses. Instead, it embarked on more experimental, often deliberately provocative ventures—ventures that were premised on the versatile fictional functions of such indeterminacies. Financial instability therein operated as an expression of emotional, moral, or social insecurity. What this study furthermore outlines, in fact, is that nineteenth-century financial plots were crucial to the formation of new narrative structures not simply because of the temptations of speculation but because of the fissures in the attempts to manage them. A turn to speculation came to function so explicitly as a symptom of instability that, in Margaret Oliphant's *Hester*, a country banker could be shown to take to stock-market shares "as another man might have flown to brandy or laudanum" (131). Beyond such unequivocal identifications of risky enterprises with the addictive and self-destructive, the plotting of incongruities in various financial arrangements transformed the fictionalization of interconnected experiences of instability. The Victorian novel tapped into diverse discourses while becoming increasingly self-reflexive, underscoring the fact that the evolving narratives of speculation were by no means monolithic or a mere reflection of economic change. In one of the most complex fictionalizations of the intrinsically speculative definition of paper currencies, numbered banknotes help disclose the real murderer in Mary Braddon's *Aurora Floyd*. A ghost is out for compound interest in Charlotte Riddell's *The Uninhabited House*, and the railway to the moon in Ellen Wood's *Adam Grainger* takes the self-destructive allure of such speculative projects to its extremes.

As a shaping force in fiction that connects widely divergent novels, the representation of financial speculation as a metonymy for a speculative society thus describes overlapping trajectories. The speculator as a recognizable literary figure stands in for a welter of cultural, social, and personal emotional issues. From such early references to misguided financiers as can be found in Henry Siddons's *Virtuous Poverty* of 1804, in which Doublepop asserts that he "did not *mean* it" when he "ruined a great many others" as well as himself (3:144–45), to the sorting out of degrees of risk in Oliphant's *Hester* at the end of the century, the emergence of the professional stockbroker and his projection onto the untrained amateur chart a preoccupation with reliability that pivots on the narrative potential of its slippages. Actively plotting stock-market villains become more multifaceted and more easily typecast. Their emotional and moral as well as financial instabilities become realized by topoi involving buildings (and their collapses), vehicles (and their crashes), and projections onto foreign spaces.

Within a narrative discourse of finance that forges linkages between subgenres, these structural metaphors and specific motifs are variously adapted, generating a field of mutual influence. In Jane Austen's *Sanditon*, mobility generated by estate speculation is already rendered manifest in a physical crash, deserted ancestral homes, empty houses for rent, and overstocked shops. Subsequently, two parallel trajectories traverse what may best be pictured as intersecting circles of subgenres. Financial fiction of the century's first decades emerges from a common pool of narratives about a speculative economy and society, comprising thinly fictionalized essays of economic journalism, while increasingly intersecting with traditional plotlines structured by inheritance, courtship, and (mercenary) marriage. *Sanditon* forms the partly parodic product of such overlaps with economic writing, fictional and nonfictional, by Thomas Surr among others, and established property plots, including Austen's own earlier works. Austen's more widespread, less focused influence on fashionable society fiction by women writers can then be seen to parallel their likewise ambiguous relationship with male dandy novels. These trajectories' revealing complications can be rendered visible as affinities between silver-fork fiction's two versions, or manifestations. They cut across the chronological progression from Surr to Austen and from Austen to female silver-fork novelists as well as from early financial journalism to some of the most straightforwardly realized, chiefly cautionary stock-market narratives, including MacFarlane's *Railway Scrip; Or, The Evils of Speculation*, Laurence Oliphant's "Autobiography of a Joint-Stock Company (Limited)," or also parts of Lever's *Davenport Dunn*. The same decades, moreover, that propelled the growing presence of new financial plots in different forms of writing saw the emergence of distinct subgenres.

From the middle of the century onwards, cross-fertilization among literary subgenres as well as other discourses (including economic journalism or also the proto-psychological accounts of Mackay) indeed became markedly self-reflexive. Catherine Gore's late works, we have seen, illustrate intersections between such different narrative modes as silver-fork and social-problems fiction. Conversely, Gaskell pastiches "millinery fiction" to indicate that the structures of the fashionable novel need reworking if not replacement. *North and South* not only sets out to reflect concerns with economic and social change by dramatizing the conflicting demands of moral economies at home and in business. It also mines fashionable writing to redirect narrative modes. Catherine Sinclair's *Sir Edward Graham; Or, Railway Speculators* likewise forms a particularly pertinent example of such ongoing interchanges because the introduction of railway speculation into the changing world of the upper classes locates the novel itself exactly at the interstices between works by Gore (silver-fork fiction) and by Gaskell (social-problems fiction), while anticipating elements of the primarily sensational detective novel. Interstices between genres are generated by new financial plots that presage a rewriting that structures representations of stock-market villains as sensational figures. The establishment of moral economies in the conceptualization of financial accountability as a personal responsibility constitutes a widespread cultural enterprise, with all the stereotyping such a project entails. Its fictionalization, however, is increasingly invested in the charm of speculation, in the allure offered by the act of speculating as well as by the figure of the speculator. What makes stock-market villains and what renders them appealing fictional characters becomes the leading question. Although the containment of financial instability remains important, this attractiveness causes the boundaries between villains and heroes, irresponsibility and innocence, risk taking and expulsion, to become revealingly porous. If novels of the 1850s are still generally concerned with the moral dilemmas of speculators who are as much victims as culprits, the attraction of sensationalized villainy induces stock-market novels of the 1860s to redeploy established paradigms with new twists. This is why the "sensational sixties" provide a nodal point in the literary negotiation of the most influential figures and tropes associated with narratives of financial speculation.

Sensation novels without doubt produce the most captivating stock-market villains. They do more than provide revealing transitional figures that enrich the novel genre's pool of intriguing villains, however. When Braddon sets the proliferation of overtly familiar kinds of papers at the book market against the "plagiarisms of commerce" in *Charlotte's Inheritance,* she at once exposes the pervasive impact of financial speculation on society (including literary circles) and situates her own sensationalization of commerce in a tradition of fictional rewritings. Such a self-ironic conscription of various paper fictions does not stop at alignments between the book market and the stock market, of course. That the miser who learns to covet paper money in Braddon's *Aurora Floyd* is declared dangerously insane critiques finance capitalism's new instruments, while the solution of the sensational mystery turns upon a retired banker's professional knowledge and habits. Reade's *Hard Cash* employs the same suspicions about paper currencies: they are easily torn, lost, forged, and discounted. Only a monomaniacal madman could believe that they really are, intrinsically, of the value they are meant to represent. Yet the desperately chased banknotes, wrapped in a pocket book, sewn into a waistcoat, form the anthropomorphized "Hard Cash" on which depends so much in the novel. Its embodiment of both hardness (seeming solidity) and fragility (paper's brittleness) complicates the Cash's spiritualization through the receipt issued for it (its "soul"). The accumulation of papers that makes up Wilkie Collins's *The Moonstone* issues a conversion of an even harder currency (a diamond) into paper as the spoils of imperialism operate as a deliberately misleading clue to fraudulent ventures at home. In depicting the repercussions of imports from "the East" as a complex threat, both novels locate the triggering point and even the origins of actual danger at home. They constitute representative instances of the sensationalization of colonial speculation that stands in revealing contradistinction to the fictional treatment of guilty legacies in Thackeray's *The Newcomes* and Dickens's *Little Dorrit* a decade earlier. An analysis of these texts side by side casts new light on the changing representation of a specific form of speculation, propelled by an empire invested in commercial expansion. Here the overlaps between different ways of plotting financial speculation become particularly manifold. The centrality of foreign transactions causes these novels of the 1850s and 1860s to be grouped together, while intersecting with their projection onto internal colonization. Increasingly, metaphors coined by a preoccupation with foreign finances additionally eschew easy streamlining.

As new detective plots capitalize on the narrative potential offered by established plotlines as false clues, in fact, they engender some of the most self-reflexive engagements with the competition between opposing literary trends. Wood's *The Shadow of Ashlydyat* and Trollope's *Can You Forgive Her?* both reveal, in distinctly different ways, the most threatening speculator as an insider. When financial speculation itself stands in for the market forces of a speculative economy, moreover, it underpins the self-defense of the popular producer of sensation. In Oliphant's *At His Gates*, clichés are reorganized with a self-reflexivity that locates the novel at the interstices of the popular detective novel and of ambiguously anti-sensational domestic fiction. While engaging with the possibilities of endorsing competing trends for the sake of their popularity, *At His Gates* at the same time prefigures the reworking of ossified stereotypes in Oliphant's later novel *Hester*. Literary sensationalism indisputably makes the most of any cataclysmic crises (financial panics prominently among them), yet the integration of its most popular plotlines into domestic realism additionally prompts us to rethink the zones of intersection between evolving subgenres and the function of financial plotlines for what can revealingly be pictured as areas of agreement within genre formations.

The representation of financial speculation identifies overlaps between diametrically opposed narrative modes. In the century's most intricate engagements with literary shifts, what can usefully be pictured as intersections between different subgenres not only accounts for much of their complexities, but also facilitates a remapping of even their outwardly most representative examples in translating cultural anxieties into narrative form: landed estates and lady's names circulating in the market; aristocrats looking for openings among the committees of shareholders; redefinitions of the domestic Gothic by anti-sensational writers; the artist victimized as speculator. Victorian stock-market novels extricate marital and inheritance plots from increasingly clichéd structures to tie them instead to a growing fascination with self-deceived and deceiving speculators as well as with writers and artists caught up in the same speculative economy. A critical analysis of the formation and transformation of these plotlines hence also unearths developments of the novel genre that stress the significance of noncanonical works for a reconsideration of literary influence across subgenres. Finance capitalism has provided new plots, shaping the form as well as the content of the Victorian novel. Simultaneously, it has been instrumental in creating the sheer proliferation of narratives, and it is only by beginning to analyze this markedly different engagement with changing plot structures in detail that we are able to realize the full significance of these developments of literary culture.

Notes

Introduction

1. On the swindler John Sadleir see Norman Russell, *The Novelist and Mammon: Literary Responses to the World of Commerce in the Nineteenth Century* (Oxford: Clarendon, 1986), 134–35, and Barbara Gates, *Victorian Suicide: Mad Crimes and Sad Histories* (Princeton: Princeton University Press, 1988), 65–70. On Melmotte and George Hudson see G. R. Searle, *Morality and the Market in Victorian Britain* (Oxford: Clarendon, 1998), 80–81. Other novels of the fifties that take up the cultural myth of George Hudson, the "Railway King," include Robert Bell's *The Ladder of Gold* (1850) and Emma Robinson's *The Gold-Worshippers* (1851). Less thinly disguised, Dickens's Merdle has been described as "a very different man from Hudson, gloomy and retiring where Hudson was flamboyant and forceful; a fraud who perishes by his own hand where Hudson was merely a gross mismanager of accounts who went to his grave in 1871 with a crowd of mourners, while the great bell of York Minster was tolled in tribute" (Russell, 132). See also Jennifer Carnell on the different way in which Braddon worked Sadleir's suicide into fiction, *Three Times Dead* (*The Literary Lives of Mary Elizabeth Braddon* [Hastings: Sensation Press, 2000], 158).

2. John Butt, "The Topicality of *Little Dorrit*," *University of Toronto Quarterly* 29 (1959): 8.

3. Undoubtedly, fictional businessmen, their strategies, and moral dilemmas can be useful as a reflection of the businesses of a past era. In *The Cash Nexus: Money and Power in the Modern World, 1700–2000* (New York: Basic Books, 2001), Niall Ferguson takes a much contested parliamentary seat that continuously creates

problems in Trollope's Palliser novels as a diagnostic term to describe the changes electoral economics underwent in the nineteenth century (217-19).

4. Gillian Beer, *Open Fields: Science in Cultural Encounter* (Oxford: Oxford University Press, 1996), 173.

5. Ibid.

6. John Louis Digaetani, "Introduction," *Money: Lure, Lore, and Literature* (Westport: Greenwood, 1994), xv-xix.

7. John Vernon, *Money and Fiction: Literary Realism in the Nineteenth and Early Twentieth Century* (Ithaca: Cornell University Press, 1984), 7.

8. Cedric Watts, *Literature and Money: Financial Myth and Literary Truth* (New York: Harvester Wheatsheaf, 1990), 3.

9. Ibid., 12.

10. Gail Turley Houston, *From Dickens to Dracula: Gothic, Economics, and Victorian Fiction* (Cambridge: Cambridge University Press, 2005), 1. Anna Maria Jones has similarly remarked "that the economic realm was sensationalized by Victorians and in Victorian realism" at a time when the British economic system came to depend more on the stock market (*Problem Novels: Victorian Fiction Theorizes the Sensational Self* [Columbus: The Ohio State University Press, 2007], 65).

11. Barbara Weiss, *The Hell of the English: Bankruptcy and the Victorian Novel* (Lewisburg: Bucknell University Press, 1986), 17, 20.

12. Jeff Nunokawa, *The Afterlife of Property: Domestic Security and the Victorian Novel* (Princeton: Princeton University Press, 1994), 7, 122. Simon James has similarly diagnosed inheritance as the primary fictive strategy of the "classic" novel. In earlier fiction, sudden inheritance as a plot resolution commonly serves to restore a desired link between moral value and economic existence in a "moral accounting" that is questioned at the mid-century (*Unsettled Accounts: Money and Narrative in the Novels of George Gissing* [London: Anthem, 2003], 6).

13. J. Jeffrey Franklin, "The Victorian Discourse of Gambling: Speculations on *Middlemarch* and *The Duke's Children*," *English Literary History* 61.4 (1994): 918.

14. Paul Delany, *Literature, Money and the Market from Trollope to Amis* (Basingstoke: Palgrave, 2002), 1.

15. Peter Brooks, *Realist Vision* (New Haven: Yale University Press, 2005), 17.

16. Jonathan Rose, "Was Capitalism Good for Victorian Literature?" *Victorian Studies* 46.3 (2004): 491.

17. Patrick Brantlinger, *Fictions of State: Culture and Credit in Britain, 1694-1994* (Ithaca: Cornell University Press, 1996), chapter 4; Delany, 23. Money and fiction, Brantlinger further stresses, are both representational systems that rely on a credit system. They are interchangeable in multiple ways: "money as the fiction of gold or of absolute value; fiction as a commodity, exchangeable for money," premised on their expected exchange value (*Fictions,* 144). For an overview of different approaches to paper money's perceived intangibility see also Christina Crosby ("Financial," *A Companion to Victorian Literature and Culture,* ed. Herbert Tucker [Oxford: Blackwell, 1999], 232).

18. The pioneer studies of John Reed, Norman Russell, John Vernon, and Barbara Weiss have generated a growing field of inquiry, which the critical contributions of Patrick Brantlinger, Paul Delany, Margot Finn, Elaine Freedgood, Catherine

Gallagher, Claudia Klaver, and Mary Poovey have continued to reinvestigate and redirect. Contributions to the 2002 special issue of *Victorian Studies* on "Victorian Investments" have drawn attention to the ways in which fictional and nonfictional writing on finance took part in the production of meaning, of a symbolic as well as a material economy, within Victorian financial systems. For a good account of recent developments in the field, including an assessment of the special issue, see Jones, 62–63.

19. Mary Poovey, "Introduction," *The Financial System in Nineteenth-Century Britain* (Oxford: Oxford University Press, 2003), 1, 3.

20. Ibid. In *Making a Social Body: British Cultural Formation, 1830–1864,* Poovey refers to "a relationship of generic proximity" ([Chicago: University of Chicago Press, 1995], 2). Poovey's most recent work further underscores the importance of genre as she reads economic journalism and financial fiction as related parts of the same phenomenon. In *Genres of the Credit Economy: Mediating Value in Eighteenth- and Nineteenth-Century Britain,* she presents a detailed history of the disciplines that distinguished economic fact from imaginative fiction through a process of generic differentiation from the late seventeenth century to the 1870s (Chicago: University of Chicago Press, 2008). Equally important, Margot Finn and Catherine Gallagher have recently built on—and moved beyond—traditional economic criticism to foreground what Gallagher terms "a more sympathetic and a less platitudinous picture" of various textual practices that allows us to reassess "formal relations between literary and economic writing and studies of the historical development of literature as an economic activity" (*The Body Economic: Life, Death, and Sensation in Political Economy and the Victorian Novel* [Princeton: Princeton University Press, 2006], 3, 1). Finn has specifically suggested that the "enduring presence of extended credit in the novel (and in the historical consumer market) provided writers with a host of narrative opportunities for reading individuals' misbehaviors as 'misfortunes'" (*The Character of Credit: Personal Debt in English Culture, 1740–1914* [Cambridge: Cambridge University Press, 2003], 63). When Walter Bagehot started his articles on the money market for *The Economist,* serialized in the 1850s and published in book form in 1873, he symptomatically entitled his first contribution "Lombard Street" to emphasize the "concrete realities" of the new money business (*Lombard Street: A Description of the Money-Market* [New York: John Wiley & Sons, 1999], 1).

21. Poovey, "Introduction," 3. Elaine Freedgood speaks of textual strategies of risk management: the Victorians' cultural enterprise of constructing a safe England in a textual containment of risk was achieved with the help of elaborate constructions of "large-scale consolation and reassurance" and a "geography of risk" (*Victorian Writing about Risk: Imagining a Safe England in a Dangerous World* [Cambridge: Cambridge University Press, 2000], 2).

22. Mary Poovey, "Writing about Finance in Victorian England: Disclosure and Secrecy in the Culture of Investment," *Victorian Studies* 45.1 (2002): 33.

23. John Reed, *Victorian Conventions* (Athens: Ohio University Press, 1975), 268. Chapter 8 of Reed's seminal study focuses on "swindles" as central to the representation of finance in Victorian literature; chapter 12 provides an overview of the treatment of inheritance and other financial matters in nineteenth-century literature.

Compare John Reed, "A Friend to Mammon: Speculation in Victorian Literature," *Victorian Studies* 27 (1984): 179–202.

24. Martha Woodmansee and Mark Osteen, "Introduction," *The New Economic Criticism: Studies at the Intersection of Literature and Economics* (London and New York: Routledge, 1999), 3.

25. Ibid., 35–39.

26. James Phelan, "The Changing Profession; Narratives in Contest; or, Another Twist in the Narrative Turn," *PMLA* 123.1 (2008): 166. See also the section "Narrative Theory, 1966–2006: A Narrative" in Robert Scholes, James Phelan, and Robert Kellogg, *The Nature of Narrative*, 40th ed. (Oxford: Oxford University Press, 2006): in this "age of the Narrative Turn, an era when narrative is widely celebrated and studied for its ubiquity and importance," narrative's "power to capture certain truths and experiences" has been widely acknowledged (285), yielding new developments in narrative theory, including interdisciplinary approaches. Since the relations between the same elements (the same story) varies widely from narrative to narrative (in different discourses), the comparison of such versions across different media, or between intersecting subgenres, shows how such approaches "cast new light on literary narrative, whether by highlighting similarities, emphasizing differences, or leading to revised understandings of literary narrative itself" (289, 285).

27. Susan Griffin, *Anti-Catholicism and Nineteenth-Century Fiction* (Cambridge: Cambridge University Press, 2004), 2.

28. Ibid., 3. Jonathan Culler has likewise recently stressed that formalism does by no means necessarily reject or rule out history. What it does reject is "historical interpretation that makes the work a symptom, whose causes are to be found in historical reality," and hence, to counteract this, "we could do worse than to insist on the necessity of formalism for understanding the historicity of semiotic systems (*The Literary in Theory* [Stanford: Stanford University Press, 2007], 9–10).

29. Herbert Tucker, "Tactical Formalism: A Response to Caroline Levine," *Victorian Studies* 49.1 (2006): 86. This new formalism has been at the center of recent discussions in Victorian studies, and the present study profits from this large-scale reconsideration. Compare Caroline Levine, "Strategic Formalism: Toward a New Method in Cultural Studies," *Victorian Studies* 48.4 (2006): 625–57, and Carolyn Dever, "Strategic Aestheticism: A Response to Caroline Levine," *Victorian Studies* 49.1 (2006): 94–99.

30. Houston highlights the importance of moving beyond simplistic "cultural studies chiasms" (1), and Jones discusses the promises of a "critical turn" away from the "contextual mode" and especially "Foucault-inspired studies" (3). Jones further maintains that such studies are "guilty of erasing difference, reading all texts and contexts into a giant uniform power/knowledge edifice" (3). Delany similarly criticizes the dangers of new historicism, of that "harping on its tropes of 'complicity' and 'commodification' [which] might be caught up in an ultimately sterile re-tracing of the endless circulation of power through culture" (5). As James Eli Adams has already put it, we need to avoid the mere restaging of familiar "versions of what one might call Foucauldian melodrama" ("Recent Studies in the Nineteenth Century," *Studies in English Literature* 41.4 [2001], 858–59). He specifically warns against "the

lure of totalising explanation and to the overreaching that is always a danger for work that aspires to be interdisciplinary," emphasizing "how much of the satisfaction afforded by the best literary study derives not from the sheer conceptual reach or audacity of its enabling premises, but from the intricacy and variety with which those premises are borne out in particular encounters" (849, 879).

31. Franklin, "Gambling," 918. In *Gambling and Speculation: A Theory, a History, and a Future of Some Human Decisions* (Cambridge: Cambridge University Press, 1990), Reuven Brenner and Gabrielle Brenner trace this distinction to the "Puritan work ethic" and further suggest the suddenness as well as the sheer extent of the "winnings" as characteristic of both speculation and gambling: "Looking at the distinction from this angle, it becomes evident that one may become significantly richer by either gambling or speculating, but not by investing" (93). As Edward Chancellor puts it, "[t]he line separating speculation from investment is so thin that it has been said both that speculation is the name given to a failed investment and that investment is the name given to a successful speculation" (*Devil Take The Hindmost: A History of Financial Speculation* [New York: Plume, 2000], xi).

32. See David Itzkowitz, "Fair Enterprise or Extravagant Speculation: Investment, Speculation, and Gambling in Victorian England," *Victorian Studies* 45.1 (2002): 122–23. This partly explains the frequent projection onto the American speculator: public perception of speculation in America and Britain was structurally similar, but not identical. Itzkowitz draws on Ann Fabian's work on gambling in nineteenth-century America to show that, in both countries, the differentiation between speculation and gambling was a purging process thought necessary for the legitimization of a capitalist economy. In the United States, this process was complete by the 1860s. In Victorian Britain, the 1870s saw the reinsertion of speculation in legal and moral discourses on gambling. Compare Ann Fabian, *Card Sharps, Dream Books, and Bucket Shops: Gambling in 19th-Century America* (Ithaca: Cornell University Press, 1990), 3.

33. Harriet Martineau's *Illustrations of Political Economy*, for example, aimed to set up a broader audience for the promulgation of emergent economic theories. Published in 1832–34, her series of twenty-five novellas formed a didactic project that, as Claudia Klaver has shown, developed "individual fictional narratives around clusters of economic 'laws' or 'principles'" (*A/Moral Economics: Classical Political Economy and Cultural Authority in Nineteenth-Century England* [Columbus: The Ohio State University Press, 2003], xiv). More recently, Poovey has selected Martineau's work "to discuss a historicist mode of textual interpretation" because it "squarely occupies the generic overlap between economic and literary writing that has by now been virtually eliminated" (*Genres*, 338–39).

34. William Cobbett, *Rural Rides* (London: Dent & Sons, 1953), 319. The OED furthermore specifies speculation's distinctness from "regular trading or investment," emphasizing its "venturesome or risky nature" ("speculation, *n.*" *Oxford English Dictionary*. 2nd ed. 1989. OED Online. Oxford University Press. 7 November 2007. http://dictionary.oed.com/cgi/entry/50232763).

35. Dinah Mulock Craik, *Olive* (Oxford: Oxford University Press, 1999), 92.

36. This erasure of a potential plot of detection—explicitly suggested by a lawyer as a possible "commission—to—to hunt out this secret" (105)—parallels the novel's

treatment of the father's other secret, his affair with an amorphously described "Creole" in a rewriting of *Jane Eyre*.

37. J. Jeffrey Franklin, *Serious Play: The Cultural Form of the Nineteenth-Century Realist Novel* (Philadelphia: University of Pennsylvania Press, 1999), 62. Compare Franklin, "Gambling," 911.

38. Thomas Carlyle, *The French Revolution* (Oxford: Oxford University Press, 1989), 36. Compare Kevin McLaughlin, *Paperwork: Fiction and Mass Mediacy in the Paper Age* (Philadelphia: University of Pennsylvania Press, 2005), 1.

39. McLaughlin, 3-4.

40. Ibid., 4.

41. It is no accident, Brooks continues, that "the founder of modern linguistics, Ferdinand de Saussure, often compares language as a system to money: meaning in both systems depends on exchange value, what you get in return for what you are offering. And the great realist novelists come to understand that words, like shillings or francs, are part of a circulatory system subject to inflation and deflation, that meanings may be governed by the linguistic economies and marketplaces of which they are part" (*Realist*, 14).

42. Anthony Trollope, *The Way We Live Now* (London: Penguin, 1994), 680.

43. Karen Odden points out that the title of Lady Carbury's projected book "alludes to the mythical wheel and the wheels of the railway engine," but as she marries a journalist who puts a stop to her "irresponsible writing" shortly after the Melmotte Bubble has burst, the novel's explorations of puffery and broken promises converge ("Puffed Papers and Broken Promises: White-Collar Crime and Literary Justice in *The Way We Live Now*," *Victorian Crime, Madness and Sensation*, ed. Andrew Maunder and Grace Moore [Aldershot: Ashgate, 2004], 144). Compare Tony Tanner's excellent discussion of Trollope's equation of railway bubbles and the circulation of various papers (including gamblers' IOUs) in *The Way We Live Now* ("Trollope's *The Way We Live Now*: Its Modern Significance," *Critical Quarterly* 9.3 [1967]: 256-71).

44. Charles Reade, *Hard Cash* (London: Chatto and Windus, 1863), 82-83.

45. George Robb, *White-Collar Crime in Modern England: Financial Fraud and Business Morality, 1845-1929* (Cambridge: Cambridge University Press, 1992), 11, 31.

46. The Bubble Act of 1720 had attempted to end speculation by blocking the formation of joint-stock companies. Even after the act had been repealed in 1825, setting up a company remained a costly enterprise until the 1850s. Once the 1856 Joint Stock Companies Act recognized business organizations that consisted of a group of seven or more persons who had signed a memorandum of association, it moreover rendered bogus companies (one-man associations with six "dummies") more than merely feasible. High-risk speculation was made not only more attractive and far less risky to the individual, but also easier to enter.

47. Mary Elizabeth Braddon, *Charlotte's Inheritance* (London: Simpkin, Marshall et al., 1868), 224. Ironically, supporters of limited liability had hoped that in promoting a laissez-faire political economy, it could have been mobilized as a mechanism for democratization. As Donna Loftus has pointed out, the debates it generated focused tension between individual action and responsibility, between private ownership and public interest. Individual agency and the social organization of pro-

duction had to be rethought within the larger restructuring of the economy ("Capital and Community: Limited Liability and Attempts to Democratize the Market in Mid-Nineteenth-Century England," *Victorian Studies* 45.1 [2002]: 93–94).

48. Larry Neal, *The Rise of Financial Capitalism: International Capital Markets in the Age of Reason* (Cambridge: Cambridge University Press, 1990), 18–19.

49. Colin Nicholson, *Writing & the Rise of Finance: Capital Satires of the Early Eighteenth Century* (Cambridge: Cambridge University Press, 1994), 7–8. Houston has recently pointed out that this split might have fed into the construction of the home as a refuge from the marketplace, but this bifurcation also created instabilities that were rendered manifest in a sense of the uncanny. Houston speaks of "Gothic economies" (3).

50. Early literary engagements with paper money, Nicholson shows, personified Credit, often adapting "the rhetoric of Eve as fateful temptress" (xi). Swift, Pope, and Defoe satirized its effects, as Brantlinger has discussed in some detail (*Fictions*, 54, 121–23). Brantlinger suggests that from Defoe onwards, the "equation between financial solvency and personal salvation, at least in the secular sense of honor or credit, reputation or respectability, informs the great, canonical works of realist fiction," yet he stresses that it was in Victorian fiction that "banking on novels" became a central discourse (*Fictions*, 144). Compare Chancellor on Joseph Penso de la Vega's 1688 *Confusion de Confusiones*, written in the form of dialogue (11).

51. Thomas Shadwell, *Complete Works*, ed. Montague Summers (London: Fortune, 1927), 5: 173, 170.

52. Evidence of the staying power of such tropes as an articulation of a larger social critique, a scene from Shadwell's play was inserted as an introductory piece in Caryl Churchill's play *Serious Money* in 1987.

53. D. Morier Evans, *The History of the Commercial Crisis 1857–1858 and the Stock Exchange Panic of 1859* (New York: Kelley, 1969), v.

54. Walter Bagehot, "The Money-market No. III: What A Panic Is and How It Might Be Mitigated," cited in Houston, 1.

55. Charles Mackay, *Memoirs of Extraordinary Popular Delusions and the Madness of Crowds*, 2nd ed. (London: Office of the National Illustrated Library, 1852), 1.

56. The imagery of disease runs through Mackay's representation of speculation: "as soon as the delirium seized them" (48); a "speculating frenzy" (50).

57. D. Morier Evans, *Speculative Notes and Notes on Speculation, Ideal and Real* (London: Groombridge and Sons, 1864), 1.

58. Compare Brantlinger on Defoe's "Lady Credit" (*Fictions*, 54).

59. Laurence Oliphant, "The Autobiography of a Joint-Stock Company (Limited)," *Blackwood's Magazine* 120 (July 1876): 96–97.

60. Laurence Oliphant, *Piccadilly* (Edinburgh and London: Blackwood and Sons, 1871), 3.

61. William Harrison Ainsworth, *John Law; The Projector* (London: Chapman and Hall, 1866), 242.

62. William Harrison Ainsworth, *The South-Sea Bubble* (London: John Dicks, 1871), 30.

63. In this, the all too fortuitous ending of this clear-cut, synoptic fictionalization

of a stock-market plot illustrates the difference between closure and completion established in narrative theory. Compare James Phelan, *Reading People, Reading Plots: Character, Progression, and the Interpretation of Narrative* (Chicago: University of Chicago Press, 1989), especially 216n15.

64. Phelan, "Changing," 167.
65. Ibid.
66. Ibid.
67. Ibid.
68. George Eliot, "Silly Novels by Lady Novelists," *Westminster Review* 66 (October 1856): 442–61, Rpt. *Essays of George Eliot*, ed. Thomas Pinney, 300–324 (London: Routledge and Kegan Paul, 1963), 301.
69. Reed, "Mammon," 183. Victorian novelists, Russell similarly stresses, "were quick to condemn the New Men of commerce as unscrupulous, coarse, bloated, probably dishonest" (150), producing what Robb has more recently called an "economic demonology" of "white-collar" crime (4). Brooks has even suggested this development as a main reason why traditional property plots came to be so crucially transformed in the course of the nineteenth century: "the emergence of the cash nexus tracks a transition from inherited identity to achieved identity, that of the self-made man, or the speculator, the capitalist, the gambler—or the destitute genius—all familiar figures in the nineteenth-century novel" (*Realist*, 14).

Chapter One

1. Catherine Gore, *The Two Aristocracies* (London: Hurst and Blackett, 1857), 3:234. Ellen Moers describes the silver-fork novel as "a literature written about the exclusives, by the exclusives (or those who knew them well) and for the exclusives [...], royally supported by those who were not but wanted desperately to become exclusives: the *nouveaux riches* of post-war England" (*The Dandy: Brummel to Beerbohm* [London: Secker & Warburg, 1960], 52). Winifred Hughes speaks of a "paradoxical formula of exclusivism for the masses" that was rapidly considered a thing of the past: it allowed readers to revel in a way of life that was seen to be fading while they simultaneously helped to construct domestic ideals so that "[e]ven the most reform-minded reader could surrender himself or herself to its decadent titillations while preserving a sense of moral and class superiority" ("Silver Fork Writers and Readers: Social Contexts of a Best Seller," *Novel* 25 [1992]: 329–30). As Robin Gilmour has put it, silver-fork fiction was "a genre which contrived to have it both ways" (*The Idea of the Gentleman in the Victorian Novel* [London: Allen & Unwin, 1981], 53). Regenia Gagnier suggests that silver-fork fiction "played to status anxiety rather than class conflict, purportedly telling middle-class aspirants how the aristocracy behaved while simultaneously providing models of a new, improved bourgeois gentleman" ("Money, the Economy, and Social Class," *A Companion to the Victorian Novel*, ed. Patrick Brantlinger and William B. Thesing [Oxford: Blackwell, 2002], 60).

2. Matthew Rosa suggests that Westmacott had Colburn in mind when he wrote of "the universal speculator in paper and print" (*The Silver-Fork School: Novels of*

Notes to Chapter One

Fashion Preceding Vanity Fair [New York: Columbia University Press, 1936], 204). From 1835–41, "Colburn's Modern Standard Novelists" appeared in nineteen volumes, a venture that did much to establish both the silver-fork mode of writing and the nineteenth-century triple-decker as fashionable commodities.

3. These were derogatory terms. William Hazlitt poked fun at pretended insider reports of such mundane facts as that "the quality eat with silver forks" (*Complete Works*, ed. P. P. Howe [London: Dent, 1934], 20:146).

4. Charles Molloy Westmacott (Bernard Blackmantle), *The English Spy* (London: Sherwood, Jones, 1825), preface.

5. Catherine Gore, *The Banker's Wife; Or, Court and City* (London: Colburn, 1843), 3:165.

6. The typical dandy novel is Bulwer-Lytton's *Pelham; Or, The Adventures of a Gentleman* (1828), which has long been considered as having solidified, if not established, silver-fork formulae (Winifred Hughes, "Elegies for the Regency: Catherine Gore's Dandy Novels," *Nineteenth-Century Literature Criticism* 50.2 [1995]: 195). In *Women in Print: Writing Women and Women's Magazines From the Restoration to the Accession of Victoria* (London: Allen and Unwin Ltd., 1972), Alison Adburgham maintains that Gore's *Women As They Are or The Manners of the Day*, published anonymously in 1830, "is generally considered to have been the first of what were called 'fashionable novels' or 'silver-fork novels'—although claims are sometimes made for Theodore Hook's *Sayings and Doings*, 1824" (255).

7. Jane Austen, *Complete Novels* (Oxford: Oxford University Press, 1994), 1502. All references to Austen's novels are to this edition.

8. When James Edward Austen-Leigh first published his *Memoir of Jane Austen* in 1870, he did not even mention the fragment, while the second edition of 1871 presented a summary and brief extracts. See James Edward Austen-Leigh, *Memoir of Jane Austen* (Oxford: Clarendon, 1951), xiii, 192–206.

9. Mary Waldron even maintains that "there is nothing to suggest moral disapproval of Mr. Parker's activities—it is his self-deception that is highlighted" (*Jane Austen and the Fiction of Her Time* [Cambridge: Cambridge University Press, 1999], 159). Clara Tuite has argued that the fragment is both "[e]legiac, and written under the sign of the backward look, [. . .] a conservative lament for the landed estate" and "strangely utopic, suggesting new directions of style, possibilities of genre, and fantasies of female mobility" (*Romantic Austen: Sexual Politics and the Literary Canon* [Cambridge: Cambridge University Press, 2002], 159). This is an interesting reinterpretation of what Marilyn Butler has diagnosed as "Sanditon's perversion from its earlier natural role as fishing village and agricultural community" (*Jane Austen and the War of Ideas* [Oxford: Clarendon, 1987], 286).

10. Tuite, 100, 5.

11. Raymond Williams, *The Country and the City* (London: Chatto and Windus, 1973), 115.

12. Jane Stabler, *Burke to Byron, Barbauld to Baillie, 1790–1830* (Basingstoke: Palgrave, 2002), 192.

13. Alistair Duckworth, *The Improvement of the Estate: A Study of Jane Austen's Novels* (Baltimore: Johns Hopkins University Press, 1971), 125.

14. *Mansfield Park* (1814) and *Persuasion* (1818) are about social as well as geo-

graphical mobility and the ambiguous nostalgia it brings with it. Both novels endorse the navy as a means of, in the words of Sir Walter, the effete baronet in *Persuasion*, "bringing persons of obscure birth into undue distinction, and raising men to honours which their fathers and grandfathers never dreamt of" (1231). Compare Robert Sales, *Jane Austen and Representations of Regency England* (London: Routledge, 1996), 199.

15. David Spring has stressed how important it is to keep in mind that the majority of Austen's family (and her characters) belonged to a "pseudo-gentry" consisting of higher professionals, the clergy, retired naval officers, and also the younger branches of the gentry. They were essentially "nonlanded," owning "comparatively little" ("Interpreters of Jane Austen's Social World: Literary Critics and Historians," *Jane Austen: New Perspectives*, ed. Janet Todd [New York: Holmes & Meier, 1983], 59–60). Occupying an increasingly marginalized social space, they sometimes rented estates, lived in big houses, valued their "independence" (a regular income chiefly derived from land or an inherited fortune), and sought to imitate the landed gentry. Discussing the effects of agricultural blockades on the banking business, Robert Miles further argues that *Emma* (1816) registers a (*pace* Edward Said) "dead silence" about the stockbroking business. Seemingly isolated, Highbury is set up as emblematic of Tory ideals of an "organic" community, while it cannot really be a rural enclave, located as it is sixteen miles south of London and hence part of what is still known as the stockbroker belt. Pointing out the village's suburban location, Miles posits that Highbury, so far from forming a pastoral space, "would have been full of rentiers and stockholders" ("'A Fall in Bread': Speculation and the Real in *Emma*," *Novel* 37 [2003]: 70). See also Watts's discussion of both Austen and Cobbett in the context of the inflation during the Napoleonic Wars (138–39).

16. John Wiltshire, *Jane Austen and the Body* (Cambridge: Cambridge University Press, 1992), 9.

17. Tony Tanner, *Jane Austen* (Basingstoke: Macmillan, 1986), 255. Edward Copeland suggests that Sanditon itself is "the purest of consumer objects, almost solely an object of the imagination. Advertisements, newspapers, and word of mouth are the bricks and mortar of Mr Parker's enterprise. The world of signs completely outruns the world of things. It is the joke of the piece, of course, but also a situation that promises to mark a fatal separation between Mr Parker and his fortune" (*Women Writing about Money: Women's Fiction in England, 1790–1820* [Cambridge: Cambridge University Press, 1995], 114).

18. William Galperin has recently suggested that the body in *Sanditon* operates as a site of resistance: "a locus of such intense preoccupation that it literally provides cover from ideology of all kind" (*The Historical Austen* [Philadelphia: University of Pennsylvania Press, 2003], 13). On the commercialization of leisure more generally in *Sanditon* see Sales, 200–205.

19. In an additional irony, Lady Denham's position as the "great Lady of Sanditon" (1504) is the result of a series of well-calculated marriages. Tuite speaks of a "closet drama of inheritance" and "anti-speculation-plot," in which Lady Denham embodies a female mobility that rivals that of her dependent relative (and possible heiress), but which becomes enmeshed in the economic rivalry with Mr. Parker (173).

20. It could be argued that this fuses discourses on overconsumption and an overproductive imagination, which is further brought out by a subplot involving Sir Edward, one of Lady Denham's expectant relatives. An overdose of "more sentimental Novels than agreed with him" (1523) induces him to cast himself in the role of seducer in the style of Lovelace. He feels he ought to be exploiting the young woman's dependent position as a form of speculation.

21. Brian Southam, "A Source for *Sanditon?,*" *Collected Reports of the Jane Austen Society, 1966–75* (1977): 122.

22. Ibid.

23. Thomas Surr, *The Magic of Wealth* (London: Sidney, 1815), 1:215, 1:218, 1:263–64.

24. Thomas Surr, *Splendid Misery* (London: Hurst, 1801–2), 3:274.

25. Thomas Holcroft, *Bryan Perdue* (London: Longman, Hurst, Rees, and Orme, 1805), 3:71, 1:119.

26. Henry Siddons, *Virtuous Poverty* (London: Richard Phillips, 1804), 2:71, 3:144–45.

27. Thomas Surr, *Russell, Or, The Reign of Fashion* (London: Colburn and Bentley, 1830), 2:304, 2:306.

28. Catherine Gore, *Pin Money* (London: Colburn and Bentley, 1831), preface.

29. Rosa, 136. Hughes even speaks of the "bittersweet tone of the Cecil novels, in which Gore combines a revival of the old sparkling comedy of manners with an elegy for its irrevocable loss' ("Elegies," 192).

30. Gore's prolific output comprises Christmas books, adventure stories, and numerous plays. In 1841, she moreover began a series of articles in *Bentley's Miscellany* under the pseudonym Albany Poyntz. Recent reassessments of her novels have acknowledged that there is more to them than either a bittersweet glorification of a more flamboyant past or, alternatively, a plot of "supersession" of aristocratic Regency society by bourgeois values. See Andrew Elfenbein, "Silver-Fork Byron and the Image of Regency England," *Byromania: Portraits of the Artist in Nineteenth-and Twentieth-Century Culture,* ed. Frances Wilson (Basingstoke: Macmillan, 1999), 79.

31. See Russell, 4.

32. Lyn Pykett, "A Woman's Business: Women and Writing, 1830–80," *An Introduction to Women's Writing: From the Middle Ages to the Present Day,* ed. Marion Shaw (London: Prentice Hall, 1998), 157–58.

33. April Kendra, "Gendering the Silver Fork: Catherine Gore and the Society Novel," *Women's Writing* 11.1 (2004): 27–28. Hilary Schor has further suggested that one way to retrieve some of the "incredibly diverse" literary forms of the 1830s that have been "largely lost to literary history" is to "read the novels of the 1840s through the genres of the 1330s" ("Fiction," *A Companion to Victorian Literature and Culture,* ed. Herbert Tucker [Oxford: Blackwell, 1999], 325, 330).

34. Catherine Gore, *Mothers and Daughters* (London: Colburn and Bentley, 1831), 1:118. The "whole business [of marriage is] looked upon as a speculation" (2:96), so that at one point, an upstart's interest in one daughter is even said to have "fallen two and a half per cent" (3:209). In "The Special License," included in *The Fair of May Fair* (1832), a fashionable lady is similarly tempted "to hazard bolder measures,—attempt a season's dash,—and speculate on a wider scale," and a mother's

"speculations for her daughter are too notorious" (Catherine Gore, *The Fair of May Fair* [London: Colburn and Bentley, 1832], 3:307, 3:352.).

35. As Reed has already rightly pointed out, the recurring "equation of money and marriage markets was common throughout the century, but it becomes especially acute when associated with the risky world of speculation" ("Mammon," 187).

36. Catherine Gore, *Peers and Parvenus* (London: Colburn, 1846), 3:92.

37. Moers, 41. Compare Rosa, 18n3.

38. Brantlinger, *Fictions*, 145.

39. Rosa, 122.

40. Louis Cazamian, *The Social Novel in England 1830–1850: Dickens, Disraeli, Mrs Gaskell, Kingsley*, trans. Martin Fido (London: Routledge & Kegan Paul, 1973), 40.

41. Catherine Sinclair, *Sir Edward Graham: Or, Railway Speculators* (London: Longman, Green, and Longmans, 1849), x.

42. As Reed has already pointed out, the uncontrolled railway speculations "focused attention on the danger of extensive speculation, a danger quickly recorded in novels" ("Mammon," 184).

43. Elizabeth Gaskell, *North and South* (Oxford: Oxford University Press, 1998), 302–3.

44. Catherine Sinclair, *Holiday House* (Edinburgh: William Whyte, 1839), vii.

45. By contrast, Sir Edward and Lord Edenthorpe are, in different ways, released. Emily, tricked into bigamy by Fitzroy, is exiled to Paris as one of the standard refuges for impecunious aristocrats, while Fitzroy himself goes mad and is appropriately kept in the rooms originally meant for the wrongfully incarcerated lord.

46. *Ruth* (1853) already attempts to fuse social critique with the rewriting of fashionable fiction. Its "employment of the popularly recognised homologies between a forged document and an illegitimate child" moreover highlights the effects of various forms of "unlicensed" activities, as Natalka Freeland has analyzed in "Ruth's Perverse Economies: Women, Hoarding, and Expenditure," *English Literary History* 70.1 (2003): 214. With its middle-class heroine, it has been argued, *North and South* presents an improved exploration of the complexities of class conflict, especially compared to *Mary Barton* (1848), Gaskell's first social-problems novel. But see Pearl Brown, "From Elizabeth Gaskell's *Mary Barton* to her *North and South*: Progress or Decline for Women?" *Victorian Literature and Culture* 28.2 (2000), for a reassessment of analyses that "typically conclude" that *North and South* is the stylistically and ideologically more mature work (345). In the mock-pastoral *Cousin Phillis* (1863), railways do not only exist on paper, so that exemplary engineers have "no thought for the shareholders' interests" ([London: Penguin, 1995], 7), whereas in the sensational *A Dark's Night Work* (1863), "the sudden bursting of a bubble speculation" exposes muddled accounts ([Oxford: Oxford University Press, 1992], 40).

47. Late exponents of what Eliot derided as novels of "the mind-and-millinery species" have been dismissed as outmoded, unfashionable accounts of outdated literary and social fashions. Winifred Hughes has suggested that such "millinery" fiction should be seen as a lineal descendent of early silver-fork fiction ("Mindless

Millinery: Catherine Gore and the Silver Fork Heroine," *Dickens Studies Annual* 25 [1996]: 159), while Pykett maintains that Eliot referred to the silver-fork genre as a whole ("Business. 157). Although Gaskell recommended silver-fork writers to a French publisher when asked for a list of works with an estimate of "the place which the different novelists hold in England," it was clear that she did not think very highly of this subgenre (Elizabeth Gaskell, *Further Letters of Mrs Gaskell*, ed. John Chapple & Alan Shelston [Manchester: Manchester University Press, 2000], 126).

48. Eliot, "Silly," 301–2.

49. Asa Briggs, ' Samuel Smiles: The Gospel of Self Help," *Victorian Values: Personalities and Perspectives in Nineteenth-Century Society*, ed. Gordon Marsden (London: Longman, 1998), 103.

50. J. Kestner, *Protest and Reform: The British Social Narrative by Women, 1827–1867* (London: Methuen, 1985), 184. Compare "The Author of John Halifax," *British Quarterly Review* 44 (1866): 32–58, on Halifax's qualities as "derived from *ladies* and *gentlemen* who had been his remote ancestors. [Craik] does depict a noble nature and an unselfish life; but seeing that John Halifax did begin the world as a poor friendless boy, she might have allowed us to think that such a development was possible to man as man." (42–43, cited in Kestner, 184).

51. Dinah Mulock Craik, *John Halifax, Gentleman* (London: J. M. Dent & Sons, 1906), 1. The novel climaxes in the financial crisis of the mid-twenties, "this terrible 1825" (8), "the panic year [in which] commerce, in its worst form, started into sudden and unhealthy overgrowth. Speculations of all kinds sprung up like fungi, out of dead wood, flourished a little, and dropped away" (308). Kestner has traced the time scheme in some detail, comparing it also with Jewsbury's *Marian Withers* (1851), a novel that likewise rewrites silver-fork clichés of the aristocracy: "*John Halifax* opens in 1794 when Fletcher finds Halifax. By 1800 he goes to live at Enderley, commuting to work at Norton Bury. In 1812 Halifax introduces power looms to his mill, in conjunction with the Luddites, the battle of Badajoz, and the assassination of Perceval in the Commons. As in Jewsbury's novel, which Craik certainly read, the 1825 speculations mania plays a significant part in Halifax's life" (183).

52. Margaret's realization that the industrial North may have more of interest pivots on her caution to the unemployed worker Higgins that he should reconsider his plan to seek work in the South. The comparative "dullness of the life" (306) results in a general lack of "speculation," as the people of the South generally "don't care to meet to talk over thoughts and speculations, even of the weakest, wildest kind" (306). Margaret here refers to intellectual speculation, yet her choice of terminology constitutes an important indicator of her changed attitude towards the North. The role Margaret's brother Frederick has taken in a mutiny to stand up against injustice, for which he would hang if he ever returned to England, needs to be seen as yet another example of risk taking. It parallels the workers' strike. In addition, that Frederick settles down happily as a junior partner of a Spanish merchant house abroad counterbalances Margaret's marriage to a manufacturer: "Margaret smiled a little, and then sighed as she remembered afresh her old tirades against trade. Here was her preux chevalier of a brother turned merchant, trader!" (344).

53. Reed takes Emma Robinson's *The Gold Worshippers* as an example of a thinly plotted novel that illustrates the narrative structures commonly used at the time.

One of many novels based on the career of one of the most notorious railway magnates, George Hudson, it also shows how the young widow Mrs. Sparkleton "speculates in love and marriage much as she does in railway shares" ("Mammon," 187).

54. Reed, "Mammon," 187n20.

55. Watts, 146.

56. Brown, 349.

57. Watts, 147.

58. Brown proceeds to point out that it is three men, not Margaret herself, who determine her future. Her guardian provides the legacy. One suitor, Henry Lennox, makes the appropriate legal arrangements to invest it in a third man's enterprise (349–50).

Chapter Two

1. Charles Dickens, *A Christmas Carol* (London: Oxford University Press, 1966), 17, 60.

2. Audrey Jaffe, "Spectacular Sympathy: Visuality and Ideology in Dickens's *A Christmas Carol*," *PMLA* 109.2 (1994): 255.

3. Charles Dickens, "Convict Capitalists," *All the Year Round* 59 (9 June 1860): 202. This critique is voiced even more emphatically in a companion article by John Hollingshead, "Very Singular Things in the City," published in *All the Year Round* a month later. It firmly lays the blame on "men of position, of means, and reputation" who are directly responsible for railway swindles by "fill[ing] the chairs of amateur auditorship, for dinners, small patronage, and trifling fees" (*All the Year Round* 64 [14 July 1860]: 326).

4. Financial speculation recurs in Dickens's fiction, and I shall analyze its most fully realized literary investigation in *Little Dorrit* in chapter 3. "Them things as is always a-goin' up and down, in the City" already figure briefly in *The Pickwick Papers* ([Oxford: Oxford University Press, 1998], 661). *Nicholas Nickleby* features more than one death by speculation in a world replete with proliferating companies, including the often cited United Metropolitan Improved Hot Muffin and Crumpet Baking and Punctual Delivery Company: one Godfrey Nickleby is introduced at the novel's opening as "seriously revolving in his mind a little commercial speculation of insuring his life next quarter-day, and then falling from the top of the Monument by accident" (Charles Dickens, *Nicholas Nickleby* [London: Oxford University Press, 1950], 2). Nicholas Nickleby senior dies of the shock occasioned by the failure of his speculations, whereas his brother Ralph hangs himself at the end of the novel. It is left to the next generation, to the Nicholas Nickleby of the title, to engage with commerce in a personally and socially responsible fashion, divorced from the risky speculations that are exorcised with his uncle's suicide. With its invocation of the suddenly enriched returnee as escaped convict, *Great Expectations* renders current anxieties with "convict capitalists" literal, and it is by launching Mr. Wickfield "into imprudent and ill-judged speculations" that Uriah Heep, the arch-sneak of *David Copperfield*, spawns "meshes" made up of "alarming and falsified accounts of the estate" as well as of a "miscellaneous catalogue of unscrupulous chicaneries" to entrap

his former employer (*David Copperfield* [Oxford: Oxford University Press, 1999], 737). *Our Mutual Friend* most extensively takes up circulating papers as a recognizable metaphor for a widespread condition. Compare Poovey, *Body*, chapter 8.

5. Charles Dickens, *Our Mutual Friend* (London: Oxford University Press, 1952), 114.

6. Anthony Trollope, *Can You Forgive Her?* (Oxford: Oxford University Press, 1999), 2:390.

7. In fact, if Trollope satirized Dickens's dust mounds by shrinking them to a farmer's inflated dunghills, guano and bios are at the root of important financial speculations in the later *The Prime Minister*.

8. As John Sutherland has discussed in some detail, fictional criminals became cleverer in the mid-century and "this founded a line of antiheroes which begins with Fosco—who discourses with scientists on equal terms—and leads to that strange contradiction, the academically distinguished arch-criminal like 'Professor' Moriarty and 'Doctor' Nikola. Before 1850 the liaison between erudition and low crime would have seemed freakish" ("Wilkie Collins and the Origins of the Sensation Novel," *Wilkie Collins to the Forefront: Some Reassessments*, ed. Nelson Smith and R. Terry [New York: AMS, 1995], 76).

9. Patrick Brantlinger, *The Reading Lesson: The Threat of Mass Literacy in Nineteenth-Century British Fiction* (Bloomington: Indiana University Press, 1998), 2.

10. Ibid.

11. Clare Pettitt, *Patent Inventions: Intellectual Property and the Victorian Novel* (Oxford: Oxford University Press, 2004), 1.

12. Pettitt, 4. Dickens, among other popular writers, deliberately broke through the "sharp divide between the categories of literary and mechanical invention" to extend the debate to the conceptualization of mental labor more generally (Pettitt, 2). Architecture in *Martin Chuzzlewit* and engineering in *Little Dorrit*, it has amply been discussed, became a means of expressing Dickens's grievance over the absence of international copyright law to protect his books from being pirated in the United States. See Gerhard Joseph's detailed discussion in "Charles Dickens, International Copyright, and the Discretionary Silence of *Martin Chuzzlewit*," *The Construction of Authorship: Textual Appropriation in Law and Literature* ed. Martha Woodmansee and Peter Jaszi (Durham: Duke University Press, 1995), 259–270, and "Construing the Inimitable's Silence: Pecksniff's Grammar School and International Copyright," *Dickens Studies Annual* 22 (1993): 121–36. In *Little Dorrit*, creative labor is addressed through the counterpoint of a dilettante painter (Gowan) and an inventor (Doyce) in two overlapping subplots, but as Pettitt has pointed out, labor is effaced in the factory's description, and as a static stereotype, Doyce fails to present a model of creativity (196, 202).

13. "Manufacture of Novels," *Athenaeum* (16 February 1867): 221–22. Braddon was accused of plagiarism and of denying that she had, under a pseudonym, undertaken hack jobs for the penny press. Her ventures into "penny bloods" came to light when *Diavola* was reprinted as *Nobody's Daughter* "by the author of *The Black Band*" in the United States, and there acknowledged as the work of Miss Braddon. Now Braddon had been careful to release penny fiction under the pseudonym of Lady Caroline Lascelles, and this disclosure threw up a number of issues about popular

serial fiction. The anonymous critic started a "squabble [that] raised a question concerning an English novelist who would act prudently in publishing without delay her part in the transactions that have raised a Grub Street tempest on the other side of the Atlantic" (221). Extended over several issues of the *Athenaeum*, subsequent debates gave rise to personal insults. Braddon was, in fact, more than once caught up in copyright disputes and plagiarism cases. Her magazine, *Belgravia*, established in 1866, was from its very beginnings implicated in copyright and plagiarism disputes, as it duplicated part of the title of *Belgravia: a Magazine of Fashion and Amusement*, entered into the Register of Copyrights three years earlier.

14. "Not At All A New Novel," *Pall Mall Gazette* (28 February 1867): 8. This article focused on Wood's similar recycling of previously serialized fiction in slightly adapted novel form, published under a different title. Subsequent articles engaged with Wood's response to the allegations. See "Our Naughty Novelist," *Pall Mall Gazette* (6 March 1867): 10.

15. Mary Elizabeth Braddon, *The Doctor's Wife* (Oxford: Oxford University Press, 1998), 253. A toning-down of Gustave Flaubert's famous novel of adultery, *Madame Bovary*, *The Doctor's Wife* not only sports a sympathetically presented sensation writer and partly exonerates an addicted reader, but it also uses a sensational narrative involving forgery as a subplot.

16. In a striking inversion of the relationship between established and emergent plotlines of Victorian financial fiction, Philip Sheldon considers inheritance less certain than speculation in shares: "The whole business of heir-at-law hunting seemed to the stockbroker a very vague and shadowy piece of work, as compared to the kind of speculation that was familiar to him" (53). His attitude encapsulates the completion of a central shift in the Victorian novel's financial plots.

17. Mary Elizabeth Braddon, *Eleanor's Victory* (Leipzig: Tauchnitz, 1863), 2:55.

18. Ellen Wood, *Lord Oakburn's Daughters* (London: Bentley and Son, 1889), 115.

19. In Braddon's *John Marchmont's Legacy* (1863), speculation on inheritance is similarly outlined as the beginning of a criminal career. Paul Marchmont has so long calculated on "[t]he remote chance of that inheritance [that] had hung before him ever since his boyhood, a glittering prize, far away in the distance, but so brilliant as to blind him to the brightness of all nearer chances," that he ultimately resorts to more active schemes, including abduction (Mary Elizabeth Braddon, *John Marchmont's Legacy* [Oxford: Oxford University Press, 1999)], 456). Braddon's *The Lady's Mile* (1866) sees a successful capitalist's son ruined by "A Commercial Earthquake" ([London: Simpkin, Marshall, Hamilton, Kent, 1892], chapter 33); *Birds of Prey* (1867) shows how an upstart trade on "that appearance of respectability which, in a world where appearance stands for so much, is in itself a kind of capital" to set himself up as one of "your ultra-respectable men" ([London: Maxwell, 1867], 17, 142).

20. On the stockjobber as the devil compare Brantlinger, *Fictions*, 57.

21. Ellen Wood, *The Shadow of Ashlydyat* (London: Macmillan, 1900), 9, 170.

22. Although Wood's novels generally endorse the establishment of a middle-class presence in what might otherwise be reduced to a decaying estate, sympathy increasingly rests with the displaced themselves in an often ambiguous take

on ideologies of both work and domesticity. *Mildred Arkell,* first serialized in 1854, although only published in book form in 1865, for example, is set in "the days gone by" when "this feeling of exclusiveness, this line of demarcation, if you will, was far more conspicuous than it is now; it was indeed carried to a pitch that would now scarcely be believed in" ([London: Ward, Lock, & Co, n d.], 9). At the same time, however, the novel maps out a panorama of shabby-gentility and *nouveau riche* vulgarity. *Red Court Farm* (1868) similarly depicts an "exclusive" gentry society in counterpoint to those whose "early associations were not of the silver-fork school" ([Leipzig: Tauchnitz, 1868], 1:173).

23. Audrey Jaffe, "Trollope in the Stock Market: Irrational Exuberance and *The Prime Minister,*" *Victorian Studies* 45.1 (2002): 45. Although Jaffe refers specifically to *The Prime Minister,* the hesitating speculators of the early-1860s perhaps even more explicitly exemplify the "jittering" that characterizes emotional instability and shifting moral standards. They display "not the unwavering certainty of the clear moral line but rather the jittery peaks and valleys of the stock-market graph" (58).

24. Jenny Davidson has recently reassessed hypocrisy's redefinition as a condemned practice of deceit from the late eighteenth century onwards, distinct from earlier discourses on polite manners (*Hypocrisy and the Politics of Politeness* [New York: Cambridge University Press, 2004], *passim*).

25. John Halperin, *Trollope and Politics: A Study of the Pallisers and Others* (London: Macmillan, 1977), 48, 46.

26. Ibid., 48.

27. Juliet McMaster, *Trollope's Palliser Novels: Theme and Pattern* (London: Macmillan, 1978), 20, 23. Deborah Denenholz Morse speaks of the "sham romanticism" of the "counterfeit romantic George" (*Women in Trollope's Palliser Novels* [London: UMI Research Press, 1987], 13, 27).

28. Ibid., 8.

29. Halperin, 45. This is very different from the embezzling clerk's expatriation in Australia after he has duly served his prison sentence at the end of Trollope's earlier *The Three Clerks.* I shall return to the novel's reallocation of domestic space and its moral economies in chapter 4.

30. Mary Elizabeth Braddon, *Aurora Floyd* (Oxford Oxford University Press, 1999), 230.

31. Herbert Spencer, *Social Statics* (London: John Chapman, 1851), 396.

32. Ibid.

33. Richard Mallen, "George Eliot and the Precious Mettle of Trust," *Victorian Studies* 44.1 (2001): 46.

34. Mallen reassesses the significance of Britain's mixed currency in George Eliot's two "gold fables": "Brother Jacob" and *Silas Marner.* The latter, he argues, maps three phases of trust: religious faith, commercial trust, and "a revitalized trust" Mallen links to modernity (54). But compare Jeff Nunokawa's reading of the novel's "fairy-tale telling of the labour theory of value": Eliot "works overtime to discredit the affiliation between money and bodies" through the "miser's two bodies" ("The Miser's Two Bodies: *Silas Marner* and the Sexual Possibilities of the Commodity," *The Mill on the Floss* and *Silas Marner,* ed. Nahem Yousaf and Andrew Maunder [Houndmills, Basingstoke: Palgrave, 2002], 180–82).

35. Robb, 4.

36. Poovey has shown that the term economy "initially referred to the management of a household, with all of the financial, ethical, and domestic responsibilities that an early modern household entailed" (*Body*, 6). The eighteenth century yoked it to the political; nineteenth-century moral economies revived its significance at home.

37. Garrett Stewart, "Narrative Economies in *The Tenant of Wildfell Hall*," *New Approaches to the Literary Art of Anne Brontë*, ed. Julie Nash and Barbara Suess (Aldershot: Ashgate, 2001), 82.

38. George Eliot, *Middlemarch* (Oxford: Oxford University Press, 1998). Introduced as "the philanthropic banker" (82), Bulstrode is not one of the "coarse hypocrites" who consciously affect beliefs (581). He is genuinely convinced by the virtue of his very acquisitiveness, but ultimately exposed as a "speckilating fellow" (102) who has made his fortune through fraud as well as ruthlessness in business. As Pykett has argued, Eliot was perceived as a contrast to the prolific lady novelists of the time, and this may additionally explain Braddon's evocation of Eliot's novels (Lyn Pykett, *The "Improper" Feminine: The Women's Sensation Novel and the New Woman Writing* [London: Routledge, 1992], 3). But if the Softy is Braddon's answer to transformed misers like Silas, Aurora's "folly" is also the gender-reversed story of Godfrey Cass's "secret marriage, which was a blight on his life. It was an ugly story of low passion, delusion, and waking from delusion" (George Eliot, *Silas Marner* [Oxford: Oxford University Press, 1998], 29).

39. Mellish can be seen as a compensation for Aurora's bad bargain. He is himself a secure investment, and that ensures him his due reward after all: "People who were strangers to him ran after and served him *on speculation,* knowing instinctively that they would get ample reward for their trouble [italics added]" (58). This forms one of the most intriguing adaptations of the prevailing preoccupation with financial speculation in Victorian literature. In marked contrast to this embodiment of trustworthy investment, Conyers the gambler gets nothing back. There is no recompense, and for the only time in the novel that the overarching metaphor on bargains and repayments encompasses ultimate payment after death, he is shown to have invested very little in that particular fund: "there was not one who shed a tear for him; there was not one who could say, 'That man once stepped out of his way to do me a kindness; and may the Lord have mercy upon his soul!'" (298).

40. The servant setting himself up as a lord in disguise is a reference to Bulwer-Lytton's *The Lady of Lyons* (1838). Aurora curses the writer as his play "helped to make [her] what [she] was" (281).

41. As Pykett has stressed, all of Braddon's novels revolve on a secret, but bigamy and an accusation of having murdered the first husband link the two heroines especially together (*Feminine*, 86).

42. Mary Elizabeth Braddon, *Lady Audley's Secret* (Peterborough: Broadview, 2003), 168.

43. Compare Richet Drouet, "'Taming the Shrew': Melodrama and the Representation of Desire in *Lady Audley's Secret* and *Aurora Floyd*," *Cahiers Victoriens & Edouardiens* 59 (2004): 63–74; Robert Dingley, "Mrs. Conyers's Secret: Decoding Sexuality in *Aurora Floyd*," *Victorian Newsletter* 95 (1999): 16–18.

44. Karl Marx, *Capital*, trans. Ben Fowkes (Harmondsworth: Penguin, 1976), 1:255. Compare Matthew Rowlinson's reassessment of Marxist, psychoanalytical, and formalist interpretations of (fictional) misers. He diagnoses "the generalized misrecognition of money" as a "basic principle of narrative organization" in *The Old Curiosity Shop*, in which a gambler is wrongly suspected of being a miser ("Reading Capital with Little Nell," *The Yale Journal of Criticism* 9 [1996]: 373).

45. Anthony Trollope, *The Last Chronicle of Barset* (London: Penguin, 2002), 807, 18.

Chapter Three

1. The two plots of *Martin Chuzzlewit* map out a juxtaposition of imported and exported speculators, as has amply been argued. An extreme version of the economic system at home, in which "smartness" seems "American for forgery" (Charles Dickens, *Martin Chuzzlewit* [Oxford: Clarendon, 1982], 265), the large-scale scam in America exposes the emigrant's expectations. Compare Diana Archibald, *Domesticity, Imperialism, and Emigration in the Victorian Novel* (Columbia: University of Missouri Press, 2002), 143–46.

2. Although the "lands of the Empire" could represent "an idyllic retreat, an escape from debt or shame, or an opportunity for making a fortune," the "idea of rural England" as home, Williams suggests, most powerfully contrasted with "the tropical or arid places of actual work; its sense of belonging, of community, idealised by contrast with the tensions of colonial rule and the isolated alien settlement" (281). It was this very dichotomy that Edward Said's *Orientalism* sought to expose and his *Culture and Imperialism* traced further in European cultural productions.

3. Franco Moretti, *Atlas of the European Novel* (London: Verso, 1999), 27.

4. Charles Dickens, *Little Dorrit* (Oxford: Oxford University Press, 1953), 400.

5. Elizabeth Gaskell, *Cranford* (Oxford: Oxford University Press, 1998), 3.

6. Raphael Samuel, *Theatres of Memory: Past and Present in Contemporary Culture* (London: Verso, 1994), 74.

7. Wilkie Collins, *The Moonstone* (London: Penguin, 1998), 94.

8. William Makepeace Thackeray, *The Newcomes* (London: Penguin, 1996), 732.

9. Gordon Ray speaks of the "clannishness" of the "self-contained Anglo-Indian social group" in which Thackeray grew up. Although Thackeray left India very young, Anglo-Indians in Britain remained closely knit by "ties of blood, shared experience, common interest, and like assumptions" (*Thackeray: The Uses of Adversity, 1811–1846* [London: Oxford University Press, 1955], 19–20).

10. William Makepeace Thackeray, *Vanity Fair* (Oxford: Oxford University Press, 1983), 27.

11. Weiss, 69.

12. Weiss describes the failure of an Indian agency-house in 1834 as "almost certainly the inspiration for Colonel Newcome's disaster with the Bundelcund Bank" (15). Ray suggests that even while the details of the financial catastrophe that affected Thackeray cannot be clearly established, "it seems reasonable to suppose that

the bulk of [the] estate was lost in the collapse of the great Indian agency-houses that took place at this period" (162). The cycle "began with the failure of Palmer and Company for £5,000,000 in 1830, and ended with the failure of Cruttenden and Company for £1,350,000, in 1834" (162). The Thackerays' involvement with one single agency-house is reflected in the misguided loyalty Colonel Newcome displays for the Bundelcund Bank (Ray, 162). See Ray's discussion of Thackeray's brief foray into bill discounting (159–60).

13. William Makepeace Thackeray, *The Great Hoggarty Diamond* (London: Oxford University Press, n.d.), 13–14, 67.

14. Daniel Thorner, *Investment in Empire: British Railway and Steam Shipping Enterprise in India, 1825–1849* (Philadelphia: University of Pennsylvania Press, 1950), 2.

15. "Mulligatawny, *n.*" *The Oxford English Dictionary.* Draft Revision. Mar. 2003. *OED Online.* Oxford University Press. 1 July 2006. http://dictionary.oed.com/cgi/entry/00317917.

16. Outlining the varying functions of orientalism in Thackeray's writing, J. Russell Perkin has traced revealing parallelisms between those involved in financial speculation who are at the same time connected to "the Orient": Rumman Loll, the money-lending wine merchants Moss and Sherrick, whose Jewishness is identified with a largely undifferentiated "East," and also Barnes Newcome, who is repeatedly likened to the equally dandified merchant prince on the one hand and ruthless moneylenders on the other ("Thackeray and Orientalism: *Cornhill to Cairo* and *The Newcomes*," *English Studies in Canada* 16.3 [1990]: 304). Sherrick's daughter, moreover, marries Clive's maternal uncle, the Reverend Honeyman, and emigrates to India. There clearly is more than one linkage between dubious businessmen in London and commerce with India. Brantlinger has suggested that Thackeray's investigation of the bank failure breaks down once he "displaces financial fraudulence onto the oriental (if not quite 'Hebrew') machinations of one person, the sinister Rummun Loll" (*Fictions*, 156). Although Brantlinger speaks of "Thackeray's resentful racism," he situates the novel's financiers among a list of fictional characters who bring in dubious capital or credit from abroad, from Magwitch's offstage Australia in *Great Expectations* to the proliferation of Melmotte's origins in *The Way We Live Now* (*Fictions*, 156, 45).

17. As Jeff Nunokawa has pointed out, it is driven by the law of exchange to the extent that when "the mother of a guilt-ridden heir observes that he regards the hard-got family fortune as so much 'plunder' that must be renounced, she describes more than filial ingratitude; she describes the general economy of the novel" (*Afterlife*, 8). Claudia Klaver has added that these accounts are "rigged," so that for Mrs. Clennam, the credit column will always exceed the debit column, inviting the amassing of more debts to strike a balance ("Natural Values and Unnatural Agents: *Little Dorrit* and the Mid-Victorian Crisis in Agency," *Dickens Studies Annual* 28 [1999], 23). Philip Collins has similarly diagnosed Mrs. Clennam's paralysis as the symptom of a "mysterious illness" caused by self-incarceration and the need for punishment as part of a moralized exchange economy (*Dickens and Crime*, 3rd ed. [New York: St Martin's, 1962, 1994], 281–82).

18. George Holoch, "Consciousness and Society in *Little Dorrit*," *Victorian Studies* 21 (1978): 337.

19. Grace Moore, *Dickens and Empire: Discourses of Class, Race and Colonialism in the Works of Charles Dickens* (Aldershot: Ashgate, 2004), 16.

20. Moore links the novel's critique of "how not to do it" and "Nobody's Fault" to the Crimean War (1854–56), one of the most notorious wars of imperialist history and one of the major medical disasters of the nineteenth century (16–17).

21. Christopher Herbert has discussed Victorian (mis)readings of the taboo with reference to the linkage the novel makes between "filthy lucre," the South Sea Gods at home in an apparently diseased London, and the magical name of Merdle, which is connected to the proverbial dirtiness of money through the fecal pun on the name itself ("Filthy Lucre: Victorian Ideas of Money," *Victorian Studies* 44.2 [2002], 185–213). Nunokawa has similarly suggested that "[t]he circle of gain and loss that makes any acquisition a kind of debt in *Little Dorrit* is like the exotic cultures where Western anthropologists find in primitive or archaic circuits of giving and getting the logic of exchange hard at work far away from the regions of the commodity form" (*Afterlife*, 8).

22. Jeremy Tambling, "Opium, Wholesale, Resale, and for Export: On Dickens and China, Part I," *Dickens Quarterly* 21.1 (2004): 35. Ironically, the same system prompts Arthur to take the responsibility upon himself when his losses in the Merdle enterprises threaten to cause his new business partner's bankruptcy. His methods—writing to the papers and turning himself in—are peculiarly ineffective.

23. The perceptual distance between *Mansfield Park* and *Little Dorrit* spans the Opium Wars, the "opening" of China, and the shift from a Romantic aesthetics of curiosity to the mid-century juxtaposition of orientalist Chinomanie and commercial preoccupation. The heroine of *Mansfield Park* can go on an imaginary "trip" (568) to Lord Macartney's China. It is an educational venture and creates a space for dreamy escape, reached through the reading of travel accounts, autobiography, and poetry in the tellingly named "East room." As such, it is identified with Fanny's "nest of comforts" (568) where she can retire, as her cousin puts it, from domestic persecution: "*You* in the meanwhile will be taking a trip into China, I suppose. How does Lord Macartney go on?" (570). By contrast, the novel's "dead silence" on the slave trade has been seen as evidence of a preoccupation with differentiated spaces of alterity and imperialist cultural productions ever since Edward Said's influential analysis reinscribed the novel within geopolitical discourses of its time (Edward Said, *Culture and Imperialism* [London: Chatto & Windus, 1993], 73). For detailed discussions of the problematic see Susan Fraiman, "Jane Austen and Edward Said: Gender, Culture, and Imperialism," *Critical Inquiry* 21.4 (1995): 805–21.

24. What exactly Arthur proposes, or whether there is a workable alternative to be proposed at all, is tantalizingly unclear. Ronald Thomas suggests that it may be read either as "a call for more aggressive speculation or a warning of its dangers" ("Spectacle and Speculation: The Victorian Economy of Vision in *Little Dorrit*," *Dickens, Europe and the New Worlds*, ed. Anny Sadrin [London: Macmillan, 1999], 41–42). Wenying Xu maintains that the "total silence about Arthur's twenty formative years in China is an anomaly in *Little Dorrit*" ("The Opium Trade and *Little*

Dorrit: A Case of Reading Silences," *Victorian Literature and Culture* 25.1 [1997]: 54). Xu goes further to suggest that the novel "is ordered by concealing the disorders that permeated the Sino-British relationship" (54).

25. Tambling argues that it remains unclear "whether the 'thirty years ago' that the novel refers to in its first line relates to 1825, so that Clennam is to be presumed to have been in Canton from 1805 to 1825, or whether Dickens thinks of Clennam as a China trader over the period 1835 to 1855" (35).

26. Xu, 55. Xu locates Arthur's twenty years in China roughly between 1805 and 1825. His father was sent there shortly after his son's birth, probably around 1786. His business could therefore "only have been located outside the city walls of Canton since the British were not allowed to enter the interior of the country until after China lost the war in 1842. Since almost no manufactured goods were sold to China and there is no indication that the Clennams had any factory in Britain, they could be either selling Indian cotton or opium" (56).

27. Thomas, 40. Drawing attention to the tendency of the novel's Italy to melt into familiar London spaces, specifically the Marshalsea, for which Little Dorrit feels such an ambiguous nostalgia, Thomas stresses that Venice stands in for the British Empire "as the centre of a certain kind of world commerce based on financial speculation" (36). Tambling similarly suggests that Dickens's Marseilles "may be an allegory, or displacement of Canton" (38) since commercial settlements in both Canton (Guangzhou) and Marseilles had been established in the course of European colonialism. In *The Powers of Distance: Cosmopolitanism and the Cultivation of Detachment,* Amanda Anderson similarly emphasizes the significant redeployment of the contest between "the not always compatible values [to say the least] of nationalism and cosmopolitanism" ([Princeton: Princeton University Press, 2001], 63). Far from being simply "anti-cosmopolitan," the novel explores the contribution of different cosmopolitan standpoints to a reinvigoration of corrupt Britain. Anderson focuses on Little Dorrit's vision of Rome (89).

28. As Susan Schoenbauer Thurin reminds us in *Victorian Travelers and the Opening of China,* "[a]s a rule, foreign merchants traveled little in China. They were notorious for not learning the language and avoiding the Chinese population. To some extent these patterns were a response to the treaty-port regulations in that foreign businesses and housing were confined to the concession areas" ([Athens: Ohio University Press, 1999], 60).

29. Daniel Born, *The Birth of Liberal Guilt in the English Novel: Charles Dickens to H. G. Wells* (Chapel Hill: University of North Carolina Press, 1995), 29.

30. Moore, 17.

31. As Ross Dabney has already pointed out in *Love and Property in the Novels of Dickens,* when Little Dorrit destroys the codicil that proclaims her entitlement to part of the Clennam estate, it is essentially a renunciatory gesture, a triumph of love over money (*Love and Property in the Novels of Dickens* [London: Chatto & Windus, 1967], 123–24). Nunokawa has further argued that this renunciation makes her "safe property" and "exempt from the rule of exchange," although the allegorical connection to acquisition is qualified by financial metaphors of surplus value (*Afterlife,* 14, 32). Klaver pinpoints an additional complication: Amy Dorrit may suggest herself as the antidote to speculative economic relations, but as a moral touchstone,

she is grounded in a separate-spheres ideology that is compromised, first, because Amy earns a living and hence does not stay in the domestic sphere, and second, because the "dynamic of individual responsibility and irresponsibility" is collapsing ("Values," 31, 19–20). And yet, the novel's "antispeculation alternative" ("Values," 32) operates in that love itself is reasserted as a "charm," as the real magic, unqualified by economic exchange. As Gates has pointed out, it does prevent the speculator's self-destruction: in her study of suicide in Victorian Britain, Gates stresses that Arthur Clennam falls "ill in both body and spirit, almost as Merdle did. Only the love of Little Dorrit restores Dickens's hero to health, sanity, and relative unconcern over money" (67).

32. Brantlinger, *Fictions*, 144.

33. Herbert, 189.

34. Ibid., 186.

35. Karl Marx, *Economic and Philosophic Manuscripts of 1844*, trans. Martin Milligan (Progress: Moscow, 1959), 129, cited in Herbert, 194. Compare Herbert on Freud's analysis of the symbolic equivalence of money and excrement (186–87).

36. Thorner, 45. In what is still one of the most informative discussions of British investment in Indian railways, Thorner analyzes how from the speculative notions advanced in 1844, "railways for India had become, by 1845, a serious matter occupying the concern of the highest officers of the East India Company in London and of the ranking government officials in far-off India" (119).

37. It did not need the revival of interest in sensation fiction for Reade's importance in the cultural discourses on insane asylums (and the fluid definitions of sanity) to be acknowledged. Controversial at the time, *Hard Cash* was conceived as a novel with a purpose. As Malcolm Elwin has put it, it was "a 'sensation' or 'purpose' novel of the type first made fashionable by Dickens" (*Charles Reade: A Biography* [London: Jonathan Cape, 1931], 166). It was directly based on the case of a young man named Fletcher who had been certified insane because he had become a financial hazard in the firm in which his father was a partner. Unlike Hardie's completely innocuous son in *Hard Cash*, young Fletcher had been a spendthrift who had claimed £35,000 from the company. Fletcher escaped from the asylum in which he had been wrongly confined and won the case of Fletcher v. Fletcher in July 1859 (Elwin, 166).

38. For an excellent overview of "the variety of methods critics now use to read Collins," see Tamar Heller, *Dead Secrets: Wilkie Collins and the Female Gothic* (New Haven: Yale University Press, 1992), 5, and on the epistemological as well as psychoanalytical implications of the novel's "several careful investigations and an apparent study of inhibited sexuality" compare Alexander Welsh, *George Eliot and Blackmail* (Cambridge, MA: Harvard University Press, 1985), 25–26. For a more recent analysis see Timothy Carens, "Outlandish English Subjects in *The Moonstone*," in *Reality's Dark Light: The Sensational Wilkie Collins*, ed. Maria Bachman and Don Richard Cox (Knoxville: University of Tennessee Press, 2003), 239–65. Although there is no mention of *The Moonstone*, see Gautam Chakravarty, *The Indian Mutiny and the British Imagination* (Cambridge: Cambridge University Press, 2005) on the "Indian Mutiny" as "the vulgate of late-nineteenth century British expansionism" (1) and on the general interest both Dickens and Wilkie Collins took in the rebellion.

Albert Pionke has linked *The Moonstone* not only to the Mutiny, but also to European revolutions and Chartists agitation through "the use of allusive dating," since both Rachel Verinder's birthday party and the theft of the diamond take place in 1848 (*Plots of Opportunity: Representing Conspiracy in Victorian England* [Columbus: The Ohio State University Press, 2004], 93). Reading the novel side by side with earlier representations of the rebellion, Pionke suggests that in appropriating "the rhetoric of conspiracy surrounding the Mutiny and revers[ing] its imperialistic implications," Collins "forces readers to reexamine Britain's role in the Mutiny" (80–81).

39. See Ilana Blumberg's excellent analysis of Miss Clack's own perverted credit system in "Collins's Moonstone: The Victorian Novel as Sacrifice, Theft, Gift, and Debt," *Studies in the Novel* 37.2 (2005): 162–86. Miss Clack's distribution of her evangelical tracts operates on a twofold credit system: she amasses points in heaven and creates debts for which she expects to be repaid by those on whom she bestows her spiritual riches. Blumberg also speaks of the description of Miss Clack's "dissemination of tracts as a kind of anti-robbery" as she is seen to slip into the house, leaving her treasures in choice places (172).

40. Blumberg, 169, 183. Blumberg further links the novel's exploration of ethical difficulties of textual and material exchange to "the under-legislated world of mid-nineteenth-century authorship and publication, exchange," which "seemed to Collins and not a few of his contemporaries to be fraught with ethical danger and practical loss" (163).

41. Deirdre David terms it a "gratifying ending wherein the diamond is restored to its original location and disruptive Indians who have invaded the domestic space of a Yorkshire country-house are put back where they belong on Britain's imperial map" ("Empire, Race, and the Victorian Novel," *A Companion to the Victorian Novel*, ed. Patrick Brantlinger and William B. Thesing [Oxford: Blackwell, 2002], 94). As David emphasizes elsewhere, *The Moonstone* illustrates "that nineteenth-century novels do not need exotic settings to characterize their pervasive representation of imperialism's structure and effects" ("Children of Empire: Victorian Imperialism and Sexual Politics in Dickens and Kipling," *Gender and Discourse in Victorian Literature and Art*, ed. Antony Harrison and Beverly Taylor [DeKalb: Northern Illinois University Press, 1992], 125).

Chapter Four

1. Whether outlandish imports or self-made men arising from the equally suspect dark continent of urban slums, Montague, Melmotte, Merdle, and Lopez are nevertheless all foreign bodies penetrating the City and often Parliament as well.

2. Earlier fiction chiefly drew on Continental villains to take advantage, first, of the xenophobia bred by the Napoleonic Wars and then of the Austrian-Hungarian Empire's role in the Italian struggle for unification (the *Risorgimento*). "*Der Große Krach*" ("the great crash") that followed in the wake of the World Exhibition of 1873 guaranteed Vienna's prevalent association with proud display of wealth and financial failure.

3. "Romance in Business," *Blackwood's Magazine* 131 (March 1882): 239.

4. Ibid., 241, 231.

5. Although Trollope was to create in Madame Max Goesler, an English-born businesswoman from Vienna who ultimately marries the Irish hero of *Phineas Finn* (1869) and *Phineas Redux* (1874), a fascinatingly complex character, Melmotte and Lopez came to embody the indeterminately foreign business partner with connections abroad.

6. Ellen Wood *Adam Grainger* (Leipzig: Tauchnitz, 1876), 81.

7. Robert Bell, *The Ladder of Gold* (London: Richard Bentley, 1850), 1:274.

8. Oscar Wilde, *An Ideal Husband* (London: A&C Black, 1993), 11.

9. Joseph Bristow, "Dowdies and Dandies: Oscar Wilde's Refashioning of Society Comedy," *Modern Drama* 37.1 (1994): 2.

10. Anthony Trollope, *The Three Clerks* (Oxford: Oxford University Press, 1989), 21.

11. Elizabeth Wilson, *The Sphinx in the City: Urban Life, the Control of Disorder, and Women* (London: Virago, 1991), 6, 46.

12. Mary Augusta Ward [Mrs. Humphrey], *Robert Elsmere* (Oxford: Oxford University Press, 1987), 150.

13. T. W. H. Crosland, *The Suburbans* (London: John Long, 1905), 80. The architectural historian Geoffrey Tyack speaks of the constructed middle-class suburb as "perhaps the most original contribution of nineteenth-century London to urban civilisation" (*James Pennethorne and the Making of Victorian London* [Cambridge: Cambridge University Press, 1992], 310). Sharon Marcus's study of nineteenth-century Paris and London provides perhaps the most extensive account of the failure of the domestic ideal of single-family houses in Victorian Britain, a failure, she argues, that contrasts with the Parisian apartment house. The latter's negotiation of communal and private space overshadows the suburb in the study itself, thereby only convincing us further of suburbia's most confining aspects. See Sharon Marcus, *Apartment Stories: City and Home in Nineteenth-Century Paris and London* (Berkeley: University of California Press, 1999), 4. Anne Humphery refers to the division into margin and centre that still continues to shape work on the Victorian city ("Knowing the Victorian City: Writing and Representation," *Victorian Literature and Culture* 30 [2002]: 604). Suburbia remains obscure within these binaries or is glossed over quickly as a (failed) project to combine city and country. Compare Richard Stein, "Recent Work in Victorian Urban Studies," *Victorian Studies* 45.2 (2003): 319–31.

14. Wilkie Collins, *Basil* (Oxford: Oxford University Press, 1990), 32, 158.

15. As the *OED* reminds us, as the "country lying immediately outside a town or city," suburbs had been described in English from ca. 1380 onwards. Suburbia, however, is a "quasi-proper name" for London's suburbs and largely a nineteenth-century construction ("suburb, *n.*" *The Oxford English Dictionary*. 2nd ed. 1989. *OED Online*. Oxford University Press. 21 Jan. 2005. http://dictionary.oed.com/cgi/entry/50241270; "Suburbia, *n.*" *Oxford English Dictionary*. 2nd ed. 1989. *OED Online*. Oxford University Press. 21 Jan. 2005. http://dictionary.oed.com/cgi/entry/502412740). At a time when continental capitals like Paris or Vienna saw redevelopments that revived the bourgeoisie's attraction to inner spaces of the city,

Britain's industrial cities—Manchester in their lead—set up models for middle-class suburbanization.

16. H. J. Dyos and D. A. Reeder, "Slums and Suburbs," *The Victorian City: Images and Realities,* edited by H. J. Dyos and Michael Wolff (London: Routledge, 1973), 362, 371–72. In *Victorian Suburb: A Study of the Growth of Camberwell,* Dyos similarly stresses the significance of speculative builders for suburban architecture, and vice versa: "labourers and mechanics, servants and publicans, shopkeepers and merchants" invested capital in suburban speculation, frequently forfeiting it all in what became notorious as a "history of bad workmanship and bad debts" ([Leicester: Leicester University Press, 1973] 123, 85).

17. George Sala, "Dumbledowndeary," *Household Words* 5 (19 June 1852): 312.

18. Ibid., 314–15.

19. T. M. Thomas, "A Suburban Connemara," *Household Words* 2 (8 March 1851): 562–65. See Lara Whelan, "Unburying Bits of Rubbish: Deconstruction of the Victorian Suburb Ideal," *Literary London,* http://homepages.gold.ac.uk/london-journal/whelan.html. Whelan offers a detailed "deconstruction" of what she terms the "Victorian suburb ideal."

20. "Suburbanity," *The Spectator* (12 April 1884): 483.

21. Gail Cunningham re-views the disturbance of mundane suburbia through "the distinctively suburban targeting of the Martian invaders" ("Houses in Between: Navigating Suburbia in Late Victorian Writing," *Victorian Boundaries.* Special issue of *Victorian Literature and Culture* [2004]: 431). The explosion in suburban living "had disturbed and fractured identities," so that for writers of the *fin-de-siècle,* "the new suburban "houses in between" had become imaginatively central" (421, 433).

22. Arthur Conan Doyle, *Sherlock Holmes: Selected Stories* (Oxford: Oxford University Press, 1998), 89, 88.

23. Compare Lynne Hapgood, "The Literature of the Suburbs," *Journal of Victorian Culture* 5.2 (2000): 289; *Margins of Desire: The Suburbs in Fiction and Culture, 1880–1925* (Manchester: Manchester University Press, 2005), 44–48.

24. Arthur Conan Doyle, *Beyond the City: An Idyll of a Suburb* (London: Everett, 1912), 8.

25. Todd Kuchta, "Semi-Detached Empire: Suburbia and Imperial Discourse in Victorian and Edwardian Britain," *Nineteenth-Century Prose* 32.2 (2005): 66–67, 173.

26. George Gissing, *The Nether World* (Brighton: Harvester, 1974), 248, 273–74.

27. Charles Dickens, *Dombey and Son* (Oxford: Clarendon, 1974), 65. J. R. Kellett has praised the novel for its vivid descriptions of the slum-like suburbs springing up around railway junctions or termini: a "type of no-man's land created by speculative building in the areas between railway sidings and industrial users on the outer fringe of an urban central district" ("The Railway as an Agent of Internal Change in Victorian Cities," *The Victorian City: A Reader in British Urban History, 1820–1914,* ed. R. J. Morris, and Richard Rodger [London: Longman, 1993], 192). For Dombey, the suburban spaces of his son's working-class nurse (the wife of a stoker) as well as of his scheming confidential clerk seem as remote from his own townhouse and office as the foreign countries on which his business primarily rests. Compare Jeff Nunokawa, "For Your Eyes Only: Private Property and the Oriental Body in *Dombey*

and Son," *Macropolitics of Nineteenth-Century Literature: Nationalism, Exoticism, Imperialism,* ed. Jonathan Arac and Harriet Ritvo (Philadelphia: University of Pennsylvania Press, 1991), 138–58.

28. A. MacFarlane's *Railway Scrip; Or, The Evils of Speculation* (London: Ward & Lock, 1856), 134–35.

29. Charles Lever, *Davenport Dunn* (Boston: Little, Brown, and Co, 1902), 1:51–52.

30. Reed has pointed out that, although the bill had been designed to attract English investors to Ireland, the overwhelming number of purchasers were Irish—"suggestions in Lever's novel notwithstanding" (Reed, *Conventions,* 181).

31. William Booth, *In Darkest England and The Way Out* (London: Salvation Army, 1890), 9.

32. Ibid., 11–12. Booth himself admitted that this extended analogy "becomes wearisome when it is pressed too far" (12).

33. Ibid., 144.

34. H. M. Hyndman, *General Booth's Book Refuted* (London: Justice Printery, 1890), 4.

35. Anthony King, "Excavating the Multicultural Suburb: Hidden Histories of the Bungalow," *Visions of Suburbia,* edited by Roger Silverstone (London and New York: Routledge, 1997), 55–85.

36. John Archer, "Colonial Suburbs in South Asia, 1700–1850, and the Spaces of Modernity," *Visions of Suburbia,* edited by Roger Silverstone (London and New York: Routledge, 1997), 26–54.

37. George and Weedon Grossmith, *The Diary of a Nobody* (London: J. M. Dent & Sons, 1962), 246. Hapgood sees the novel as one of the most enduring testimonies to the popularity of suburban satire of the "clerk class" against which aspiring middle- and lower-middle-class readers could define themselves (*Margins,* 189).

38. Charles Dickens, *Great Expectations* (Oxford: Clarendon, 1993), 193–95.

39. Welsh, 82.

40. John Tosh. *A Man's Place: Masculinity and the Middle-Class Home in Victorian England* (New Haven: Yale University Press, 1999), 32.

41. Charlotte Riddell, *The Race for Wealth* (Leipzig: Tauchnitz, 1866), 194.

42. J. Sheridan LeFanu, *In A Glass Darkly* (London: Lehmann, 1947).

43. Roy Porter points out that by the 1880s, the places in Britain with the largest population increase were London railway suburbs that had been constructed to remove the working and lower-middle classes out from inner-city slums to the suburbs (*London: A Social History* [Harvard: Harvard University Press, 1995], 234).

44. This denotes Alaric Tudor as one of the few speculating heroes who are punished by the law in Victorian fiction. This is despite the fact that, unlike so many sensational stock-market villains, he never moves beyond white-collar crime, and his fiscal irresponsibility is the result of moral frailty alone, not of any interesting villainous scheme.

45. As Archibald points out, "Norman is traditional and solid; Tudor rises to great heights and falls just as far; and Woodward lives in the countryside and represents an idyllic life outside the city" (72).

46. Wilkie Collins, *Armadale* (Oxford: Oxford University Press, 1990), 453.

47. Wilkie Collins's first successful sensation novel *Basil* starts with a young gentleman's idle impulse to ride omnibuses as his entry into what he views as exotic lower-middle-class life. The crash of his social tourism paves the way for a suburban Gothic that mediates between eighteenth-century Gothic castles and the "architectural uncanny" of urban modernity. Anthony Vidler suggests that this makes the uncanny a quintessential bourgeois fear (*The Architectural Uncanny: Essays in the Modern Unhomely* [Cambridge, Mass: MIT Press, 1992], 3–4). Compare Julian Wolfreys's discussion of "the spectralisation of the gothic" (*Victorian Hauntings: Spectrality, Gothic, the Uncanny and Literature* [Basingstoke: Palgrave, 2002], 7–10). In Collins's novel about vivisection, *Heart and Science* (1883), the enigmatic scientist conducts experiments at the outskirts of London: "Nobody seems to know much about him. He has built a house in a desolate field—in some lost suburban neighbourhood that nobody can discover" (*Heart and Science* [Peterborough: Broadview, 1996], 97). When he blows up his laboratory, it is with the "intermittent shriek of a railway whistle in the distance [as] the only sound that disturbed the quiet of the time" (322–23). The most lurid scenes of *The Law and the Lady* (1875) likewise take place in a "great northern suburb of London," "a dingy brick labyrinth of streets," where a condemned villa houses a madman who defies the "speculators in this new neighbourhood" ([London: Penguin, 1998], 188–89).

48. A recent revival of interest has also drawn new attention to her autobiographical fictionalization of the struggles of women writers in *A Struggle for Fame* (1883). See Linda Peterson, "Charlotte Riddell's *A Struggle for Fame*: Myths of Authorship, Facts of the Market," *Women's Writing* 11.1 (2004): 99–116.

49. Charlotte Riddell, *George Geith of Fen Court* (London: Warne, 1870), 1.

50. Charlotte Riddell, *Mitre Court: A Tale of the Great City* (London: Bentley, 1885), 67.

51. As Julian Wolfreys has pointed out, Riddell "bemoans the indiscriminate, often wholesale, architectural destruction of 'beautiful' buildings" (*Writing London: The Trace of the Urban Text from Blake to Dickens* [New York: St. Martin's, 1998], 21).

52. Charlotte Riddell, *City and Suburb* (London: Skeet, 1861).

53. *Home, Sweet Home* (1873) symptomatically describes suburbia as a transitional space for a professional singer from the country, who trains in "its counterfeit the suburbs" before conquering London society and eventually gaining her reward in a country house on which her "childish gaze used to fasten itself in curiosity and in awe" ([Berlin: Asher, 1873], 2:96, 1:333).

54. Charlotte Riddell, *Mortomley's Estate* (London: Hutchinson, 1874), 1.

55. Riddell's bitterest novel, *Mortomley's Estate* draws heavily on her husband's bankruptcy. A patent agent, Joseph Hadley Riddell petitioned the bankruptcy court for liquidation in 1871.

56. Wolfreys speaks of "the spectralisation of the gothic": "Exorcised from its haunted houses, the spectral-gothic takes on its most *unheimlich* aspects," as its "recirculation" manifests itself "in ever stranger articulations of revenant alterity" (*Victorian*, 7–11).

57. Marcus, 12, 122.

58. Charlotte Riddell, *The Haunted River & Three Other Ghostly Novellas* (Mountain Ash: Sarob, 2001), 87.

59. Lara Whelan, "Between Worlds: Class Identity and Suburban Ghost-stories, 1850 to 1880," *Mosaic* 35.1 (2002): 134. In many suburban ghost stories, the "exorcist" is a middle-class male who successfully manages the threat of the undomesticated (the supernatural).

60. Margaret Oliphant, *Hester* (Oxford: Oxford University Press, 2003), 395.

61. Ellen Wood, "In the Dead of Night," *Argosy* 17–18 (1 January–1 December 1874): 18. This defended stockbroker is significantly successful, reliable, responsible, saves a squire from ruin, and against all expectations of the usual fictional speculators, refuses to profit from the land he has bought "entirely on speculation" (251) after a mine is discovered on it. Still, he is wary of disclosing his occupation: what would the squire "think and say if he knew that it was by speculation, pure and simple, that I earn my bread and cheese" (251).

62. The heroines of New Woman writing work as clerks, telegraph, or typewriter girls. Sarah Grand's *The Beth Book* (1897) shows Beth making money with needlework, writing, and oratory, and in *The Winged Victory* (1916), lacemaking literally means business. Mary Ward's novels include an actress in *Miss Bretherton* (1884), a violinist in *Robert Elsmere* (1888), a painter in *The History of David Grieve* (1892), and a district nurse in *Marcella* (1894). Representations of the New Woman in fiction by male authors such as Trollope's "The Telegraph-Girl" (1877) and Grant Allen's *The Type-Writer Girl* (1897) likewise deal explicitly with women in offices.

63. Charles James Scotter, *Lost in a Bucket-Shop: A Story of Stock Exchange Speculation* (London: Field & Tuer, 1890), 4.

64. In Charlotte Yonge's *The Clever Woman of the Family* (1865), an absconded speculator's camouflage as a clergyman operates as a catalyst to expel the heroine's misdirected ambitions, and *The Trial* (1864) delineates a fever-infested swamp highly reminiscent of the promised city of Eden in *Martin Chuzzlewit*. Similarly referencing, in a sleight-of-hand manner, the failure of "goodness knows what speculations" as the way of "those Yankees," *The Pillars of the House* (1873) uses "successful speculations and hair's-breath escapes" abroad to throw the primacy of the home into sharp relief ([London: Macmillan and Co, 1875], 2:108–9, 1:126). It is in a doubly critical take on financial plots that the heroine of Eliza Lynn Linton's *The Rebel of the Family* (1880) works as a clerk in the Post-Office Savings Bank, while bankruptcy through speculation is conjured up as a—fraudulent, fictitious—narrative to exact financial assistance from a wealthy industrialist, who revealingly spurns this attempt.

65. Compare Joseph O'Mealy, "Rewriting Trollope and Yonge: Mrs. Oliphant's *Phoebe Junior* and the Realism Wars," *Texas Studies in Literature and Language* 39.2 (1997): 125; O'Mealy's "Scenes of Professional Life: Mrs. Oliphant and the New Victorian Clergyman," *Studies in the Novel* 23 (1991): 247. Laurie Langbauer similarly stresses that "Oliphant tackles not just sensationalism, but drawing-room comedy, Tractarian conversion, electioneering, and so on," stringing together literary commonplaces that reveals them as such (*Novels of Everyday Life: The Series in English Fiction, 1850–1930* [Ithaca: Cornell University Press, 1999], 64–65).

66. Speculation plots fulfill changing narrative functions in Oliphant's novels. In *Miss Marjoribanks* (1866), it is simply with a stab at the whimsicality of scandal mongering that it is considered "a great deal more likely that he speculates" than that an adventurer has invested his money more securely, and whenever he leaves

Carlingford abruptly, it is suspected that "he had speculated, and lost money." Yet it is Lucilla Marjoribanks's father after whose sudden death it is "found out that everything named in [his will] had disappeared like a bubble" (Margaret Oliphant, *Miss Marjoribanks* [London: Penguin, 1998], 317, 141, 404). In *Phoebe, Junior* (1876), a clergyman's check fraud perhaps the most overtly dismantles the paradigms of sensational detective fiction. Compare O'Mealy, "Rewriting," passim; Elsie Michie, "Buying Brains: Trollope, Oliphant, and Vulgar Victorian Commerce," *Victorian Studies* 44.1 (2001): 77–97, especially 79.

67. Margaret Oliphant, "The Stockbroker at Dinglewood," *Cornhill Magazine* (September 1868): 311.

68. Henry Mansel, "Sensation Novels," *Quarterly Review* 113 (1863): 501. Brantlinger has already pointed out that sensation novelists "paradoxically discovered that they were making fictions out of the stuff that filled the newspapers every day" and that Charles Reade freely acknowledged that some of his works were "inspired by the *Times*" ("What Is 'Sensational' about the 'Sensation Novel'?" *Nineteenth-Century Fiction* 37.1 [1982]: 9–10).

69. Margaret Oliphant, *At His Gates* (London: Tinsley Brothers, 1872), 2:135.

70. Rev. of *At His Gates,* by Mrs Oliphant. *Athenaeum* (28 September 1872): 401.

71. Gates, *Suicide,* 57–59.

72. Most memorably, Dickens's *Our Mutual Friend* has the main protagonist resurface under a different name while the investigations into his supposed death continue. In Oliphant's use of this device, the missing body likewise leaves all the more space for the newspapers' ghoulish feasting on a dead man who cannot be traced.

73. Oliphant's persistent image as "the Victorian woman as literary workhorse" whose level of productivity has long been seen to have "guaranteed mediocrity or worse" (O'Mealy, "Scenes," 245) is reflected in her own descriptions of struggling painters and writers. From her early writing onwards, Oliphant chose visual representation to reflect her literary art. The narrative of a failing writer as that of "an artist, more probably of talent than of genius" in *The Quiet Heart* (1854), for example, already anticipates the more poignant thematization of such a failure in *At His Gates* nearly twenty years later (Vineta and Richard Colby, *The Equivocal Virtue: Mrs Oliphant and the Victorian Marketplace* [Hamden, Conn.: Archon Books, 1966], 21).

74. Anthony Trollope, *The Prime Minister* (Oxford: Oxford University Press, 1999), 2:52.

75. Representing an inherent self-destructiveness of economic and/or social systems, the list of suicidal speculators in nineteenth-century fiction ranges from the fashionable young man in Siddons's *Virtuous Poverty* via such offstage cases as Thornton senior to Merdle, Melmotte, and Lopez, including also those parasuicides who, like Nicholas Nickleby's father, just take to their beds to die after their speculations have failed. In Arthur Conan Doyle's "The Stock-Broker's Clerk" (1893) in *The Memoirs of Sherlock Holmes,* stock-market suicide functions as a narrative cliché.

76. As Robert Polhemus has already pointed out, Trollope saves "his real venom for the staunch old guard [...], the Conservative Party who put Melmotte up for office, and the rest of the Establishment. He makes it painfully clear how much worse they are than the Jews and the parvenus" (*The Changing World of Anthony*

Trollope [Berkeley: University of California Press, 1968], 192–93). See also McMaster on Trollope's ambiguous dissection of bigotry (110). Much has been written on Trollope's representations of Americans and specifically American women, although Marie Melmotte is rewritten as the ambiguous Marie Goesler (Madame Max). Madame Max has often been dismissed as simply one of Trollope's "extended portraits of Jewesses," a representation of "the Victorian woman liberationist and her reductio ad absurdum, the Jewess'" (Charles Blinderman, "The Servility of Dependence: The Dark Lady in Trollope," *Images of Women in Fiction: Feminist Perspectives*, ed. Susan Koppelman Cornillon [Bowling Green, Ohio: Bowling Green University Popular Press, 1972], 63, 55). In a particularly negative reading, she has even been called "one of the most repulsive characters in fiction," such a scheming intruder into highlife that "hardly anything could redeem [Phineas] from the charge implicit in his marriage" (Rebecca West, *The Court and the Castle: A Study of the Interactions of Political and Religious Ideas in Imaginative Literature* [London: Macmillan, 1958], 121–22). Elizabeth Epperly has suggested that "Trollope, carried away as he probably was by his own creation, manages the writing in the novel so that it is Madame Max who seems to change" ("From the Borderlands of Decency: Madame Max Goesler," *Victorians Institute Journal* 15 [1987]: 25).

77. Headon Hill, *Guilty Gold: A Romance of Financial Fraud and City Crime* (London: Pearson, 1896), 16.

78. Russell, 153.

79. Petri Liukkonen, "Anthony Trollope," *Author's Calendar*, 27 June 2005. http://www.kirjasto.sci.fi/trollope.htm; Robb, 102, 4.

80. Most critics agree on the swindler's American connections, if not origins, in *The Way We Live Now* (Russell, 149–50; Robb, 99–102), yet primarily to accentuate a common alignment between "American-ness" and social, financial, and also ethnic indeterminacy. In her recent study of emigration in Victorian fiction, Archibald suggests that Melmotte's "nationality is hidden, yet hinted to be American," while his daughter is "identified as an American only in passing" (163–64). Delany stresses that the "vagueness of Melmotte's identity is precisely the point" (26). Gagnier calls Melmotte the "[c]orporate center of 'the way we live now,'" but she also emphasizes that he is "silent, inarticulate among Trollope's brilliant dialogues, almost without content," which is to an extent why he so suitably embodies "the pure form of the power of credit to transform human lives" (49).

81. Ouida [Marie Louise de la Ramee], *The Massarenes* (London: Sampson Low, Marston et al., 1897), 154.

82. Delany has suggested that Melmotte "commits suicide in the honorable style of an antique Roman" (3).

83. Talia Schaffer, *The Forgotten Female Aesthetes: Literary Culture in Late-Victorian England* (Charlottesville: University Press of Virginia, 2000), 127. In "The Origins of the Aesthetic Novel: Ouida, Wilde, and the Popular Romance," *Wilde Writings: Contextual Conditions*, ed. Joseph Bristow (Toronto: University of Toronto Press, 2003), Schaffer further contrasts Ouida's dandies with those of "[e]arlier silver-fork novels" (214–15).

Bibliography

Adams, James Eli. "Recent Studies in the Nineteenth Century." *Studies in English Literature* 41.4 (2001): 827–79.
Adburgham, Alison. *Women in Print: Writing Women and Women's Magazines from the Restoration to the Accession of Victoria.* London: Allen and Unwin, 1972.
Ainsworth, William Harrison. *John Law; The Projector.* 1864. London: Chapman and Hall, 1866.
———. *The South-Sea Bubble.* London: John Dicks, 1871.
Alborn, Timothy L. *Conceiving Companies: Joint-Stock Politics in Victorian England.* London and New York: Routledge, 1998.
Anderson, Amanda. *The Powers of Distance: Cosmopolitanism and the Cultivation of Detachment.* Princeton: Princeton University Press, 2001.
Arac, Jonathan and Harriet Ritvo, eds. *Macropolitics of Nineteenth-Century Literature: Nationalism, Exoticism, Imperialism.* Philadelphia: University of Pennsylvania Press, 1991.
Archer, John. "Colonial Suburbs in South Asia, 1700–1850, and the Spaces of Modernity." *Visions of Suburbia.* Ed. Roger Silverstone, 26–54. London and New York: Routledge, 1997.
Archibald, Diana C. *Domesticity, Imperialism, and Emigration in the Victorian Novel.* Columbia: University of Missouri Press, 2002.
Armstrong, Frances. *Dickens and the Concept of Home.* Ann Arbor: UMI Research Press, 1990.
Austen, Jane. *Complete Novels.* Oxford: Oxford University Press, 1994.
Austen-Leigh, James Edward. *Memoir of Jane Austen.* 1870. 2nd ed. 1871. Ed. R. W. Chapman. Oxford: Clarendon, 1951.

Bibliography

"The Author of John Halifax." *British Quarterly Review* 44 (1866): 32–58.

Bachman, Maria and Don Richard Cox, eds. *Reality's Dark Light: The Sensational Wilkie Collins*. Knoxville: University of Tennessee Press, 2003.

Bagehot, Walter. *Lombard Street: A Description of the Money-Market*. 1873. New York: John Wiley & Sons, 1999.

Beer, Gillian. *Open Fields: Science in Cultural Encounter*. Oxford: Oxford University Press, 1996.

Bell, Robert. *The Ladder of Gold*. London: Richard Bentley, 1850.

Blinderman, Charles. "The Servility of Dependence: The Dark Lady in Trollope." *Images of Women in Fiction: Feminist Perspectives*. Ed. Susan Koppelman Cornillon, 55–67. Bowling Green, Ohio: Bowling Green University Press, 1972.

Blumberg, Ilana. 'Collins's Moonstone: The Victorian Novel as Sacrifice, Theft, Gift, and Debt." *Studies in the Novel* 37.2 (2005): 162–86.

Booth, William. *In Darkest England and The Way Out*. London: Salvation Army, 1890.

Born, Daniel. *The Birth of Liberal Guilt in the English Novel: Charles Dickens to H. G. Wells*. Chapel Hill: University of North Carolina Press, 1995.

Braddon, Mary Elizabeth. *Lady Audley's Secret*. 1862. Ed. Natalie Houston. Peterborough: Broadview, 2003.

———. *Aurora Floyd*. 1863. Ed. P. D. Edwards. Oxford: Oxford University Press, 1999.

———. *Eleanor's Victory*. Leipzig: Tauchnitz, 1863.

———. *John Marchmont's Legacy*. 1863. Ed. Toru Sasaki and Norman Page. Oxford: Oxford University Press, 1999.

———. *The Doctor's Wife*. 1864. Ed. Lyn Pykett. Oxford: Oxford University Press, 1998.

———. *The Lady's Mile*. 1866. London: Simpkin, Marshall, Hamilton, Kent, 1892.

———. *Birds of Prey*. London: Maxwell, 1867.

———. *Charlotte's Inheritance*. London: Simpkin, Marshall, Hamilton et al., 1868.

Brantlinger, Patrick. "What Is 'Sensational' about the 'Sensation Novel'?" *Nineteenth-Century Fiction* 37.1 (1982): 1–28.

———. *Fictions of State: Culture and Credit in Britain, 1694–1994*. Ithaca: Cornell University Press, 1996.

———. *The Reading Lesson: The Threat of Mass Literacy in Nineteenth-Century British Fiction*. Bloomington: Indiana University Press, 1998.

Brantlinger, Patrick and William B. Thesing, eds. *A Companion to the Victorian Novel*. Oxford: Blackwell, 2002.

Brenner, Reuven and Gabrielle A. Brenner. *Gambling and Speculation: A Theory, a History, and a Future of Some Human Decisions*. Cambridge: Cambridge University Press, 1990.

Briggs, Asa. "Samuel Smiles: The Gospel of Self Help." *Victorian Values: Personalities and Perspectives in Nineteenth-Century Society*. Ed. Gordon Marsden, 101–13. London: Longman, 1998.

Bristow, Joseph. "Dowdies and Dandies: Oscar Wilde's Refashioning of Society Comedy." *Modern Drama* 37.1 (1994): 53–70.

———, ed. *Wilde Writings: Contextual Conditions*. Toronto: University of Toronto Press, 2003.

Brooks, Peter. *Reading for the Plot: Design and Intention in Narrative*. Oxford: Clarendon, 1984.
———. *Realist Vision*. New Haven: Yale University Press, 2005.
Brown, Pearl L. "From Elizabeth Gaskell's *Mary Barton* to her *North and South*: Progress or Decline for Women?" *Victorian Literature and Culture* 28.2 (2000): 345–58.
Bulwer-Lytton, Edward. *Pelham; Or, Adventures of a Gentleman*. 1828. London: Routledge and Sons, 1875.
Butler, Marilyn. *Jane Austen and the War of Ideas*. Oxford: Clarendon, 1987.
Butt, John. "The Topicality of *Little Dorrit*." *University of Toronto Quarterly* 29 (1959): 1–10.
Butt, John and Kathleen Tillotson. *Dickens at Work*. London: Methuen, 1957.
Carens, Timothy. "Outlandish English Subjects in *The Moonstone*." *Reality's Dark Light: The Sensational Wilkie Collins*. Ed. Maria Bachman and Don Richard Cox, 239–65. Knoxville: University of Tennessee Press, 2003.
Carlyle, Thomas. *The French Revolution*. Oxford: Oxford University Press, 1989.
Carnell, Jennifer. *The Literary Lives of Mary Elizabeth Braddon: A Study of her Life and Work*. Hastings: Sensation Press, 2000.
Cazamian, Louis. *The Social Novel in England 1830–1850: Dickens, Disraeli, Mrs Gaskell, Kingsley*. Trans. Martin Fido. London: Routledge & Kegan Paul, 1973.
Chakravarty, Gautam. *The Indian Mutiny and the British Imagination*. Cambridge: Cambridge University Press, 2005.
Chancellor, Edward. *Devil Take The Hindmost: A History of Financial Speculation*. New York: Plume, 2000.
Childers, Joseph. "*Nicholas Nickleby*'s Problem of *Doux Commerce*." *Dickens Studies Annual* 25 (1996): 49–66.
Cobbett, William. *Rural Rides*. London: Dent & Sons, 1953.
Colby, Vineta, and Richard Colby. *The Equivocal Virtue: Mrs Oliphant and the Victorian Marketplace*. Hamden, Conn.: Archon Books, 1966.
Collins, Philip. *Dickens and Crime*. 3rd ed. New York: St Martin's, 1994.
Collins, Wilkie. *Basil*. 1852. Ed. Dorothy Goldman. Oxford: Oxford University Press, 1990.
———. *Armadale*. 1866. Ed. Catherine Peters. Oxford: Oxford University Press, 1990.
———. *The Moonstone*. 1868. Ed. Sandra Kemp. London: Penguin, 1998.
———. *The Law and the Lady*. 1875. Ed. David Skilton. London: Penguin, 1998.
———. *Heart and Science*. 1883. Ed. Steve Farmer. Peterborough: Broadview, 1996.
Copeland, Edward. *Women Writing about Money: Women's Fiction in England, 1790–1820*. Cambridge: Cambridge University Press, 1995.
Cornillon, Susan Koppelman, ed. *Images of Women in Fiction: Feminist Perspectives*. Bowling Green, Ohio: Bowling Green University Press, 1972.
Cotsell, Michael. "The Book of Insolvent Fates: Financial Speculation in *Our Mutual Friend*." *Dickens Studies Annual* 13 (1984): 125–42.
Craik, Dinah Mulock. *Olive*. 1850. Ed. Cora Kaplan. Oxford: Oxford University Press, 1999.
———. *John Halifax, Gentleman*. 1856. London: J. M. Dent & Sons, 1906.

Crosby, Christina. "Financial." *A Companion to Victorian Literature and Culture*. Ed. Herbert Tucker, 225–43. Oxford: Blackwell, 1999.

Crosland, T. W. H. *The Suburbans*. London: John Long, 1905.

Culler, Jonathan. *Literary Theory: A Very Short Introduction*. 1997. Oxford: Oxford University Press, 2000.

———. *The Literary in Theory*. Stanford: Stanford University Press, 2007.

Cunningham, Gail. "Houses in Between: Navigating Suburbia in Late Victorian Writing." *Victorian Boundaries*. Special issue of *Victorian Literature and Culture* (2004): 421–34.

Dabney, Ross. *Love and Property in the Novels of Dickens*. London: Chatto & Windus, 1967.

David, Deirdre. "Children of Empire: Victorian Imperialism and Sexual Politics in Dickens and Kipling." *Gender and Discourse in Victorian Literature and Art*. Ed. Antony Harrison and Beverly Taylor, 124–42. DeKalb: Northern Illinois University Press, 1992.

———. "Empire, Race, and the Victorian Novel." *A Companion to the Victorian Novel*. Ed. Patrick Brantlinger and William B. Thesing, 84–100. Oxford: Blackwell, 2002.

Davidson, Jenny. *Hypocrisy and the Politics of Politeness*. New York: Cambridge University Press, 2004.

Delany, Paul. *Literature, Money and the Market from Trollope to Amis*. Basingstoke: Palgrave, 2002.

Dever, Carolyn. "Strategic Aestheticism: A Response to Caroline Levine." *Victorian Studies* 49.1 (2006): 94–99.

Dickens, Charles. *The Pickwick Papers*. 1837. Ed. James Kinsley. Oxford: Oxford University Press, 1998.

———. *Nicholas Nickleby*. 1839. Ed. Sybil Thorndike. London: Oxford University Press, 1950.

———. *A Christmas Carol*. 1843. London: Oxford University Press, 1966.

———. *Martin Chuzzlewit*. 1844. Ed. Margaret Cardwell. Oxford: Clarendon, 1982.

———. *Dombey and Son*. 1848. Ed. Alan Horsman. Oxford: Clarendon, 1974.

———. *David Copperfield*. 1850. Ed. Nina Burgis. Oxford: Oxford University Press, 1999.

———. *Little Dorrit*. 1857. Ed. Lionel Trilling. Oxford Oxford University Press, 1953.

———. "Convict Capitalists." *All the Year Round* 59 (9 June 1860): 201–4.

———. *Great Expectations*. 1861. Ed. Margaret Cardwell. Oxford: Clarendon, 1993.

———. *Our Mutual Friend*. 1865. Ed. Salter Davies. London: Oxford University Press, 1952.

Digaetani, John Louis, ed. *Money: Lure, Lore, and Literature*. Westport: Greenwood, 1994.

Dingley, Robert. "Mrs. Conyers's Secret: Decoding Sexuality in *Aurora Floyd*." *Victorian Newsletter* 95 (1999): 16–18.

Doyle, Arthur Conan. *Beyond the City: An Idyll of a Suburb*. London: Everett, 1912.

———. *Sherlock Holmes: Selected Stories*. 1928. Oxford: Oxford University Press, 1998.

Drouet, Richet S. "'Taming the Shrew': Melodrama and the Representation of Desire in *Lady Audley's Secret* and *Aurora Floyd*." *Cahiers Victoriens & Edouardiens* 59 (2004): 63–74.

Duckworth, Alistair. *The Improvement of the Estate: A Study of Jane Austen's Novels.* Baltimore: Johns Hopkins University Press, 1971.

Dyos, H. J. *Victorian Suburb: A Study of the Growth of Camberwell.* Leicester: Leicester University Press, 1973.

Dyos, H. J. and D. A. Reeder. "Slums and Suburbs." *The Victorian City: Images and Realities.* Ed. H. J. Dyos, and Michael Wolff, 359–86. London and Boston: Routledge & Kegan Paul, 1973.

Dyos, H. J. and Michael Wolff, eds. *The Victorian City: Images and Realities.* London and Boston: Routledge and Kegan Paul, 1973.

Elfenbein, Andrew. "Silver-Fork Byron and the Image of Regency England." *Byromania: Portraits of the Artist in Nineteenth-and Twentieth-Century Culture.* Ed. Frances Wilson, 77–92. Basingstoke: Macmillan, 1999.

Eliot, George. "Silly Novels by Lady Novelists." *Westminster Review* 66 (October 1856): 442–461. Rpt. *Essays of George Eliot.* Ed. Thomas Pinney, 300–324. London: Routledge and Kegan Paul, 1963.

———. *Silas Marner.* 1861. Ed. Terence Cave. Oxford: Oxford University Press, 1998.

———. *Middlemarch.* 1872. Ed. David Carroll. Oxford: Oxford University Press, 1998.

Elwin, Malcolm. *Charles Reade: A Biography.* London: Jonathan Cape, 1931.

Epperly, Elizabeth R. "From the Borderlands of Decency: Madame Max Goesler." *Victorian Institute Journal* 15 (1987): 25–35.

Evans, D. Morier. *Speculative Notes and Notes on Speculation, Ideal and Real.* London: Groombridge and Sons, 1864.

———. *The History of the Commercial Crisis 1857–1858 and the Stock Exchange Panic of 1859.* New York: A. M. Kelley. 1969.

Fabian, Ann. *Card Sharps, Dream Books, and Bucket Shops: Gambling in 19th-Century America.* Ithaca: Cornell University Press, 1990.

Ferguson, Niall. *The Cash Nexus: Money and Power in the Modern World, 1700–2000.* New York: Basic Books, 2001.

Finn, Margot C. *The Character of Credit: Personal Debt in English Culture, 1740–1914.* Cambridge: Cambridge University Press, 2003.

Flanders, Judith. *Inside the Victorian Home: A Portrait of Domestic Life in Victorian England.* New York: Norton, 2003.

Fraiman, Susan. "Jane Austen and Edward Said: Gender, Culture, and Imperialism." *Critical Inquiry* 21.4 (1995): 805–21.

Franklin, J. Jeffrey. "The Victorian Discourse of Gambling: Speculations on *Middlemarch* and *The Duke's Children*." *English Literary History* 61.4 (1994): 899–921.

———. *Serious Play: The Cultural Form of the Nineteenth-Century Realist Novel.* Philadelphia: University of Pennsylvania Press, 1999.

———. "Anthony Trollope Meets Pierre Bourdieu: The Conversion of Capital as Plot in the Mid-Victorian British Novel." *Victorian Literature and Culture* 31.2 (2003): 501–21.

Freedgood, Elaine. *Victorian Writing about Risk: Imagining a Safe England in a Dangerous World.* Cambridge: Cambridge University Press, 2000.

Freeland, Natalka. "Ruth's Perverse Economies: Women, Hoarding, and Expenditure." *English Literary History* 70.1 (2003): 197–221.

Gagnier, Regenia. "Money, the Economy, and Social Class." *A Companion to the Victorian Novel.* Ed. Patrick Brantlinger and William B. Thesing, 48–66. Oxford: Blackwell, 2002.

Gallagher, Catherine. *The Body Economic: Life, Death, and Sensation in Political Economy and the Victorian Novel.* Princeton: Princeton University Press, 2006.

Galperin, William. *The Historical Austen.* Philadelphia: University of Pennsylvania Press, 2003.

Gaskell, Elizabeth. *Cranford.* 1853. Ed. Elizabeth Porges Watson. Oxford: Oxford University Press, 1998.

———. *North and South.* 1855. Ed. Angus Easson. Oxford: Oxford University Press, 1998.

———. *A Dark Night's Work and Other Stories.* 1863. Oxford: Oxford University Press, 1992.

———. *Cousin Phillis.* 1863. London: Penguin, 1995.

———. *Further Letters of Mrs Gaskell.* Ed. John Chapple and Alan Shelston. Manchester: Manchester University Press, 2000.

Gates, Barbara T. *Victorian Suicide: Mad Crimes and Sad Histories.* Princeton: Princeton University Press, 1988.

Gilbert, Pamela. "Ouida and the other New Woman." *Victorian Women Writers and the Woman Question.* Ed. Nicola Diane Thompson, 170–88. Cambridge: Cambridge University Press, 1999.

Gilmour, Robin. *The Idea of the Gentleman in the Victorian Novel.* London: Allen and Unwin, 1981.

Gissing, George. *The Nether World.* 1889. Ed. John Goode. Brighton: Harvester, 1974.

Gore, Catherine. *Pin Money.* London: Colburn and Bentley, 1831.

———. *Mothers and Daughters.* London: Colburn and Bentley, 1831.

———. *The Fair of May Fair.* London: Colburn and Bentley, 1832.

———. *The Banker's Wife; Or, Court and City.* London: Colburn, 1843.

———. *Peers and Parvenus.* London: Colburn, 1846.

———. *The Two Aristocracies.* London: Hurst and Blackett, 1857.

Griffin, Susan M. *Anti-Catholicism and Nineteenth-Century Fiction.* Cambridge: Cambridge University Press, 2004.

Grossmith, George and Weedon Grossmith. *The Diary of a Nobody.* 1892. London: J. M. Dent & Sons, 1962.

Halperin, John. *Trollope and Politics: A Study of the Pallisers and Others.* London: Macmillan, 1977.

Hapgood, Lynne. "The Literature of the Suburbs." *Journal of Victorian Culture* 5.2 (2000): 287–310.

———. *Margins of Desire: The Suburbs in Fiction and Culture, 1880–1925.* Manchester: Manchester University Press, 2005.

Harrison, Antony and Beverly Taylor, eds. *Gender and Discourse in Victorian Literature and Art.* DeKalb: Northern Illinois University Press, 1992.

Hayden, Dolores. *Building Suburbia: Green Fields and Urban Growth, 1820–2000.* New York: Pantheon Books, 2003.

Hazlitt, William. *Complete Works.* Ed. P. P. Howe. London: Dent, 1934.

Heller, Tamar. *Dead Secrets: Wilkie Collins and the Female Gothic.* New Haven: Yale University Press, 1992.

Herbert, Christopher. "Filthy Lucre: Victorian Ideas of Money." *Victorian Studies* 44.2 (2002): 185–213.

Hill, Headon. *Guilty Gold: A Romance of Financial Fraud and City Crime.* London: Pearson, 1896.

Holcroft, Thomas. *Memoirs of Bryan Perdue.* London: Longman, Hurst, Rees, and Orme, 1805.

Hollingshead, John. "Very Singular Things in the City." *All the Year Round* 64 (14 July 1860): 325–26.

Hollington, Michael, ed. *Charles Dickens: Critical Assessments.* Mountfield: Helm Information, 1995.

Holoch, George. "Consciousness and Society in *Little Dorrit.*" *Victorian Studies* 21 (1978): 335–51.

Holway, Tatiana. "The Game of Speculation: Economics and Representation." *Dickens Quarterly* 9 (1992): 103–14. Rpt. in *Charles Dickens: Critical Assessments Vol. 2.* Ed. Michael Hollington, 328–40. Mountfield: Helm Information, 1995.

House, Humphrey. *The Dickens World.* London: Oxford University Press, 1960.

Houston, Gail Turley. *From Dickens to Dracula: Gothic, Economics, and Victorian Fiction.* Cambridge: Cambridge University Press, 2005.

Hughes, Winifred. "Silver Fork Writers and Readers: Social Contexts of a Best Seller." *Novel* 25 (1992): 328–347.

———. "Elegies for the Regency: Catherine Gore's Dandy Novels." *Nineteenth-Century Literature* 50.2 (1995): 189–209.

———. "Mindless Millinery: Catherine Gore and the Silver Fork Heroine." *Dickens Studies Annual* 25 (1996): 159–76.

Humphery, Anne. "Knowing the Victorian City: Writing and Representation." *Victorian Literature and Culture* 30 (2002): 601–12.

Hyndman, H. M. *General Booth's Book Refuted.* London: Justice Printery, 1890.

Itzkowitz, David C. "Fair Enterprise or Extravagant Speculation: Investment, Speculation, and Gambling in Victorian England." *Victorian Studies* 45.1 (2002): 121–48.

Jackson, Russell. Introduction to Oscar Wilde, *An Ideal Husband.* 2nd ed. 1899. Ed. Russell Jackson. London: A&C Black, 1993.

Jaffe, Audrey. "Spectacular Sympathy: Visuality and Ideology in Dickens's *A Christmas Carol.*" *PMLA* 109.2 (1994): 245–65.

———. "Trollope in the Stock Market: Irrational Exuberance and *The Prime Minister.*" *Victorian Studies* 45.1 (2002): 43–64.

James, Simon. *Unsettled Accounts: Money and Narrative in the Novels of George Gissing.* London: Anthem, 2003.

Jay, Elisabeth. *Mrs Oliphant: "A Fiction to Herself": A Literary Life.* Oxford: Clarendon, 1995.

Jones, Anna Maria. *Problem Novels: Victorian Fiction Theorizes the Sensational Self.* Columbus: The Ohio State University Press, 2007.

Joseph, Gerhard. "Construing the Inimitable's Silence: Pecksniff's Grammar School and International Copyright." *Dickens Studies Annual* 22 (1993): 121–36.

———. "Charles Dickens, International Copyright, and the Discretionary Silence of *Martin Chuzzlewit*." *The Construction of Authorship: Textual Appropriation in Law and Literature*. Ed. Martha Woodmansee and Peter Jaszi, 259–70. Durham: Duke University Press, 1995.

Kellett, J. R. "The Railway as an Agent of Internal Change in Victorian Cities." *The Victorian City: A Reader in British Urban History, 1820–1914*. Ed. R. J. Morris and Richard Rodger, 181–208. London and New York: Longman, 1993.

Kendra, April. "Gendering the Silver Fork: Catherine Gore and the Society Novel." *Women's Writing* 11.1 (2004): 25–38.

Kestner, J. *Protest and Reform: The British Social Narrative by Women, 1827–1867*. London: Methuen, 1985.

King, Anthony. "Excavating the Multicultural Suburb: Hidden Histories of the Bungalow." *Visions of Suburbia*. Ed. Roger Silverstone. London and New York: Routledge, 1997.

Klaver, Claudia. "Natural Values and Unnatural Agents: *Little Dorrit* and the Mid-Victorian Crisis in Agency." *Dickens Studies Annual* 28 (1999): 13–43.

———. *A/Moral Economics: Classical Political Economy and Cultural Authority in Nineteenth-Century England*. Columbus: The Ohio State University Press, 2003.

Kuchta, Todd. "Semi-Detached Empire: Suburbia and Imperial Discourse in Victorian and Edwardian Britain." *Nineteenth-Century Prose* 32.2 (2005): 163–98.

Langbauer, Laurie. *Novels of Everyday Life: The Series in English Fiction, 1850–1930*. Ithaca: Cornell University Press, 1999.

Le Fanu, J. Sheridan. *In a Glass Darkly*. 1872. Ed. V. S. Pritchett. London: Lehmann, 1947.

Letwin, Shirley Robin. *The Gentleman in Trollope: Individuality and Moral Conduct*. Cambridge, Mass.: Harvard University Press, 1982.

Lever, Charles. *Davenport Dunn: A Man of Our Day*. 1857–59. Boston: Little, Brown and Company, 1902.

Levine, Caroline. "Scaled Up. Writ Small: A Response to Carolyn Dever and Herbert F. Tucker." *Victorian Studies* 49.1 (2006): 100–105.

———. "Strategic Formalism: Toward a New Method in Cultural Studies." *Victorian Studies* 48.4 (2006): 625–57.

Liukkonen, Petri. "Anthony Trollope." *Author's Calendar*. 27 June 2005. http://www.kirjasto.sci.fi/trollope.htm.

Loftus, Donna. "Capital and Community: Limited Liability and Attempts to Democratize the Market in Mid-Nineteenth-Century England." *Victorian Studies* 45.1 (2002): 93–120.

Lootens, Tricia. *Lost Saints: Silence, Gender, and Victorian Literary Canonization*. Charlottesville: University Press of Virginia, 1996.

MacFarlane, A. *Railway Scrip. Or, The Evils of Speculation*. London: Ward & Lock, 1856.

Mackay, Charles. *Memoirs of Extraordinary Popular Delusions and the Madness of Crowds*. 2nd ed. 1841. London: Office of the National Illustrated Library, 1852.

Mallen, Richard D. "George Eliot and the Precious Mettle of Trust." *Victorian Studies* 44.1 (2001): 41–75.

Mansel, Henry. "Sensation Novels." *Quarterly Review* 113 (1863): 501.
"Manufacture of Novels." *Athenaeum* (16 February 1867): 221–22.
Marcus, Sharon. *Apartment Stories: City and Home in Nineteenth-Century Paris and London*. Berkeley: University of California Press, 1999.
Marsden, Gordon, ed. *Victorian Values: Personalities and Perspectives in Nineteenth-Century Society*. London: Longman, 1998.
Marx, Karl. *Economic and Philosophic Manuscripts of 1844*. Trans. Martin Milligan. Progress: Moscow, 1959.
———. *Capital*. Trans. Ben Fowkes. Harmondsworth: Penguin, 1976.
Maunder, Andrew and Grace Moore, eds. *Victorian Crime, Madness and Sensation*. Aldershot: Ashgate, 2004.
McLaughlin, Kevin. *Paperwork: Fiction and Mass Mediacy in the Paper Age*. Philadelphia: University of Pennsylvania Press, 2005.
McMaster, Juliet. *Trollope's Palliser Novels: Theme and Pattern*. London: Macmillan, 1978.
Michie, Elsie B. "Buying Brains: Trollope, Oliphant, and Vulgar Victorian Commerce." *Victorian Studies* 44.1 (2001): 77–97.
Miles, Robert. "'A Fall in Bread': Speculation and the Real in *Emma*." *Novel* 37 (2003): 66–85.
Mintz, Steven. *A Prison of Expectations: The Family in Victorian Culture*. New York: New York University Press, 1983.
Moers, Ellen. *The Dandy: Brummel to Beerbohm*. London: Secker & Warburg, 1960.
Moore, Grace. *Dickens and Empire: Discourses of Class, Race and Colonialism in the Works of Charles Dickens*. Aldershot: Ashgate, 2004.
Moretti, Franco. *Atlas of the European Novel*. London: Verso, 1999.
Morris, R. J. and Richard Rodger, eds. *The Victorian City: A Reader in British Urban History, 1820–1914*. London and New York: Longman, 1993.
Morse, Deborah Denenholz. *Women in Trollope's Palliser Novels*. London: UMI Research Press, 1987.
"Mulligatawny, n." *The Oxford English Dictionary*. Draft Revision. Mar. 2003. OED Online. Oxford University Press. 1 July 2006. http://dictionary.oed.com/cgi/entry/00317917.
Nash, Julie and Barbara Suess, eds. *New Approaches to the Literary Art of Anne Brontë*. Aldershot: Ashgate, 2001.
Nayder, Lillian. *Wilkie Collins*. London: Prentice Hall, 1997.
Neal, Larry. *The Rise of Financial Capitalism: International Capital Markets in the Age of Reason*. Cambridge: Cambridge University Press, 1990.
Nicholson, Colin. *Writing & the Rise of Finance: Capital Satires of the Early Eighteenth Century*. Cambridge: Cambridge University Press, 1994.
"Not At All A New Novel." *Pall Mall Gazette* (28 February 1867): 8–9.
Nunokawa, Jeff. "For Your Eyes Only: Private Property and the Oriental Body in *Dombey and Son*." *Macropolitics of Nineteenth-Century Literature: Nationalism, Exoticism, Imperialism*. Ed. Jonathan Arac and Harriet Ritvo, 138–58. Philadelphia: University of Pennsylvania Press, 1991.
———. *The Afterlife of Property: Domestic Security and the Victorian Novel*. Princeton: Princeton University Press, 1994.

———. "The Miser's Two Bodies: *Silas Marner* and the Sexual Possibilities of the Commodity." *The Mill on the Floss* and *Silas Marner*. Ed. Nahem Yousaf and Andrew Maunder, 162–87. Houndmills, Basingstoke: Palgrave, 2002.

Odden, Karen. "Puffed Papers and Broken Promises: White-Collar Crime and Literary Justice in *The Way We Live Now*." *Victorian Crime, Madness and Sensation*. Ed. Andrew Maunder and Grace Moore, 135–45. Aldershot: Ashgate, 2004.

Oliphant, Laurence. *Piccadilly: A Fragment of Contemporary Biography*. 1866. Edinburgh and London: Blackwood and Sons, 1871.

———. "The Autobiography of a Joint-Stock Company (Limited)." *Blackwood's Magazine* 120 (July 1876): 96–122.

Oliphant, Margaret. "Modern Novelists—Great and Small." *Blackwood's Magazine* 77 (May 1855): 554–68.

———. "Sensational Novels." *Blackwood's Magazine* 91 (May 1862): 564–80. Rpt. *Varieties of Women's Sensation Fiction: 1855–1890: Sensationalism and The Sensation Debate*. Ed. Andrew Maunder, 8–15. London: Pickering & Chatto, 2004.

———. *Miss Marjoribanks*. 1866. London: Penguin, 1998.

———. "The Stockbroker at Dinglewood." *Cornhill Magazine* (September 1868): 311–43.

———. *At His Gates*. London: Tinsley Brothers, 1872.

———. *Hester*. 1883. Ed. Philip Davies and Brian Nellist. Oxford: Oxford University Press, 2003.

O'Mealy, Joseph. "Scenes of Professional Life: Mrs Oliphant and the New Victorian Clergyman." *Studies in the Novel* 23 (1991): 245–61.

———. "Review of *The Novels of Mrs Oliphant: A Subversive View of Traditional Themes*, by Margarete Rubik, and *Margaret Oliphant: Critical Essays On A Gentle Subversive*, ed. D. J. Trela." *Victorian Studies* 39.2 (1996): 249–51.

———. "Rewriting Trollope and Yonge: Mrs Oliphant's *Phoebe Junior* and the Realism Wars." *Texas Studies in Literature and Language* 39.2 (1997): 125–38.

Ouida [Marie Louise de la Ramee]. *The Massarenes*. London: Sampson Low, Marston et al., 1897.

"Our Naughty Novelist." *Pall Mall Gazette* (6 March 1867): 10.

Perkin, J. Russell. "Thackeray and Orientalism: *Cornhill to Cairo* and *The Newcomes*." *English Studies in Canada* 16.3 (1990): 297–313.

Peterson, Linda H. "Charlotte Riddell's *A Struggle for Fame*: Myths of Authorship, Facts of the Market." *Women's Writing* 11.1 (2004): 99–116.

Pettitt, Clare. *Patent Inventions: Intellectual Property and the Victorian Novel*. Oxford: Oxford University Press, 2004.

Phelan, James. *Reading People, Reading Plots: Character, Progression, and the Interpretation of Narrative*. Chicago: University of Chicago Press, 1989.

———. "The Changing Profession; Narratives in Contest; or, Another Twist in the Narrative Turn." *PMLA* 123.1 (2008): 166–75.

Pionke, Albert. *Plots of Opportunity: Representing Conspiracy in Victorian England*. Columbus: The Ohio State University Press, 2004.

Polhemus, Robert M. *The Changing World of Anthony Trollope*. Berkeley: University of California Press, 1968.

Poovey, Mary. *Making a Social Body: British Cultural Formation, 1830–1864*. Chicago: University of Chicago Press, 1995.
———. "Writing about Finance in Victorian England: Disclosure and Secrecy in the Culture of Investment." *Victorian Studies* 45.1 (2002): 17–41.
———, ed. *The Financial System in Nineteenth-Century Britain*. Oxford: Oxford University Press, 2003.
———. *Genres of the Credit Economy: Mediating Value in Eighteenth- and Nineteenth-Century Britain*. Chicago: University of Chicago Press, 2008.
Porter, Roy. *London: A Social History*. Harvard: Harvard University Press, 1995.
Pykett, Lyn. *The "Improper" Feminine: The Women's Sensation Novel and the New Woman Writing*. London: Routledge, 1992.
———. "A Woman's Business: Women and Writing, 1830–80." *An Introduction to Women's Writing: From the Middle Ages to the Present Day*. Ed. Marion Shaw, 149–76. London: Prentice Hall, 1998.
Rance, Nicholas. *Wilkie Collins and Other Sensation Novelists: Walking the Moral Hospital*. Basingstoke: Macmillan, 1991.
Ray, Gordon. *Thackeray: The Uses of Adversity, 1811–1846*. London: Oxford University Press, 1955.
Reade, Charles. *Hard Cash*. London: Chatto and Windus, 1863.
Reed, John. *Victorian Conventions*. Athens: Ohio University Press, 1975.
———. "A Friend to Mammon: Speculation in Victorian Literature." *Victorian Studies* 27 (1984): 179–202.
Review of *At His Gates*, by Mrs Oliphant. *Athenaeum* (28 September 1872): 400–401.
Riddell, Charlotte. *City and Suburb*. London: Skeet, 1861.
———. *The Race for Wealth*. Leipzig: Tauchnitz, 1866.
———. *George Geith of Fen Court*. 1864. London: Warne, 1870.
———. *Home, Sweet Home*. Berlin: Asher, 1873.
———. *Mortomley's Estate*. London: Hutchinson, 1874.
———. *Mitre Court: A Tale of the Great City*. London: Bentley, 1885.
———. *The Haunted River & Three Other Ghostly Novellas*. Ed. Richard Dalby. Mountain Ash: Sarob Press, 2001.
Robb, George. *White-Collar Crime in Modern England: Financial Fraud and Business Morality, 1845–1929*. Cambridge: Cambridge University Press, 1992.
"Romance in Business." *Blackwood's Magazine* 131 (March 1882): 221–45.
Rosa, Matthew Whiting. *The Silver-Fork School: Novels of Fashion Preceding Vanity Fair*. New York: Columbia University Press, 1936.
Rose, Jonathan. "Was Capitalism Good for Victorian Literature?" *Victorian Studies* 46.3 (2004): 489–501.
Rowlinson, Matthew. "Reading Capital with Little Nell." *The Yale Journal of Criticism* 9 (1996): 347–80.
Ruskin, John. *Works*. Ed. E. T. Cook and Alexander Wedderburn. London: George Allen, 1905.
Russell, Norman. *The Novelist and Mammon: Literary Responses to the World of Commerce in the Nineteenth Century*. Oxford: Clarendon, 1986.
Sadrin, Anny, ed. *Dickens, Europe and the New Worlds*. London: Macmillan, 1999.

Said, Edward. *Culture and Imperialism*. London: Chatto & Windus, 1993.
Sala, George. "Dumbledowndeary." *Household Words* 5 (19 June 1852): 312–17.
Sales, Roger. *Jane Austen and Representations of Regency England*. London: Routledge, 1996.
Samuel, Raphael. *Theatres of Memory: Past and Present in Contemporary Culture*. London: Verso, 1994.
Schaffer, Talia. *The Forgotten Female Aesthetes: Literary Culture in Late-Victorian England*. Charlottesville: University Press of Virginia, 2000.
———. "The Origins of the Aesthetic Novel: Ouida, Wilde, and the Popular Romance." *Wilde Writings: Contextual Conditions*. Ed. Joseph Bristow, 212–29. Toronto: University of Toronto Press, 2003.
Scholes, Robert, James Phelan, and Robert Kellogg. *The Nature of Narrative*. 40th ed. Oxford: Oxford University Press, 2006.
Schor, Hilary. "Fiction." *A Companion to Victorian Literature and Culture*. Ed. Herbert Tucker, 323–38. Oxford: Blackwell, 1999.
Scotter, Charles James. *Lost in a Bucket-Shop: A Story of Stock Exchange Speculation*. London: Field & Tuer, 1890.
Searle, G. R. *Morality and the Market in Victorian Britain*. Oxford: Clarendon, 1998.
Shadwell, Thomas. *Complete Works*. Ed. Montague Summers. London: Fortune, 1927.
Sicher, Efraim. *Rereading the City, Rereading Dickens: Representation, the Novel, and Urban Realism*. New York: AMS, 2003.
Siddons, Henry. *Virtuous Poverty*. London: Richard Phillips, 1804.
Silverstone, Roger, ed. *Visions of Suburbia*. London and New York: Routledge, 1997.
Sinclair, Catherine. *Holiday House*. 1839. Edinburgh: William Whyte, 1849.
———. *Sir Edward Graham: Or, Railway Speculators*. London: Longman, Green, and Longmans, 1849.
Smalley, Donald, ed. *Anthony Trollope: The Critical Heritage*. London: Routledge, 1999.
Smiles, Samuel. *Self-Help; With Illustrations of Character, Conduct and Perseverance*. New York: Harper, 1870.
Smith, Nelson and R. Terry, eds. *Wilkie Collins to the Forefront: Some Reassessments*. New York: AMS, 1995.
Southam, Brian. "A Source for *Sanditon*?" *Collected Reports of the Jane Austen Society, 1966–75* (1977): 122.
Spencer, Herbert. *Social Statics*. London: John Chapman, 1851.
Spring, David. "Interpreters of Jane Austen's Social World: Literary Critics and Historians." *Jane Austen: New Perspectives*. Ed. Janet Todd, 53–72. New York: Holmes & Meier, 1983.
Stabler, Jane. *Burke to Byron, Barbauld to Baillie, 1790–1830* Basingstoke: Palgrave, 2002.
Stein, Richard L. "Recent Work in Victorian Urban Studies." *Victorian Studies* 45.2 (2003): 319–31.
Stewart, Garrett. "Narrative Economies in *The Tenant of Wildfell Hall*." *New Ap-

proaches to the Literary Art of Anne Brontë. Ed. Julie Nash and Barbara Suess, 75–102. Aldershot: Ashgate, 2001.

"Suburb, *n.*" *The Oxford English Dictionary.* 2nd ed. 1989. *OED Online.* Oxford University Press. 21 Jan. 2005. http://dictionary.oed.com/cgi/entry/50241270.

"Suburbanity." *The Spectator* (12 April 1884): 483.

"Suburbia, *n.*" *Oxford English Dictionary.* 2nd ed. 1989. *OED Online.* 21 Jan. 2005. http://dictionary.oed.com/cgi/entry/50241274.

Surr, Thomas. *Splendid Misery.* London: Hurst, 1801–2.

———. *The Magic of Wealth.* London: Sidney, 1815.

———. *Russell; Or, The Reign of Fashion.* London: Colburn and Bentley, 1830.

Sutherland, John. "Wilkie Collins and the Origins of the Sensation Novel." *Wilkie Collins to the Forefront: Some Reassessments.* Ed. Nelson Smith and R. Terry, 75–90. New York: AMS, 1995.

Tambling, Jeremy. "Opium, Wholesale, Resale, and for Export: On Dickens and China, Part I." *Dickens Quarterly* 21.1 (2004): 28–43.

Tanner, Tony. "Trollope's *The Way We Live Now:* Its Modern Significance." *Critical Quarterly* 9.3 (1967): 256–71.

———. *Jane Austen.* Basingstoke: Macmillan, 1986.

Taylor, Jenny Bourne. *In the Secret Theatre of the Home: Wilkie Collins, Sensation Narrative, and Nineteenth-Century Psychology.* London: Routledge, 1988.

Terry, R. C. *Victorian Popular Fiction, 1860–80.* London: Macmillan, 1983.

Thackeray, William Makepeace. *The Great Hoggarty Diamond.* 1841. Ed. George Saintsbury. London: Oxford University Press, n.d.

———. *Vanity Fair.* 1848. Ed. John Sutherland. Oxford: Oxford University Press, 1983.

———. *The Newcomes.* 1855. Ed. David Pascoe. London: Penguin, 1996.

Thomas, Ronald. "Spectacle and Speculation: The Victorian Economy of Vision in *Little Dorrit.*" *Dickens, Europe and the New Worlds.* Ed. Anny Sadrin, 34–46. London: Macmillan, 1999.

Thomas, T. M. "A Suburban Connemara." *Household Words* 2 (8 March 1851): 562–65.

Thompson, Nicola Diane. "Responding to the Woman Questions: Rereading Noncanonical Victorian Women Novelists." *Victorian Women Writers and the Woman Question.* Ed. Nicola Diane Thompson, 1–23. Cambridge: Cambridge University Press, 1999.

———, ed. *Victorian Women Writers and the Woman Question.* Cambridge: Cambridge University Press, 1999.

Thorner, Daniel. *Investment in Empire: British Railway and Steam Shipping Enterprise in India, 1825–1849.* Philadelphia: University of Pennsylvania Press, 1950.

Thurin, Susan Schoenbauer. *Victorian Travelers and the Opening of China, 1842–1907.* Athens: Ohio University Press, 1999.

Tosh, John. *A Man's Place: Masculinity and the Middle-Class Home in Victorian England.* New Haven: Yale University Press, 1999.

Trollope, Anthony. *The Three Clerks.* 1857. Ed. Graham Handley. Oxford: Oxford University Press, 1989.

———. *Can You Forgive Her?* 1865. Ed. Andrew Swarbrick. Oxford: Oxford University Press, 1999.

———. *The Last Chronicle of Barset.* 1867. Ed. Sophia Gilmartin. London: Penguin, 2002.

———. *The Way We Live Now.* 1875. Ed. Frank Kermode. London: Penguin, 1994.

———. *The Prime Minister.* 1876. Ed. Jennifer Uglow. Oxford: Oxford University Press, 1999.

Tucker, Herbert, ed. *A Companion to Victorian Literature and Culture.* Oxford: Blackwell, 1999.

———. "Tactical Formalism: A Response to Caroline Levine." *Victorian Studies* 49.1 (2006): 85–93.

Tuite, Clara. *Romantic Austen: Sexual Politics and the Literary Canon.* Cambridge: Cambridge University Press, 2002.

Tyack, Geoffrey. *James Pennethorne and the Making of Victorian London.* Cambridge: Cambridge University Press, 1992.

Van, Annette. "Realism, Speculation, and the Gold Standard in Harriet Martineau's *Illustrations of Political Economy.*" *Victorian Literature and Culture* 34 (2006): 115–29.

Vernon, John. *Money and Fiction: Literary Realism in the Nineteenth and Early Twentieth Century.* Ithaca: Cornell University Press, 1984.

Vidler, Anthony. *The Architectural Uncanny: Essays in the Modern Unhomely.* Cambridge, Mass: MIT Press, 1992.

Vrettos, Athena. *Somatic Fictions: Imagining Illness in Victorian Culture.* Stanford: Stanford University Press, 1995.

Wagner, Tamara S. "The Miser's New Notes and the Victorian Sensation Novel: Plotting the Magic of Paper Money." *Literature and Money.* Special issue of *Victorian Review* 31.2 (2005): 79–98.

———. "Speculators at Home in the Victorian Novel: Making Stock-Market Villains and New 'Paper Fictions.'" *Victorian Literature and Culture* 36.1 (2008): 43–62.

———. "London's Great Starfish: The Construction of Mid-Victorian Suburban Fiction." *Cahiers Victoriens & Edouardiens* 69 (2009): 151–67.

Waldron, Mary. *Jane Austen and the Fiction of her Time.* Cambridge: Cambridge University Press, 1999.

Ward, Mary Augusta [Mrs Humphrey]. *Robert Elsmere.* 1888. Oxford: Oxford University Press, 1987.

Watts, Cedric. *Literature and Money: Financial Myth and Literary Truth.* New York: Harvester Wheatsheaf, 1990.

Weiss, Barbara. *The Hell of the English: Bankruptcy and the Victorian Novel.* Lewisburg: Bucknell University Press, 1986.

Welsh, Alexander. *George Eliot and Blackmail.* Cambridge, Mass.: Harvard University Press, 1985.

West, Rebecca. *The Court and the Castle: A Study of the Interactions of Political and Religious Ideas in Imaginative Literature.* London: Macmillan, 1958.

Westmacott, Charles Molloy [Bernard Blackmantle]. *The English Spy: An Original Work, Characteristic, Satirical, and Humorous.* London: Sherwood, Jones, 1825.

Whelan, Lara. "Between Worlds: Class Identity and Suburban Ghost-stories, 1850 to 1880." *Mosaic* 35.1 (2002): 133–48.

———. "Unburying Bits of Rubbish: Deconstruction of the Victorian Suburb Ideal." *Literary London: Interdisciplinary Studies in the Representation of London*

1.2 (2003). 1 May 2004. http://homepages.gold.ac.uk/london-journal/whelan.html.

Wilde, Oscar. *An Ideal Husband*. 1899. 2nd ed. Ed. Russell Jackson. London: A&C Black, 1993.

Williams, Raymond. *The Country and the City*. London: Chatto and Windus, 1973.

Wilson, Elizabeth. *The Sphinx in the City: Urban Life, the Control of Disorder, and Women*. London: Virago, 1991.

Wilson, Frances, ed. *Byromania: Portraits of the Artist in Nineteenth- and Twentieth-Century Culture*. Basingstoke: Macmillan, 1999.

Wiltshire, John. *Jane Austen and the Body*. Cambridge: Cambridge University Press, 1992.

Wolfreys, Julian. *Writing London: The Trace of the Urban Text from Blake to Dickens*. New York: St. Martin's, 1998.

———. *Victorian Hauntings: Spectrality, Gothic, the Uncanny and Literature*. Basingstoke: Palgrave, 2002.

Wood, Ellen. *The Shadow of Ashlydyat*. 1863. London: Macmillan, 1900.

———. *Lord Oakburn's Daughters*. 1864. London: Bentley and Son, 1890.

———. *Mildred Arkell*. 1865. London: Ward, Lock, & Co., n.d.

———. *The Red Court Farm*. Leipzig: Tauchnitz, 1868.

———. "Out in the Streets." *Argosy* 10 (December 1870): 496–515.

———. "In the Dead of Night." *Argosy* 17–18 (1 January–1 December 1874).

———. *Adam Grainger*. Leipzig: Tauchnitz, 1876.

Woodmansee, Martha and Peter Jaszi, eds. *The Construction of Authorship: Textual Appropriation in Law and Literature*. Durham: Duke University Press, 1995.

Woodmansee, Martha and Mark Osteen. "Taking Account of the New Economic Criticism." *The New Economic Criticism: Studies at the Intersection of Literature and Economics*. Ed. Martha Woodmansee and Mark Osteen, 3–50. London and New York: Routledge, 1999.

———, eds. *The New Economic Criticism: Studies at the Intersection of Literature and Economics*. London and New York: Routledge, 1999.

Xu, Wenying. "The Opium Trade and *Little Dorrit*: A Case of Reading Silences." *Victorian Literature and Culture* 25.1 (1997): 53–56.

Yonge, Charlotte M. *The Pillars of the House*. 1873. London: Macmillan and Co., 1875.

Yousaf, Nahem and Andrew Maunder, eds. *The Mill on the Floss* and *Silas Marner*. Houndmills, Basingstoke: Palgrave, 2002.

Index

absconder, 71, 127, 147–48, 150, 156–57, 159–60, 162–63, 207
accounting: moral, 94, 102–3, 105, 124, 180n12
Adam Bede (Eliot), 83
Adam Grainger (Wood), 127–28, 174
Ainsworth, Harrison, 21–24. See also *Mississippi Bubble*; *The South Sea Bubble*
Allen, Grant: *The Type-Writer Girl*, 207n62
Anglo-Indian, 28, 91, 95, 197n9
anthropomorphism, 9, 19, 114–15, 176
Armadale (Collins), 141
At His Gates (Oliphant, M.), 131, 151–59, 177, 200n73
Augustan satire, 15
Aurora Floyd (Braddon), 27, 78–88, 174, 176
Austen, Jane, 25, 33–39, 43, 47, 107, 135, 174–75, 196n15. See also *Emma*; *Mansfield Park*; *Persuasion*; *Pride and Prejudice*; *Sanditon*
"Autobiography of a Joint-Stock Company (Limited)" (Oliphant, L.), 18–19

Bagehot, Walter, 16, 181n20
bank failure, 15, 22, 52, 63, 93, 97, 99, 116, 159, 198. *See also* bankruptcy
The Banker's Wife (Gore), 25, 33, 44–48, 50
banknote, 2, 27, 42, 64, 79–80, 84–88, 99, 114, 145–46, 174, 176. *See also* paper money
bankruptcy, 4–5, 20, 36, 47, 57–58, 78, 95, 101, 127, 142, 144, 148, 150, 153, 155, 199n22, 206n55, 207n64
Basil (Collins), 133, 206n47
Bell, Robert: *The Ladder of Gold*, 128, 179n1
bigamy, 84, 86, 190n45, 196n41
bildungsroman, 55
bill of exchange, 9–10
Birds of Prey (Braddon), 62, 64–65, 194n19
blackmail, 20, 81–82, 129

Index

Bleak House (Dickens), 105, 136
bookkeeping: and ethics, 105, 111, 124. *See also* accounting
Booth, William: *In Darkest London and the Way Out*, 136–37, 205n32
Braddon, Mary Elizabeth, 10, 14, 27, 62, 64–66, 78–79, 83–84, 110, 141, 174, 176, 179n1, 193–94n13, 196n38, 196n41. See also *Aurora Floyd; Birds of Prey; Charlotte's Inheritance; The Doctor's Wife; Eleanor's Victory; John Marchmont's Legacy; Lady Audley's Secret; The Lady's Mile*
bribery, 81–82, 119
Brontë, Charlotte: *Jane Eyre*, 183–84n36
"Brother Jacob" (Eliot), 195n34
building speculation, 28, 120, 130–32, 135–37, 141
Bulwer-Lytton, Edward: *The Lady of Lyons*, 196n40; *Pelham*, 187n6
Burney, Frances: *Camilla*, 39
Byronic, 43, 73

Can You Forgive Her? (Trollope), 27, 62, 66–68, 72–78, 87, 165, 177; based on *The Noble Jilt*, 74
capitalism, 14; credit, 85; finance, 2, 7, 13–14, 36, 68, 70, 90, 94, 139, 176, 178
Carlyle, Thomas: *The French Revolution*, 11
Cecil (Gore), 43, 189n29
Cecil, The Peer (Gore), 43, 189n29
Chambers, Robert, 136
Charlotte's Inheritance (Braddon), 14, 64–66, 176
A Christmas Carol (Dickens), 61, 80, 141
Churchill, Caryl: *Serious Money*, 185n52
City and Suburb (Riddell), 138, 142
Cobbett, William: *Rural Rides*, 9
Colburn, Henry, 32, 42, 186n2

Collins, Wilkie, 10, 28, 89–90, 94, 120–21, 125, 132–33, 141, 153, 176, 201–2n38, 202n39, 202n40, 206n47. See also *Armadale; Basil; Heart and Science; The Law and the Lady; The Moonstone; The Woman in White*
Conan Doyle, Arthur, 134, 193n8, 208n75
copyright, 64–65, 193n12, 194n13
cosmopolitan, 107–8, 124, 127, 165, 167, 200n27
counterfeit, 11, 81–82, 195n27, 206n53
courtship: as plot structure, 4, 22, 26, 31, 40, 48, 52, 58, 144–45, 152, 154–55, 163, 174
Cousin Phillis (Gaskell), 190n46
Craik, Dinah Mulock, 9, 57, 147, 191nn50–51. See also *John Halifax, Gentleman; Olive*
Cranford (Gaskell), 52, 91–94
credit, 14–18, 27, 40, 75, 82, 84, 88, 95, 98, 105, 112, 124, 164, 180n17, 181n20, 185n50, 202n39, 209n80; capitalism, 85; and debt, 82, 87, 103; system, 14, 180n17, 202n39. *See also* debt; economy: and credit
creditworthiness, 3, 27, 80–83, 88
Crosland, T. W. H.: *The Suburbans*, 132
currency: and unreliability, 5, 79; and value, 23, 109, 113, 121, 176. *See also* paper currency

dandy, 15, 33, 42–43, 69, 95, 175, 187n6
A Dark Night's Work (Gaskell), 190n46
David Copperfield (Dickens), 86–87, 192–93n4
debt, 20–21, 42, 71, 75, 82, 87, 103, 110–11, 121, 123, 125, 127, 135, 144–45; debt-credit system, 82, 87, 103; debt-ridden, 21, 23, 124; imprisoned for, 105, 112; legacy of, 46, 62, 103, 110, 112, 123–24; as metaphor, 82, 98, 99, 103, 105,

110–12, 121, 131, 198n17, 199n21, 202n39
debtors' prison, 104, 113. See also Marshalsea
Defoe, Daniel: Robinson Crusoe, 73, 109, 185n50, 185n58
detection: as plot structure, 9–10, 28, 69, 79, 84, 89–90, 93, 104–6, 108, 110, 115, 122, 125, 144, 152, 155, 177, 183n36. See also detective fiction
detective: amateur, 69, 103; professional, 17, 86, 105, 150
detective fiction, 17, 25, 51, 94, 136, 175, 177, 208n66
Dickens, Charles, 3, 20, 27–28, 46, 61–62, 66, 80, 83, 86–87, 89–91, 103, 105–7, 127, 134, 136–38, 141, 171, 176, 179n1, 192n3, 192n4, 193n7, 193n12, 200n25, 200n27, 200n31, 201n31, 201–2n38, 204n27, 208n72. See also Bleak House; A Christmas Carol; David Copperfield; Dombey and Son; Great Expectations; Hard Times; Little Dorrit; Martin Chuzzlewit; Nicholas Nickleby; The Old Curiosity Shop; Oliver Twist; Our Mutual Friend; The Pickwick Papers
The Doctor's Wife (Braddon), 65, 141, 194n15
Dombey and Son (Dickens), 134–35, 204n27
doppelganger, 43, 69, 108, 141
double, 26, 28, 43, 45, 60, 69, 85–86, 96, 102, 107, 119, 144, 159, 162, 165–66. See also doppelganger; double life; doubling
double life, 67, 69, 71, 125
doubling, 45, 69, 108, 144, 159

East India Company, 14, 21, 93, 96–97, 107, 116, 121, 201n36
economic journalism. See finance journalism

economics: cf authorship, 5; as discipline, 6, 7; and elections, 180n3; laissez-faire, 61
economy: and credit, 2, 5, 12, 64, 67, 80, 85; definition of, 14, 196n36; of the household, 14, 93, 159, 163; moral, 45, 49, 57–58, 63, 69, 79–80, 82–83, 91, 123, 125, 128–29, 131, 139, 146, 175, 195n29, 196n36, 198n17; speculative, 165, 174, 177, 183n32
Eleanor's Victory (Braddon), 66
Eliot, George 25–26, 55, 66, 80, 82–83, 87, 190n47, 191n47, 195n34, 196n38. See also Adam Bede; "Brother Jacob"; Middlemarch; Silas Marner
embezzlement, 120, 139
Emma (Austen), 188n15
epistemological uncertainty, 2, 7, 201n38
Evans, D. Morier, 15–18, 23–24
exclusivism, 44, 97, 186n1, 195n22

The Fair of May Fair (Gore), 189–90n34
Fielding, Henry: Tom Jones, 72
finance journalism, 6, 10, 17, 175; economic journalism, 21, 42, 174–75, 181n20
financial crisis, 3, 13–15, 20–24, 33, 40, 97, 118, 127, 150, 155, 160, 191n51
financial panic, 14–18, 24, 32, 199, 135, 177, 191n51
financial scandal, 3, 148, 155
fiscal responsibility, 6, 9, 14, 28, 56–58, 63, 68, 92, 101–2, 111
Flaubert, Gustave: Madame Bovary, 194n15
forgery, 71, 75, 83, 86, 92, 125, 141, 165–66, 176, 190n46, 194n15, 197n1
fraud, 7, 12, 14, 19, 64, 67, 71, 116, 120, 133, 148, 196n38, 208n66. See also scam; swindle

French Revolution, 11, 14

gambling, 8–10, 26, 35, 42, 44, 56–57, 65, 67, 70–71, 73–74, 81, 86, 144, 162, 164, 167–68, 183n31, 183n32, 184n43, 196n39, 197n44; anti-gambling rhetoric, 9
Gaskell, Elizabeth, 26, 46, 48, 51–52, 55, 57–59, 91–92, 94, 114, 175, 190n46, 191n47. See also *Cousin Phillis*; *Cranford*; *A Dark Night's Work*; *Mary Barton*; *North and South*; *Ruth*
George Geith of Fen Court (Riddell), 142
ghost story, 28, 142–43, 145–46, 207n59
Gissing, George: *The Nether World*, 134
gold standard, 11, 80, 87, 114
Gore, Catherine, 25–26, 32–33, 43–48, 50, 170, 175, 189nn29–30. See also *The Banker's Wife*; *Cecil*; *Cecil, The Peer*; *The Fair of May Fair*; *Men of Capital*; *The Moneylender*; *Mothers and Daughters*; *Peers and Parvenus*; *Stokeshill Place*; *The Two Aristocracies*; *Women As They Are*
Gothic: domestic, 69, 86, 124, 177; and finance, 127, 142, 180n10, 185n49; suburban, 28, 130, 137, 139, 141, 206n47, 206n56; traditional, 41, 141, 143, 206n47
Grand, Sarah, 207n62
Great Expectations (Dickens), 66, 137–38, 192n4, 198n16
The Great Hoggarty Diamond (Thackeray), 3, 97
Grossmith, George and Weedon: *The Diary of a Nobody*, 137

Hard Cash (Reade), 13, 28, 83, 89, 91–92, 94, 113–21, 125, 176, 201n37

Hard Times (Dickens), 83
Hazlitt, William, 32, 187n3
Heart and Science (Collins), 206n47
Hester (Oliphant, M.), 29, 130–31, 146, 159–63, 173–74, 177
Hill, Headon: *Guilty Gold*, 165
Holcroft, Thomas, 42
Holiday House (Sinclair), 49
Home, Sweet Home (Riddell), 206n53
Hook, Theodore, 42, 187n6
Hudson, George 179n1, 191–92n54

imperialism: and commerce, 91, 100, 117, 169; and expansion, 36, 91, 132, 136–37, 169, 176
In the Dead of Night (Wood), 147, 207n61
indeterminacy, 2, 12, 14–15, 21, 23, 26–27, 62–63, 73–74, 79, 89–91, 94, 99, 108, 116, 125–28, 130, 164–67, 173, 209n80; and foreignness, 146, 163–65, 203n5; and identity, 3, 108, 117, 163–65, 171
Industrial Revolution, 14
industrialization, 55
inheritance: of guilt, 36, 46, 58, 70, 91, 93, 96, 101–13, 121–25, 134, 144, 169, 176, 198n17; as plot structure, 3–4, 6, 13, 22–23, 26, 31, 34–35, 42, 46, 48, 58–60, 66–67, 70, 72, 79, 83–85, 101–4, 110, 112, 121–23, 143–45, 171, 174, 177, 180n12, 181n23, 188n19; speculation on, 65–66, 72, 111, 194n16, 194n19
intertextuality, 10, 17, 24, 27, 48, 156
investment: as defined against speculation, 8, 10, 56, 60, 183n31

Jewsbury, Geraldine: *Marian Withers*, 191n51
John Halifax, Gentleman (Craik), 57, 191nn50–51
John Law, The Projector (Ainsworth), 21

John Marchmont's Legacy (Braddon), 194n19
joint-stock companies, 18–19, 52, 102, 151–52, 155, 175, 184n46

Lady Audley's Secret (Braddon), 84
The Lady's Mile (Braddon), 194n19
Last Chronicle of Barset (Trollope), 87
Law, John, 16, 21–22. *See also* Mississippi Bubble
The Law and the Lady (Collins), 206n47
LeFanu, J. Sheridan: *In A Glass Darkly*, 139
Lever, Charles: *Davenport Dunn*, 132, 135, 175, 205n30
Lillo, George, 40–41
limited liability, 14, 22, 184n47
Linton, Eliza Lynn, 207n64
Little Dorrit (Dickens), 3, 10, 27–28, 46, 89, 91, 94, 101–13, 125, 127, 171, 176, 179n1, 192n4, 193n12, 199n21, 199n22, 199n23, 200n27, 200–201n31, 202n1
Lord Oakburn's Daughters (Wood), 66

MacFarlane, A.: *Railway Scrip*, 135, 175
Mackay, Charles, 16, 21, 175, 185n56
The Magic of Wealth (Surr), 25, 39–41
Mansfield Park (Austen), 107, 187–88n14, 199n23
marriage market, 8–10, 26, 43–44, 53, 59, 80–81, 110, 161–62, 190n35
Marshalsea, 104, 112, 127, 200n27. *See also* debtors' prison
Martin Chuzzlewit (Dickens), 3, 20, 90, 164, 193n12, 197n1, 202n1, 207n64, 208n75
Martineau, Harriet, 183n33
Marx, Karl, 85, 114
Mary Barton (Gaskell), 190n46
The Massarenes (Ouida), 29, 130–31, 163, 167–72

Men of Capital (Gore), 44
Middlemarch (Eliot), 66, 83, 196n38
Mildred Arkell (Wood), 194–95n22
mimesis. *See* realism
miser, 64, 78–88, 115, 119–20, 176, 195n34, 196n38, 197n44
Miss Marjoribanks (Oliphant, M.), 207–8n66
Mississippi Bubble, 13, 16, 21, 118, 128
Mitre Court (Riddell), 142
mobility, 34, 36, 130, 132, 174, 187n9, 188n14, 188n19; social, 44, 55
The Moneylender (Gore), 44,
The Moonstone (Collins), 28, 89–91, 94, 121–25, 141, 176, 201–2n38, 202n41
Mortomley's Estate (Riddell), 142–43, 206n55
Mothers and Daughters (Gore), 44, 189n34

nabob, 28, 45, 91, 95–96, 102, 125, 149. *See also* Anglo-Indian
The Nether World (Gissing), 134
The Newcomes (Thackeray), 20, 27, 89, 91, 94–103, 125, 175
Nicholas Nickleby (Dickens), 192n4, 208n75
North and South (Gaskell), 26, 51–60, 46, 48, 175, 190n46, 191n52, 208n75

The Old Curiosity Shop (Dickens), 197n44
Oliphant, Laurence, 18–20. *See also* "Autobiography of a Joint-Stock Company (Limited)"; *Piccadilly*
Oliphant, Margaret, 10, 29, 130–31, 146–48, 151, 154, 156–59, 173–75, 177, 207n65, 207n66, 208n72, 208n73. *See also* *At His Gates*; *Miss Marjoribanks*; *Phoebe, Junior*; *The Quiet Heart*; "The Stockbroker at Dinglewood"; *Hester*

229

Index

Olive (Craik), 9–10, 147
Oliver Twist (Dickens), 140
opium, 123–24, 168; trade in, 91, 100, 107, 109, 112, 123, 200n26
Opium Wars, 100, 107, 109, 199n23
Orient, 97, 99, 102, 107–8, 123, 198n16. *See also* orientalism
orientalism, 84, 90–93, 95, 98–101, 109, 122, 132, 197n2, 198n16, 199n23
Ouida (Marie Louise de la Ramée), 29, 130, 147, 163, 167, 170–71, 209n83; See also *The Massarenes*
Our Mutual Friend (Dickens), 62, 80, 87, 193n4, 193n7, 208n72

paper currency. *See* paper money.
paper money: abstraction, 5–6, 10–12, 16, 86, 114, 119; and instability, 21, 41, 52, 64, 70, 74, 79–80, 87, 90, 92, 114–15, 174, 180n17; and magicality, 5, 12, 27, 40–41, 70, 78, 85, 87–88, 104, 107, 109, 113–24; as plot device, 5, 11, 21, 41, 78–88, 92, 176, 185n50. *See also* banknote
patent, 42, 65, 142, 206n55
Peers and Parvenus (Gore), 44
Persuasion (Austen), 72, 187–88n14
Phineas Finn (Trollope), 203n5
Phineas Redux (Trollope), 203n5, 208–9n76
Phoebe, Junior (Oliphant, M.), 207–8n66
Piccadilly (Oliphant, L.), 19–20
The Pickwick Papers (Dickens), 192n4
piracy, 89, 94, 115–18, 121; as metaphor, 95, 101, 115–18, 121, 125, 193n12
plagiarism: in commerce, 63–64, 176; and the press: 64–65, 193–94n13
Pride and Prejudice (Austen), 35–36
The Prime Minister (Trollope), 62, 77, 164–65, 193n7, 202n1, 203n5, 208n75

The Quiet Heart (Oliphant, M.), 208n73

The Race for Wealth (Riddell), 138, 142–43
railway speculation, 3, 13–14, 22, 48–51, 59, 65, 98, 116, 118–19, 128, 135, 164, 174–75, 190n42, 190n46, 192n3, 201n36
Reade, Charles, 10, 13, 28, 83, 87, 89, 113–14, 116, 120, 125, 176, 201n37
realism, 5, 25, 48; domestic, 28, 44, 63–64, 69, 92, 115, 131, 140, 156, 158, 177; mimetic, 157; and mimetic representation, 21, 23, 40
Red Court Farm (Wood), 194–95n22
Regency, 13, 31–33, 40, 44, 53, 97, 118, 161, 189n30
Richardson, Samuel: *Clarissa*, 189n20
Riddell, Charlotte, 28, 130, 137–38, 142–43, 174, 206n51, 206n55. See also *City and Suburb*; *George Geith of Fen Court*; *Home, Sweet Home*; *Mitre Court*; *Mortomley's Estate*; *The Race for Wealth*; *The Uninhabited House*
risk management, 9–10, 12, 23, 26, 28, 63, 90–91, 96, 147, 164, 181n21
risk taking, 8, 26, 56, 76, 82, 146–47, 159–63, 176, 191
Robinson, Emma: *The Gold-Worshippers*, 179n1
Royal Exchange. *See* Stock Exchange
Russell (Surr), 42–43
Ruth (Gaskell), 190n46

Sadleir, John, 179n1
Sala, George, 132–33
Sanditon (Austen), 25, 33, 34–39, 47, 135, 174, 187n9, 188n17–19
scam, 1, 19, 90, 99, 117, 126, 167, 197n1
Scotter, C. J.: *Lost in a Bucket Shop*, 147

Index

self-destruction, 1, 26, 42, 57, 71, 151, 165, 174, 208n75. *See also* suicide
self-help, 8, 57, 61–62
Self-Help (Smiles), 55, 61
self-reflexivity, 2, 6–9, 12, 18, 25, 27–28, 32–33, 58, 63, 65–66, 121, 126, 128, 131, 141, 148, 151–52, 154, 159, 174–77
sensation: anti-sensational, 10, 64, 185, 177; craze for, 22, 63, 130; fiction, 10, 13–20, 22–23, 25–29, 50–51, 61–89, 91–94, 110, 115, 120, 122, 124–25, 131, 133, 141, 147–56, 160, 165, 175, 177, 194n15, 201n37, 205n44, 206n47, 207n65; and finance, 17, 22, 24–26, 28–29, 28, 50, 63, 65–66, 77, 85, 87, 131, 143, 148–51, 154, 177
sensationalism, 17, 27–28, 147–48, 150–51, 153, 157–60, 177, 207n65
sensationalization, 22, 113, 133–34, 141–42, 150, 153, 157, 176, 180n10
The Shadow of Ashlydyat (Wood), 27, 67–72, 78, 177
Shadwell, Thomas: *The Volunteers*, 15, 185n52
Siddon, Henry, 42
Silas Marner (Eliot), 80, 83, 87, 195n34
silver-fork fiction, 20, 25–26, 31–35, 39, 42–49, 52, 54–55, 59, 118, 160–61, 170–71, 175, 186n1, 187n2, 187n6, 190–91n47, 191n51, 195n22
Sinclair, Catherine, 11, 48–51, 55, 175. See also *Holiday House; Sir Edward Graham*
Sir Edward Graham (Sinclair), 48–51, 175
Smiles, Samuel, 55, 61. See also *Self-Help*
social-problems fiction, 25, 33, 43, 48, 54, 57–59, 175, 190n46
South Sea Bubble, 13, 15–16, 22, 28, 118

The South Sea Bubble (Ainsworth), 21–23
speculation definition of, 9; marital, 149. *See also* building speculation; investment; railway speculation; stock market
Spencer, Herbert, 80
stockbroker, 147–48, 150, 159, 161, 165, 174, 188n15, 194n16, 207n61
"The Stockbroker at Dinglewood" (Oliphant, M.), 131, 147–51, 154, 156
Stock Exchange, 8–9, 15, 20, 42–43, 47, 64, 78, 110, 129, 147, 160, 162; Change, 47, 74; Exchange, 18, 77, 108; Royal Exchange, 17, 23
stock-jobbing, 15
stock market, 3, 5, 8–9, 13, 15, 18, 20–21, 23, 26, 29, 34, 50, 55, 64–66, 59, 72–74, 78, 101, 117, 129, 145, 162, 176, 180n10; crash, 5, 20–23, 69, 117; fluctuations on, 13, 15, 54, 76, 98, 132, 146; graph as metaphor, 22, 68, 76, 116–17, 195n23; novel (as subgenre), 14–15, 18, 21–23, 26–27, 47, 59, 61–88, 92–93, 103–4, 126, 128–31, 135, 137, 141, 146–48, 159–60, 163, 170–71, 175–77; as metaphor, 8–10, 13, 15, 18, 26–29, 47, 56, 68–69, 71, 103–4, 186n63, 195n23; shares, 2, 5, 14, 20, 38, 47, 50, 56, 62, 64, 67–68, 75, 80, 87, 90, 92, 100, 141, 144, 163–64, 173, 177, 190n46, 192n53, 194n16; swindle, 135, 139, 148; villains (in fiction), 1–3, 15, 25–26, 31, 34, 43–44, 47, 50–51, 58, 63, 67, 70, 71–72, 77–78, 90, 110, 126, 129, 150–51, 165, 169, 174–75, 205n44. *See also* stockbroker; Stock Exchange; stock-jobbing
Stokeshill Place (Gore), 44
suburban speculation, 146, 204n16; and internal colonization, 28. *See also* building speculation; suburbanization; suburbia

231

Index

suburbanization, 130–31, 133, 142–143, 203–4n15
suburbia, 28, 89, 125, 130–34, 137–42, 203n13, 203n15, 204n21, 206n53
suicide, 20, 26, 42–43, 47, 51, 56–58, 71, 77, 111, 113, 127, 145, 153, 155, 163, 165–66, 169, 171, 179n1, 192n4, 201n31, 208n75, 209n82; failed: 20, 51, 151–53, 157, 208n75; as metaphor, 42, 50, 71, 77–78, 111, 163, 165, 171, 208n75; note, 42, 152, 155
Surr, Thomas, 25, 39–43, 174–75. See also *The Magic of Wealth; Russell*
swindle, 1, 3, 8, 48, 61, 76–77, 81, 91, 95, 97–98, 104, 121, 126–27, 129, 135, 148, 181n23, 192n3, 209n80. See also stock-market swindle

"The Telegraph-Girl" (Trollope), 207n62
Thackeray, William Makepeace, 3, 20, 27, 89, 91, 95, 97, 100, 125, 176, 197n9, 197–98n12, 198n16. See also *The Great Hoggarty Diamond; The Newcomes; The Tremendous Adventures of Major Goliah Gahagan; Vanity Fair*
Thomas, T. M., 133
The Three Clerks (Trollope), 28, 130–32, 137, 139–42, 195n29, 205n44
The Tremendous Adventures of Major Goliah Gahagan (Thackeray), 95
Trollope, Anthony, 1, 3, 10, 12, 27–29, 62–63, 67–68, 72, 74, 77–78, 87, 127–28, 130–31, 134, 137, 139–40, 163–71, 177, 184n43, 193n7, 195n29, 203n5, 209n76. See also *Can You Forgive Her?; Last Chronicle of Barset; Phineas Finn; Phineas Redux;* "The Telegraph-Girl"; *The Three Clerks; The Way We Live Now*

The Two Aristocracies (Gore), 32, 43–44

uncanny, 109, 144, 185n49, 206n47
unheimlich, 206n56. See also uncanny
The Uninhabited House (Riddell), 28, 130–31, 142–46, 174

Vanity Fair (Thackeray), 95, 97

Ward, Mary: *Robert Elsmere*, 132, 207n62
The Way We Live Now (Trollope), 1–3, 10, 12, 29, 63, 127, 163–64, 171, 179n1, 202n1, 208n75, 209n80, 209n82
Weber, Max, 114
Wells, H. G.: *The War of the Worlds*, 134
Westmacott, Charles Molloy: *The English Spy*, 32
Wilde, Oscar: *An Ideal Husband*, 128–30
The Woman in White (Collins), 120, 141, 193n8
Women As They Are (Gore), 187n6
Wood, Mrs. Henry (Ellen), 10, 27, 65–67, 71–72, 77, 127–28, 147, 174, 177, 194n14, 194–95n22. See also *Adam Grainger; In the Dead of Night; Lord Oakburn's Daughters; Mildred Arkell; Red Court Farm; The Shadow of Ashlydyat*

xenophobia, 93, 202n2

Yonge, Charlotte, 207n64

www.ingramcontent.com/pod-product-compliance
Lightning Source LLC
Chambersburg PA
CBHW020946230426
43666CB00005B/185